"The Land Where Two Streams Flow"

"THE LAND WHERE TWO STREAMS FLOW"

Music in the German-Jewish
Community of Israel

PHILIP V. BOHLMAN

UNIVERSITY OF ILLINOIS PRESS

Urbana and Chicago

This publication was made possible in part by a grant from the National Foundation for Jewish Culture.

This book is printed on acid-free paper.

Kösel Verlage, Munich, West Germany, has kindly granted permission to reprint Else Lasker-Schüler's "Mein blaues Klavier" [Jerusalem, 1943], from *Helles Schlafen—dunkles Wachen* (Munich: Deutscher Taschenbuch Verlag, 1981), p. 146.

Library of Congress Cataloging-in-Publication Data

Bohlman, Philip Vilas.
    The land where two streams flow : music in the German-Jewish
community of Israel / Philip V. Bohlman.
        p.   cm.
    Bibliography: p.
    Includes index.
    ISBN 0-252-01596-7 (alk. paper)
    1. Jews, German—Israel—Music—History and criticism. 2. Music—
Israel—History and criticism. I. Title.
ML345.I8B6   1989
781.75694—dc19
                                                        88-25902
                                                        CIP
                                                        MN

For
Bruno Nettl
Teacher, Colleague, Friend

Ich habe zu Hause ein blaues Klavier
Und kenne doch keine Note.

Es steht im Dunkel der Kellertür,
Seitdem die Welt verrohte,

Es spielten Sternenhände vier
— Die Mondfrau sang im Boote —
Nun tanzen die Ratten im Geklirr.

Zerbrochen ist die Klaviatür. . . . .
Ich beweine die blaue Tote.

Ach liebe Engel öffnet mir
— Ich aß vom bitteren Brote —
Mir lebend schon die Himmelstür —
Auch wider dem Verbote.

Else Lasker-Schüler, "Mein blaues Klavier"

פעמי אביב

הָיְתָה רוּחַ אַחֶרֶת, גָּבְהוּ שְׁמֵי הַשָּׁמַיִם,
וַיִּגְלוּ מֶרְחַקִּים בְּהִירִים, רַחֲבֵי יָדַיִם--
עַל-הָהָר עוֹמְדוֹת רַגְלֵי הָאָבִיב!
עַל-הַמִּגְרָשׁ עִם-שֶׁמֶשׁ אֵדִים חַמִּים מִשְׁתַּטְּחִים,
מִן-הָעֵצִים הָרְטֻבִּים פְּטוּרֵי צִיצִים מִתְפַּתְּחִים--
הָיְתָה רוּחַ אַחֶרֶת מִסָּבִיב.

עוֹד לֹא-פָרְצוּ הַנְּגֹהוֹת, אֵין עוֹד צִלְצְלֵי תְרוּעָה--
מֵאֵלֶיהָ תִתְחַפֵּשׂ שִׁירָה זַכָּה וּצְנוּעָה,
אֲרֻרוֹת רַכִּים כְּמוֹ בֹקְעִים וְעוֹלִים--
חֲבוּ כִמְעָט! וְהִתְפָּרֵץ עֹז הַחַיִּים הַחֲתוּמִים,
יָצִיץ פִּתְאֹם וְיַחְגֹּל כָּל-עֱזוּז הָעֲלוּמִים,
כָּל-הַכֹּחוֹת הַפֹּרִים, הַגְּדוֹלִים!

וּמַה-מָּתוֹק הָאוֹר וּמַה-מָּתוֹק הָרוּחַ!
פָּנִים שׂוֹחֲקוֹת בַּכֹּל, בַּאֲשֶׁר עַיִן תָּנוּחַ--
שָׁם רְעוּתָהּ לִקְרָאתָהּ מַזְהֶרֶת.
וּמִכָּל אֵלַי-כָּל חוּטוֹ זָהָב נִמְתָּחִים;
עוֹד מְעַט וְהִשְׁתַּפְּכָה בְּלִבְנַת הַפְּרָחִים
שִׁפְעַת נַעַר הַלָּזוּ וְזֶה הָעֹתֶרֶת.

עוֹד מְעַט וְהִשְׁתַּפְּכוּ בִּפְרָחִים לִבְנִים
גַּם-נְעוּרַי הַחֲדָשִׁים וַחֲלֹמוֹתַי הַיְשָׁנִים,
כִּי גַם-בָּם נָשְׁבָה רוּחַ הַשָּׁבִיב.
וּמִלְּבָבִי הַמָּלֵא כָּל-הֲגִיגִי אָשִׂיחָה,
וּבְדִמְעוֹת מַזְהִירוֹת שָׁחוֹר יָאוֹשִׁי אָדִיחָה--
הָיְתָה רוּחַ אַחֶרֶת מִסָּבִיב!

חיים נחמן ביאליק

Chaim Nachman Bialik, "Pa'ameh aviv"
("Footsteps of Spring")

CONTENTS

PREFACE

It is with a profound sense of awe and esteem that I take the title of this book from the collection of late essays (1926) that Franz Rosenzweig entitled *Zweistromland,* "the land where two streams flow." For Rosenzweig the metaphor had a complex of meanings that embodied the struggles and successes of Jewish history and society since the period after the destruction of the First Temple in Jerusalem, when the Jews of ancient Israel occupied the fertile lands surrounding the Tigris and Euphrates rivers in Mesopotamia. Their residence in a foreign land notwithstanding, the Jews used the years in the *Zweistromland* of Mesopotamia to enrich their culture, to absorb Persian, Greek, and Parthian influences and yet to assimilate these as their own. And so too, throughout Jewish history in the subsequent millennia, Jews had been forced to accommodate the streams of other cultures, while still replenishing the springs from which their own flowed. Implicit in Rosenzweig's metaphor was that the decisive triumph of Jewish history was a constant ability to negotiate between Jewish culture and another, between the self and the other, between the community and the outside world. Continual interaction and negotiation, though often marked by struggle, were nevertheless fruitful over the course of a long history, for they empowered a process of taking nourishment from the several streams that nurtured the culture of which the Jews were ineffably a part.

German-Jewish history by the early twentieth century had come to epitomize for Franz Rosenzweig his metaphor of a *Zweistromland.* He consistently addressed the contemporary world of German Jewry through the formulation of dual, sometimes dialectical, relationships: *Deutschtum und Judentum* ("Germanness and Jewishness"), *die Wissenschaft und das Leben* ("science and life"), *Liberalismus und Zionismus* ("liberalness and Zionism"), *Glauben und Wissen* ("belief and knowledge"), to cite just a few titles from his *Zweistromland* essays. The connective "and" with which Rosenzweig linked these concepts was not a means of staking out territory that could not be traversed, but of signifying an inseparability afforded by the present moment in German-Jewish history. To be German did not negate the possibility of being Jewish; to maintain religious faith did not contradict the pursuit of humanistic and scientific study; to participate fully in the life of the Jewish community did not require withdrawal from the life of the nation.

Rosenzweig's *Zweistromland* was a particularly twentieth-century realization, which is to say that he saw it as particularly auspicious and trenchant as a symbol for the Jewish community in the renascent moment that characterized the German-Jewish culture from which emerged the immigrant and ethnic community examined in this book. This was a moment when the false specter of assimilation had passed, when visions and plans for the creation of a new Jewish community could be implemented. Rosenzweig's own concept of the Jewish *Lehrhaus,* a community school in which one could study various facets of Judaism and Jewish culture, was in fact one of the institutions that took full advantage of the freshened streams flowing through the community. Many of the other institutions that benefited from the intensified cultural independence and interdependence, especially those that spurred a radical transformation of the musical life within the German-Jewish community, form the subject of the early chapters of this book.

The "land where two streams flow" that I examine in the following pages, however, extends beyond Rosenzweig's *Zweistromland,* both historically and geographically. His metaphor, nevertheless, is equally as powerful, equally as pregnant, when applied to the culture and community of Central European immigrants in Israel. Indeed, the cultural streams from which the ethnic community drew sustenance were frequently no more than a reformulation of the institutions that provided the infrastructure of the German-Jewish community. The duality of Germanness and Jewishness in Israel, for example, might assume the form of a duality between secular German-Jewishness and advocacy of Israel as a religious state. Israel, in turn, was the source of new cultural bifurcations, such as the admixture of Western and non-Western cultures, whether Ashkenazic and Sephardic Judaism or, indeed, Judaism and Islam. Significantly, just as the post-assimilation era of the early twentieth century had given Franz Rosenzweig hope for the future of his *Zweistromland,* so too did the settlement of Palestine and Israel during the 1930s and 1940s give the Central European community new faith that it could found itself on the banks of cultural streams both ancient and modern.

The musical life of the German-Jewish community fully availed itself of the cultural streams of Central Europe and then Israel. It benefited from the experiences of Jews in music outside the community and from their willingness to participate in those musical activities that were specific to the community. In Israel, German-Jewish musicians committed themselves to establishing an entirely new musical culture and to reestablishing links with Central Europe after the end of World War II. The community cultivated its revered traditions of *Lieder* and chamber music, while its composers experimented with new ways of setting classical and modern Hebrew. Although aware that the musical life of their community was not always shared by all Israelis, the German-Jewish Israelis nonetheless perceived that musical life as inextricably bound to the larger culture of the entire nation.

The tension and strife that often characterized the historical *Zweistromland* envisioned by Franz Rosenzweig has also been a factor in the music of the German-Jewish community in Israel. But also like the metaphor posited by the ever-hopeful Rosenzweig was the profit that ensued from the engagement with seemingly contradictory ideas. The opposition of secular and religious Judaism, for example, proved to engender a proliferation of musical activities, some addressing the community's attraction to a broadly based intellectual expression of its distinctive music history and others yielding new forms of religious celebration. Criticized for their unwillingness to distance themselves completely from use of the German language or performance of music favored by the Nazis, many in the Central European community quietly sequestered their concerts to include Wagnerian orchestral works or songs by Richard Strauss, while at the same time campaigning with forbearance for public acceptance of German songs with texts by the nineteenth-century Jewish poet Heinrich Heine. Whereas conflict and tension are sometimes endemic to the coexistence of the cultural streams, the multifarious alternatives that the streams make possible likewise lead to a relaxation and amelioration of potential conflict between the community and the nation of which it is a part.

The rivers in Franz Rosenzweig's metaphor for German-Jewish history, of course, eventually flowed together, conjoining before they entered the sea, just as the two cultural streams recognized by Rosenzweig had the ability to become indistinguishably one. Rosenzweig, who passed away in 1929, never had the opportunity to witness the propitious confluence that he hoped would take place. Soon after his death, moreover, this confluence — had anyone during the Holocaust been undaunted enough to imagine such a turn in the course of history — would have seemed particularly impossible, just a naive fancy of Rosenzweig's philosophical fantasy. But the experiences of the German-Jewish community in Israel were to bring about the impossible, for it was in Israel that the eventual merging of the community's cultural streams was to take place. Although the streams flowed with considerable depth in Rosenzweig's Germany, their courses had increasingly deviated in distinct and ineluctable directions. That their ultimate consummation became possible through reestablishment of the German-Jewish community in Israel was, no doubt, understood only too well by Franz Rosenzweig, for it was in Israel that the community truly could discover the land where two streams flowed.

ACKNOWLEDGMENTS

This is a book that has benefited from ideas and diverse contributions as sustaining and nurturing as the streams flowing through the *Zweistromland* of the Central European community in Israel. As with a flowing stream the sources from which these ideas have sprung are many and various, each ineffably yielding some identifiable quality to the larger body of water that exists only as the commingling of many other streams. Ultimately, this book too would not exist without the ideas of many other individuals, and to these individuals, who have given so much to this book, I am indebted in ways far greater than the confines of my acknowledgments here allow me to detail.

My port of entry to the *Zweistromland* of musical life in the German-Jewish community of Israel was fieldwork, indeed fieldwork of a distinct kind, for, more than anything else, it is what has made this book an ethnomusicological study of Western art music. My years in Israel, 1980-82 and again in the summer of 1983, were filled with interviews, participant-observer experiences, and daily contact with the German-speaking community, a contact that has lasted until the present. I cannot name all of my consultants here, many of whose names appear in an appendix to the book. Alice Sommer Herz, however, played a role so essential to the shaping of the book's ideas that she deserves special mention. By inviting me to share in the musical life of the Central European community, Alice figuratively opened the field for my research and facilitated the writing of this book. My personal debt to all of my consultants — those whose experiences I have come to interpret in the pages of this book — is enormous, even formidable, for my fieldwork with them acquainted me with moments of history both awesome and rich, frightening and hopeful.

I was fortunate during my fieldwork in Israel to partake of the generous advice of numerous scholars. Especially helpful were Edith Gerson-Kiwi, Amnon Shiloah, and Jehoash Hirshberg, all of whom adopted me into the ethnomusicological family of Israel. Two younger ethnomusicologists at the Hebrew University, Gila Flam and Hannah Engelard, urged my work along by their collegial interest and abundant portions of friendship. My research also benefited from the marvelous collections in the Phonothèque and Jewish Music Research Centre, both located in the Jewish National and University Library, Jerusalem. My work at the Jewish Music Research Centre would have been impossible (and considerably less pleasant) had it not been for the constant assistance provided by Lea Shalem and Helen Valencia. Israel Adler's invitation to me to plumb the archives of the World Centre for Jewish Music in Palestine was especially fortuitous during the formation of the larger concepts on which I base this book, for it allowed me to focus my research on an institution that stood at the juncture between Jewish life in Central Europe and in Palestine, hence bearing witness to both cultural streams flowing through the German-Jewish community.

My fieldwork in the Federal Republic of Germany was no less dependent on the help of consultants and colleagues too numerous to list here. Still, I must thank Evi Gilles, Gérard Rosenfeld, and Joachim Hemmerle for laying the foundation for my intensive 1982 research in Mannheim. Without Karl Otto Watzinger's tireless devotion to chronicling the history of Mannheim's Jewish community my own understanding and interpretation of that history would today remain hopelessly incomplete. Hansrainer and Ute Bosbach of nearby Ramsen opened doors for this book in quite different ways, first because of the hospitality they provide year after year and, even more important, because of the new generation of German intellectuals they symbolize for me, critical in their assessment of the past and hopeful in their vision of a workable future.

For a wealth of reasons that never cease to amaze me the Deutsches Volksliedarchiv, Freiburg im Breisgau, has been one of the richest sources for perspectives on the musical life of the Jewish community of Central Europe. In 1981 I spent a convivial two months at Freiburg, assisted in my study of printed German-Jewish songbooks by Jürgen Dittmar and Barbara James. In more recent studies of the broad range of oral Jewish musical traditions in Europe, Otto Holzapfel has given unflagging help and has shared his philological acumen with me. Access to the holdings of yet another archive was also indispensable to this book, namely the Stadtarchiv Mannheim. To these archives in Freiburg and Mannheim, and to their staffs, I offer many, many thanks.

Work on this book—the initial research and the processes of writing and rewriting—was possible only because of the generous support I received from grants and fellowships. During my first year in Israel (1980-81) I was fortunate enough to receive a travel grant from the University of Illinois at Urbana-Champaign and a grant from the American Friends of the Hebrew University. Doctoral dissertation fellowships from the Fulbright-Hays Commission and the National Foundation for Jewish Culture permitted a second year of fieldwork in Israel. A fellowship from the Memorial Foundation for Jewish Culture made a return visit to Israel possible in the summer of 1983. Finally, publication of this book has benefited from a very generous subvention from the National Foundation for Jewish Culture, awarded as a result of the NFJC 1985 Post-Doctoral Publication Program. I am extremely grateful to all of these organizations, whose generosity has made this book possible.

Judith McCulloh is an Executive Editor with remarkable faith in her authors. She has shepherded this book through more stages at the University of Illinois Press than I can remember. Even in my most curmudgeonly moments she kept me going, always employing the same gentle touch. All authors should be so lucky as one of Judy's charges. It is, no doubt, the task of a copyeditor to sharpen both the prose and the thinking of an author. Carol Bolton Betts not only carried out this task with the utmost professionalism, but made it a pleasurable learning experience for me; for this, I am very grateful to Carol.

It has always been my custom to thank my parents for lifetime support. For this book, however, that gesture of acknowledgment falls still short of the thanks and appreciation that they really deserve. By attending to thousands of minor details while I was in Israel — forwarding mail, buying books, editing a few articles — my parents made two years of fieldwork seem as if there were no inconveniences whatsoever. This book itself bears witness to my mother's artistic labors, for it is she who prepared the maps and drew several other illustrations. Most important, however, my parents adopted my interests in this endeavor as their own, never letting their encouragement flag for a moment. I couldn't ask anything more from Vilas and Florence Bohlman.

It will surprise few that I have dedicated this book to Bruno Nettl. As a teacher Bruno first acquainted me with the *Zweistromland* of Central European Jewish society, a land so much a part of Bruno's own upbringing and, though he may not admit it, the incredible breadth of his ethnomusicological worldview. As a colleague Bruno has challenged me to rethink early assumptions and to engage in a ceaseless process of reformulating ideas I might too facilely hope to be immutable. As a friend Bruno has shown me that to be an ethnomusicologist requires far more than factitious career decisions, rather an insatiable desire to understand human behavior and the profound expressive meaning that music has for all human beings.

My family has been anything but patient and forbearing during the past years of research and writing. Instead, their involvement has been active and restive, always concerned that the work proceed even when I was unsure of the direction it should take. My wife, Christine, accompanied me during the early years of fieldwork, and our daughter, Andrea, was along on her first stint of field research before the age of one. Benjamin was almost two before he accompanied us on such a sojourn, but I doubt that this will prove to be too late in his life. I really cannot imagine this book without such teamwork to keep it going. Surely the book belongs also to Christine, Andrea, and Benjamin; they know this, but the reader, too, should know what a special family they really are.

"The Land Where Two Streams Flow"

Introduction

THE CONCERT-GOERS entered the small, makeshift auditorium in tacit orderliness. The chamber concert they were about to attend this Saturday afternoon was a traditional event in the week, one which this audience observed with ritualized regularity during Jerusalem's winter and spring months. Chairs had been enlisted from sundry functions throughout the Van Leer Institute, home to the Israel Academy of Arts, Letters, and Sciences, to transform the open space of the quasi-gallery temporarily into a concert hall. The chairs at that part of the hall designated as the stage faced music stands and focused on the conductor's podium in the middle of their semicircle. The remaining chairs, too, bespoke the imminence of a concert, especially as the audience took their seats after filtering in from adjoining ramps and rooms in customary response to the performers who had begun to enter from the library *cum* greenroom.

Further signifying the ritual aspect of the concert was the relatively formal attire of the audience. Almost all the men wore jackets and ties; women, when not wearing suits, at least wore dresses. Such clothing would strike some as out of place in Israeli society, where informal dress is the rule, if not the fashion; but this audience was decidedly unfashionable. The choice of clothing fitted the event at hand, the impending concert, mooring it to a tradition that all in attendance had known for years. In contrast, the small chamber orchestra gathering in the stage area was less formal, both in attire and action. Not all the men wore jackets; many were without ties; a few of the women players wore slacks.

Though frequent participants in the tradition of Sabbath afternoon chamber concerts, the performers did not project the same sense of familiarity as the audience. Apparent on this Saturday was the chamber ensemble's obvious sense of anticipation, almost nervousness. The program was new, but this was a group whose members played together almost daily. These were musicians from the symphony of the Israel Broadcasting Service (*Kol Israel*), and they were performing only a half block or so from their usual home, the Jerusalem Theatre. They knew their audience, too, for these were the subscribers to the symphony's Saturday afternoon chamber series, thereby making it financially viable. This audience represented the hard core of the symphony's supporters, and nerves would not seem to be in order.

Assuredness arrived in the person of Mendy Rodan, a Romanian-born conductor, highly respected for his interpretation of chamber works and a favorite of the audience. Silence filled the auditorium, and the listeners seemed almost spellbound in the prelude of silence ushering in the performance. Breaking the silence were rich sounds of a pianissimo. Almost antiphonally, the audience, too, broke its silence. A murmur arose and swelled like a wave, absorbing the warmth of the music, the soft sibilants of whispered German becoming momentarily one with the music.

"Schön!"

"Wie schön!"

"Unbeschreiblich schön!"

"Etwas wunderschön!"

The air of orderliness returned, the music itself dispelling any lingering nervousness as the chamber ensemble proceeded with its performance of Richard Wagner's *Siegfried Idyll.*

A concert of chamber music from the late nineteenth and early twentieth century might seem an unlikely venue for the expression of ethnicity. Yet very few of the circumstances surrounding this concert did not touch on complex questions of ethnicity. Few Israelis would fail to identify the concert behavior of the audience as typical of the German-speaking ethnic group or exceptional for the amalgam of ethnic groups constituting virtually the entirety of Israeli society. The repertory, too, at first might seem an unlikely candidate for ethnic music. Wagner, Brahms, Mahler, Schoenberg. Some would even regard the works of these composers the culmination of an era of absolute music, the very antithesis of ethnic music. But powerful values and a burden of symbolic weight had accrued to this music, so much so that no one in attendance could possibly be unaware of the cultural undertone of the concert. This was the music of the Central European ethnic group.[1]

Each of the composers and by extension their music symbolized quite different aspects of ethnicity for the audience. Arnold Schoenberg was the quintessential Central European Jewish composer of the early twentieth century. His had been a life that reaffirmed tradition through experimentation. By exploring at and beyond the outer limits of tonality, Schoenberg came to understand it better and to illumine its essence more intensely. Seemingly departing from Judaism through conversion in an age of liberal experimentation, he discovered the most profound promise for his music only through a return to the religion of his forebears late in life. Gustav Mahler had come to epitomize for this audience the creative Jewish musician pulled in myriad directions by the rapid social changes in *fin de siècle* Austria. The pressure on Mahler resulted from both internal and external causes, many of them marked by the confrontation of traditions Jewish and non-Jewish. The audience perceived in Mahler's music the feverish pace of cultural self-examination that was synonymous with their experiences in pre-Holocaust Europe. Brahms's niche in the ethnic consciousness of this audience was more nebulous, but it was exactly because he was so difficult to place that he disturbed the audience's sense of ethnicity so much. No, he was not Jewish; at least he lacked a Jewish upbringing—most in the audience could probably provide a version of accounts that one of Brahms's relatives had changed his name from Abrahamssohn to Brahms in order to ease the family's path into German society. Apocryphal anecdotes aside, the music of Brahms epitomized a German sound for many Israelis, thereby branding it with a stigma that had been lifted only in the early 1970s.

The ethnic associations of Richard Wagner were as unambiguous as they were redoubtable. To perform the music of Wagner publicly in Israel was illegal and cause for scandal, and every member in the audience was well aware—some even painfully aware—of prior attempts to do so. For many Israelis both Wagner and his music stand as symbols of the ugliest moment in German history and the millennia of Jewish suffering in the lands of the Diaspora, namely the Holocaust. For these symbols to achieve any form of sanction whatsoever through the performance of Wagner in Israel is for many Israelis unacceptable. The Wagner question long ago became a matter for public debate when various forms of pressure determined that the nation's musical organizations—particularly those supported by government subsidy—should not perform any Wagner. This proscription implicitly shifted a long-standing ethnic conflict to the concert stage, heightening the role Western art music would play as a potential symbol of ethnicity. Were Wagner universally recognized as beyond the pale of humanity, forbidding his music would seem quite superfluous. Someone, some group must perceive different meaning and value in the music of Wagner, as well as other European composers whose attitudes toward the Jews had been questionable. Some ethnic community must weigh Wagner's anti-Semitism against a different engagement of Jews with German culture. The audience listening attentively to *Siegfried Idyll* on 21 February 1981 in the Van Leer Institute represented a cross section of exactly that community.

During the decades since the Holocaust, opposition to the performance of Wagner in Israel has solidified and rallied behind the assertion of two basic issues. First, Richard Wagner was a flagrant anti-Semite who flaunted his belief that Jewish contributions were harmful to the purity of the German arts. Not only did he direct anti-Semitic invectives against Jewish musicians and artists — Mendelssohn, Meyerbeer, and Heine probably the best-known victims of such attacks — but his writings at times called for the outright destruction of Judaism; it is hardly surprising to find this call associated by the Wagner opponents with the Holocaust and extended to prohibition in Israel. Second, the Wagner opponents believe that Wagner's anti-Semitism encouraged Hitler to misuse the composer's music, thereby assigning it an order of blame for the Holocaust. It is not only the symbolic elevation of Wagner by the Nazis to which his opponents object, but the implementation of that elevation, that aggrandized Germanness, to insult and denigrate Jews through performance in the concentration camps.[2]

Those who support the performance of Wagner do not deny the charges of anti-Semitism against him. Nor do they wish to inflict emotional distress on concentration-camp survivors in Israel by exposing them to unpleasant memories. The supporters do, however, perceive a danger in the manner whereby the Wagner question has consistently arisen in public debate. Their reasoning, too, has several components. First, they object to the musical-historical lacuna that results when Wagner is systematically deleted from nineteenth-century cultural history. This artificial gap becomes more disturbing when accompanied by attempts to discredit Wagner's influence on subsequent musical developments. To pretend that his music did not exist cannot chart a new course for nineteenth-century music, it cannot ignore the reality that Wagner was an important, even beloved, part of the musical culture of German Jews. Second, the stigma attached to Wagner in Israel too often and too arbitrarily extends to other composers. Music in the German language, music whose message is inappropriately Christian, music by composers whose politics are suspect — all have fallen victim to public opinion and have been stricken from scheduled performances. The practice of proscribing at will has become yet another corollary to the objections of the pro-Wagner voices, for they interpret the ban on Wagner as a type of censorship. Censorship, in principle, has special meaning to the ethnic community because it was German censorship during the 1930s that imposed a new ghetto on Jews; indeed, the rationale employed by the Nazis to ban the music of these composers—that the music was too intimately bound to German culture—sounded little different from the claims of the anti-Wagner forces in Israel.[3] The Wagner supporters, thus, believe that Israel must rise above a tactic of ethnic exclusion used so successfully and injuriously by the Nazis.

One would not necessarily expect the Wagner question to bear equivocal ethnic associations. Many of the most adamant voices in opposition come from Central European immigrants. Few would question that German Jews were also victims of Nazi persecution and that virtually nothing was left of Jewish culture in Germany after World War II. Those directly receiving the brunt of Wagner's particular anti-Semitism were most frequently German Jews. But the association of the Wagner question with the Central European community persists. Shaping it are cultural concerns specific to the group itself and those more generally affecting Israeli society as a whole. There are those who hold that the music of Wagner accompanies, if at a distance, many other aspects that define the German ethnic community; accordingly, Wagner may be but one of a complex set of ethnic concerns, yet his role is central to those concerns. The importance of the German language in the Wagnerian *Gesamtkunstwerk* and its inseparability from certain expressions of cultural chauvinism draw attention to the persistence of German in the ethnic community. An unwillingness to abandon Wagner's music stands for the detractor as no less than an unwillingness to cast off the culture of Germany for that of Israel.

For the Central European community itself Wagner is only one aspect of a set of values that identify the traditions of Western art music as vital to the community's past and present culture. By no means is Wagner central to these values. One need but witness the rare occasions on which performances do occur and the pain taken to prevent a concert such as that featuring *Siegfried Idyll* from becoming truly public. Many in the ethnic community are only vaguely aware that Wagner performances take place at all; most are content when the performances remain covert. Indeed, had anyone imagined that there was a remote possibility that this concert at the Van Leer Institute would offend public sensitivity in Israel, the organizers would have omitted *Siegfried Idyll* and substituted an unobjectionable work.

All circumstances surrounding the concert instead suggested careful planning to ensure that the audience would include few from outside the ethnic group. The concert was part of an annual series of chamber music concerts at the institute. Its organizers come from the orchestra of the Israel Broadcasting Service, and they customarily use the occasion of the Saturday series to experiment, that is to program works that normally would not find a place in an orchestral series. As a genre, chamber music lends itself best to the unpretentious ambience of the Van Leer series. The concerts always take place at about 5:00 P.M. on Saturday afternoons, shortly before the end of the Sabbath. No advertisements for the series appear in the press, nor are extra tickets on sale at the door. Entrance, though not restricted, is usually available only to those who subscribe to the entire series or to special guests informed by word of mouth. There is rarely a prior announcement of coming programs, and many subscribers remain unaware of the exact content of a program until the afternoon of the performance itself. That the musicians and the audience share a common feeling for a concert's immediate function and broader cultural ramifications is understood by all.

It is not surprising that most subscription holders for the Van Leer series come from the Central European community, for they are the major supporters of chamber music in Israel. The Van Leer Institute lies on the border of Reḥavia, the residential district most heavily populated by the Central European immigrants. Even the location of the concerts is of considerable importance, for most subscribers, many of them lacking automobiles, are able to walk to the concerts at a time in the week when public transportation in Jerusalem is not running.

Performances of the music of Wagner and Richard Strauss, also banned in Israel, occurred several times during the 1980-81 season. Never was there discussion that such concerts sidestepped public proscription. Instead, the programs were created in such a way that the inclusion of a work by Wagner seemed inoffensive and coincidental, no more than the vehicle necessary to express some deeper meaning. The printed program of the concert including *Siegfried Idyll*, for example, announced that it was a "Concert of the Early Works of Schoenberg and the Influences on Them." With Schoenberg announced as the actual theme, complementing his *Chamber Symphony*, op. 9, with Brahms's *Quartet in A Major*, op. 26, no. 2, Mahler's *Piano Quartet in a minor*, and *Siegfried Idyll* seems not the least bit incongruous, but still hints that the choice of programming might be as much precautionary as necessitated by adherence to theme. The repertory for the concert set forth ethnic boundaries that were both general and specific, thereby eliminating as much as possible any vulnerability to external criticism.

The cultural attitudes shared by the group made internal criticism unlikely. For those attending the concert it was not really Wagner who was at issue anyway. Most important was the concert itself: the concert as a social institution; the concert as a means of furthering the musical traditions most highly valued by the ethnic community; the concert as a symbol of ethnicity. There would be many concerts in the months to come, for this was the height of the concert season. To different degrees the multitude of concerts and the differentiation of style and genre that marked the performance of Western art music in Israel would also reflect aspects of ethnicity. Some would highlight the vigor of young Israeli composers; others would rely on the specialization requisite for the performance of a single genre. Some concerts would take place in private homes; others in overflowing auditoriums. Amidst this abundance it is unlikely that a work by Wagner was heard more than once or twice more before the end of the season.

Amidst the diversity the only invariable factor was the audience. Whether large or small, the audience would have a stable and devoted core to whom each concert was far more than entertainment or the chance to hear a visiting artist from the United States. Rather, this core sought to nurture a cultural tradition with roots in the Jewish communities of nineteenth-century Germany and to cultivate new forms of expression and new patterns of continuity. In some way each performance reinforced the cultural values constituting this tradition while still permitting it to embody new values. But on a very few occasions, perhaps a mid-winter Sabbath afternoon, the music of a composer forbidden in Israel also became a component of the tradition.

The musical culture of Central European Israelis has developed with remarkable continuity despite the disruption wrought by anti-Semitism in Europe, the displacement of immigration, and the destruction of the Holocaust. This musical culture remains today one of the most visible means of identifying the ethnic group with a German cultural background and documenting its historical evolution both in Central Europe and Israel. When immigrants from Central Europe arrived in Palestine during the 1930s, they immediately entered a world that differed completely from the urban culture they had previously known. The cultural life — concerts, theater, the university — that they had enjoyed and supported so passionately was largely lacking or struggling because of only minimal public support. The German-speaking immigrants could have responded to this new world in a variety of ways. They could have joined thriving rural communal settlements, such as the kibbutz. They could have redirected their careers to adapt to the socioeconomic structure instituted by earlier immigrants. Instead, they sought to maintain relative continuity vis-à-vis the pre-immigrant culture. Confronted with the options of changing radically to adapt to the Eastern European ideal of a new Jewish state in the Levant, or themselves establishing a new cultural order based on the enlightened and emancipated society that had benefited them so profoundly since the beginning of the nineteenth century, the Central European immigrants chose the latter. In so doing, they realized a new direction for the cultural history of Palestine and later of Israel.

Although the Central European immigrants initially established a sub-society that reflected continuity, the tremendous contrast with Israeli society also necessitated changes of enormous magnitude. These changes had to answer not only to the prevailing pioneer ideology in Palestine, but also to the mounting threat to German-Jewish culture posed by the shifting political forces in Europe. External confrontation both in Europe and Palestine tempered the interaction of continuity and change.

The continuity linking immigrant to pre-immigrant cultures followed a century during which the Jewish community in Central Europe had undergone a transformation unlike anything it had witnessed since the inception of Jewish settlement in Europe. It was a transformation that arose primarily within the community itself, and it afforded a degree and form of independence unlike any experienced by European Jewry prior to the nineteenth century. The structure of German-Jewish society distinguished it both from non-Jewish society and from other Jewish groups in Europe. This structure was amply evident in the musical culture of Central European Jews and at times was most vividly expressed through the musical activity of the Jewish community.

The ethnic foundations of the Central European ethnic group are unusually complex because, in both Europe and Israel, German-speaking Jews had to interact with other ethnic groups, both Jewish and non-Jewish; a full understanding of the group is not possible without considering both patterns of ethnic interaction, with other Jews and with non-Jews. Central European Jews also differ somewhat from many immigrant groups — in Israel and elsewhere — for their social position had benefited from their engagement with the arts and cultures of non-Jewish European society, prior to immigration and then again afterward. This status had both positive and negative ramifications, which together exacerbated differences between the Central European Jews and other groups. One hallmark of this status was the active participation in and support of Western art music until certain repertories of that music came to function as symbols of ethnicity for the group itself.

Immigration from Central Europe transpired during only a few years, thereby encouraging the conditions favorable to continuity. The *aliyah germanit*, "the German wave of immigrants," occurred entirely within a six-year period from 1933 to 1939. This same concentration, nevertheless, produced considerable rupture and shock, especially as the fear and desperation of Central European Jews escalated during the final years of the decade. Still, the ability of the ethnic group to establish itself in the wake of such disruption again bears witness to the underlying force of continuity.

The processes of continuity and change often exhibit dialectical interdependence at the heart of immigrant studies. Perhaps this is due to a universal human propensity to view the present as if it were an extension of the past. If so, the immigrant is resident in two worlds, the reality of each shaping the image of the other. Distinguishing an immigrant is his own unique relation to a particular past. The Central European Israeli differs from all other Israelis because Germany and German culture are part of her personal history. Banal or simplistic as such a statement seems on the surface, its meaning in Israel has a more troublesome meaning, for the infamy of Germany in Israel remains unmatched by any other modern nation. The immigrant from Germany cannot escape this association with the past. His culture, her way of life appear to many Israelis as residues from the German culture that decimated European Jewry, hence challenging his sense of continuity with Europe like that of no other ethnic group in Israel. When the Central European immigrant strives for continuity, it is often in spite of the tremendous pressure that would have her do otherwise.

Why would the Central European immigrant maintain a pattern of relative continuity even in the face of disapproving external opinion? The answers to such a question are hardly simple, but this book must address several of them. There is one straightforward answer that consistently serves to qualify those of a thornier nature: the immigrant valued in continuity the extension of a cultural history in which the Jewish community of Central Europe was increasingly dependent on itself. During the century prior to the Holocaust, music in the community often crystallized and then became a vehicle for expressing this new autonomy. Jewish musical organizations served the community in more diverse ways; musical repertories, whether for the Jewish singing society or the synagogue chorus, underwent continual and considerable change; growing numbers of community members participated directly in community musical activities. Most important, the increasingly vigorous musical life of the Jewish community bespoke a concomitant awareness of new settlements in Palestine, and within this awareness were germinating the seeds of subsequent continuity.

With the experience of rapidly intensifying Jewish cultural awareness so immediately a part of their past, the Central European immigrants during the 1930s were not predisposed simply to start anew in Palestine. They did not quickly embrace the halutz ("pioneer") approach to settlement that prevailed among the Eastern European settlers from earlier immigrant waves. The Central Europeans set forth instead to reestablish a culture they believed to be intensely Jewish, not in the traditional, religious sense, but clearly in a modern, enlightened sense. For this they needed the city, the urbanized cultural infrastructure that had served the transformation of the Jewish community in Central Europe so effectively. Having left an urban environment, most Central European immigrants chose to settle in the cities of Palestine, even though these were hardly more than small towns in the 1930s. But the sheer mass of immigration from Central Europe would stimulate the growth of the cities and make it possible for them to support new cultural undertakings. The immigrants would populate new residential districts at the outskirts of Jerusalem, Tel Aviv, and Haifa. There, too, the immigrants would establish new economic and cultural institutions that would allow them to pursue a way of life with which they were familiar. These same institutions would quickly become synonymous with the burgeoning cities themselves, making Israel one of the most urbanized nations of the world within only a few decades.

Just as urbanization during the 1930s transformed the socioeconomic structure of Palestine, so too did it leave a profound impact on the practices of music. The musical life assumed a radically different form immediately upon the arrival of the immigrants of the German aliyah. Musical organizations modeled on those of the Central European community quickly took root, providing positions and sustenance for immigrant musicians. Accordingly, more musicians felt the attraction of a viable musical career in Palestine. Not only could professional musicians from the Jewish orchestras of Frankfurt or Berlin find positions in the nascent orchestras of Tel Aviv and Jerusalem, but the new music academies could offer student certificates to those wishing to escape Germany and study music in Palestine. The new immigrants, accustomed to attending concerts frequently and financially endowing a broad range of musical activities, soon filled the seats of concert halls in Palestine. Because the Central Europeans were eager to experience the same level of musical professionalism they had known prior to immigration, they willingly and generously supported a broad spectrum of musical ensembles, ranging from symphony orchestras to chamber groups.

The concentration of the German *aliyah* into only a few years led rapidly to the birth of an ethnic culture influenced considerably by the cultural values of the Central European immigrants. Propelled by a fervent pursuit of humanistic and artistic activity in Europe, the immigrants implanted a similar spirit at the heart of their cultural life in Palestine. The German language and literature persisted, even flourishing in some literary and intellectual circles. The immigrants were extremely active in all areas of the country's musical life and influenced that life profoundly well into the early decades of statehood.

Four leitmotifs have recurred during the half-century history of the Central European ethnic group in Israel, and I shall employ these as centers for discussion throughout this book. The first derives from the historical consciousness of the ethnic group and the various ways such a consciousness leads to the expression of cultural continuity with the former Jewish community in Central Europe. Second, soon after its arrival the Central European ethnic group instigated particularly far-reaching processes of socioeconomic change whose impact on the arts in Israel has subsequently been extensive. Third, a major achievement of the Central European immigrants was their organization of small- and large-scale institutions that enabled them to consolidate many of their own cultural activities while also influencing broader areas of Israeli society in general. Finally, the musical life of the ethnic community reflected these other domains of change by transforming Western art music — primarily compositions by Central European composers from the eighteenth and nineteenth centuries — so that it functioned as ethnic music, that is as a traditional music distinguishing the Central Europeans from other ethnic groups.

Western art music acquired the attributes of ethnic music because its diverse functions have spawned equally diverse patterns of shared behavior particular to the Central European community. In the immigrant subsociety this has meant that new musical organizations have evolved with the specific end of cultivating the art-music traditions of Central Europe. The regularly organized concerts of chamber music that take place in the home — generally known as the *Hauskonzert* or *Hausmusik* — exemplify yet another essential quality of the Central European musical culture: inclusivity rather than exclusivity. *Hausmusik* has served to protect certain ethnic values, while also opening the community's boundaries to other ethnic and social groups.

Change and diversity have therefore come to function as necessary components of the ethnicity attributable to Western art music. The Central European penchant for establishing a wide range of cultural institutions empowered the group's contributions to extend beyond the community itself. In this book I approach change as an ally of the ethnic community and its values. Change has enabled the preservation of these values, even when many external elements of tradition have disappeared. Although the musical institutions that took root during the German *aliyah* still survive, their complexion has metamorphosed significantly during the intervening half century. Whereas the music academies at first largely served students from Germany, those from all ethnic groups now attend. The Austro-German repertory has no priority and is even less important than many other repertories. More intimate music-making, especially chamber music, continues to thrive in many areas of Israel, but it does so only because of a broadened appeal to diverse ethnic groups.

The specialized and concentrated pursuit of Western art music associated with the Central European community has gradually ceased to define specific patterns of ethnicity. Concomitantly and in accordance with the passage of time, the boundaries of the community will become increasingly obscure, and within several generations they will disappear. The eventual passing of the Central European community notwithstanding, the musical culture that has grown from foundations laid during the German *aliyah* will survive as a lasting monument to the immigrant group and the traditions that it bore from Central Europe.

NOTES

1. Throughout this book the term "Central European," when it designates a Jewish ethnic group or community, refers to Jews from nations in which they spoke German and participated in a German cultural life. In addition to designating Germany and Austria, Central European in this usage includes Jews from Czechoslovakia, from German-governed areas of Eastern Europe (e.g., "Breslau" and "Danzig" in Poland), and in some cases urban Eastern European communities whose closest affinity was to a German-speaking intelligentsia. I prefer to use the adjective "German-Jewish" to qualify some aspect of the ethnic group's culture, rather than the group itself.

2. In recent years German scholars, too, have debated the painful associations of Wagner's anti-Semitism to his music; see the collection of essays in Heinz-Klaus Metzger and Rainer Riehn, eds., *Richard Wagner: Wie anti-semitisch darf ein Künstler sein?* (Munich: edition text + kritik, 1981). See also Jacob Katz, *The Darker Side of Genius: Richard Wagner's Anti-Semitism* (Hanover, N.H.: University Press of New England, 1986).

3. The channeling of anti-Semitism and persecution through censorship of the arts took numerous forms, the most significant and effective of which are the subjects of the following: Kurt Düwell, "Jewish Cultural Centers in Nazi Germany: Expectations and Accomplishments," in *The Jewish Response to German Culture: From the Enlightenment to the Second World War,* ed. Jehuda Reinharz and Walter Schatzberg (Hanover, N.H.: University Press of New England, 1985), pp. 294-316; Herbert Freeden, *Jüdisches Theater in Nazideutschland* (Tübingen: J. C. B. Mohr [Paul Siebeck] Verlag, 1964); and Erwin Lichtenstein, "Der Kulturbund der Juden in Danzig, 1933-1938," *Zeitschrift für die Geschichte der Juden* 10 (1973): 181-90.

1

The Cultural Legacy of the German *Aliyah*

Die zwei Städte meines Zweistromlandes blieben München
und Jerusalem, aber über beiden leuchtet die Schrift auf:
Denn wir haben hier keine bleibende Stadt,
sondern die zukünftige suchen wir.

THAT A CENTRAL EUROPEAN community endures in Israel is recognized
by both its members and those of other ethnic groups. The community
has changed in many ways since the major influx of immigrants from
Central Europe during the 1930s, but change has nonetheless failed to obviate
all the cultural boundaries separating the community from other parts of
Israeli society. The community's boundaries manifest themselves in different
ways, depending on the particular perspective from which one views them.
Instead of offering a neat and convenient description of the community,
internal and external viewpoints expose a complex and confusing image of
an ethnic group whose historical consciousness partakes equally of present
and past, of the modernization of present-day Israel and the volatile cultural
vigor of an often idealized former Germany, of the waters in the community's chosen land where two rivers flow.

Distinguishing the Central European community more than any other
single factor is its passionate involvement in the intellectual and artistic life
of Israel. Fine universities, scientific and humanistic contributions of world
renown, flourishing musical and literary production; to many Central Europeans these are the qualities that mold a great nation. And these are the
qualities that have grown directly from the thirst for *Bildung,* the spirit of
enlightened humanism that had come to drive the dynamo of German-
Jewish society at the time of its emancipation during the nineteenth century.[1]
The community's deeply rooted support for Israel even finds expression in
its preoccupation with the arts and education, often at the expense of the
more usual Israeli fascination with political and economic machinations.
Thus, despite a complex community structure, the Central European de-

votion to Israel's cultural life—at times reaching almost obsessive fanaticism—serves as a core of ethnic unity.

Who are the members of the Central European ethnic community? In what ways have they maintained their group's relation with the cultural life of the immigrants fleeing Europe during the 1930s? To what degree does the ethnic community of today reflect the German-Jewish culture of pre-Nazi Europe? Was, indeed, the immigrant generation really representative of German-Jewish culture at all? These are all questions whose subtle differences we must unravel if we are to understand the ways in which German-Jewish culture was transferred to and reestablished in Israel. In Europe *Bildung* had become for Jews not just a progressive attitude toward the arts, but a fundamentally new voice for Judaism itself. Central European Jews in the half century prior to the Holocaust were growing closer to, not farther away from, a new awareness of Jewish society. Moreover, the musical life of the community bore vivid and visible witness to this transformation. A renewed sense of community, however, was ill-equipped to stave off the more massive transformation of Germany itself. Ironically, the same forces that made the Jewish community more vulnerable also intensified its most salient underpinnings, making it a more tangible and viable entity. It is hardly surprising, then, that many having to flee Germany would seek to find fertile soil in Palestine in order that the renascent Jewish culture of the German urban center might again discover and tap resources increasingly denied them as 1939 approached.

In many ways, the immigrants of the 1930s represented a cross section of Central European Jewish society. One reason for the general representativeness of the immigrants was the urgency and speed with which they had to leave Germany; time for carefully derived decisions and the implementation of new careers elsewhere was simply not available. There were also reasons for this cross section that were specific to the community itself. The subsociety of Jews in Central Europe was as a whole economically very healthy. When forced to measure up against the stringent financial and employment criteria imposed on immigration by the British Mandate, few German Jews simply failed to secure entrance into Palestine. Accordingly, no single economic or professional group was effectively blocked from immigration during the entire decade. In its early years the immigrant community could depend on the presence of many, if not most, of its former structural components.

The Central European immigrants of the 1930s differed dramatically from previous immigrants to Palestine. It was not uncommon, for example, for the Eastern Europeans in earlier immigrant movements to spend years in Zionist organizations preparing to be a *ḥalutz* in Palestine, perhaps abandoning a former profession to become a kibbutznik. Responding to the precipitous rise of Nazism, the Central Europeans arrived in quite significant numbers within only a few years, hence designating the 1930s as the German immigration, the *aliyah germanit.*[2] Settlement patterns of the Central Europeans were also fundamentally different from previous immigrants. The new immigrants preferred the cities and generally felt little attraction to those areas, such as the kibbutzim, that coupled socialist attitudes toward labor with communal living patterns. The financial welfare of many Central Europeans further distinguished them. Because they were allowed to transfer considerable funds from their bank accounts, they were often financially more secure in Palestine than were earlier immigrants.[3] These funds enabled the new immigrants to establish small businesses or even to incorporate larger ones together with other German immigrants. Finally, because the Central Europeans arrived as a more representative cross section of their society, their immigrant community retained much of its previous infrastructure. That this would not necessarily produce a "Little Germany" was already implicit prior to immigration; that it would not yield to the prevailing *ḥalutz* philosophy was explicit.

Three periods subdivide the German *aliyah* according to the relative difficulty of departure from Europe and the changing legal restrictions on entrance into Palestine: 1933-35; 1936-38; and 1939-45. Immigration statistics available for the periods differ considerably, depending on the accessibility of reliable numbers and on the censuses one cites. The British government and the Jewish Agency, for example, often generated conflicting statistics, both bodies, of course, to protect their own interests. The German component in the total immigration during the 1930s was approximately 50,000, of which some 80 percent held German citizenship.[4] Still, German-speaking Jews accounted for only about 20 percent of all immigrants during the 1930s.[5] Throughout the first two periods of the *aliyah* German immigration remained fairly steady because the severe quotas leveled by the Mandate affected the group less than others. German immigrants constituted approximately 50 percent of all those classified as either "capitalists" (individuals with at least 1,000 Palestine pounds) or "students." Thus, it was not sheer quantity that distinguished the German immigrants, but their involvement in professions only sparsely represented in previous immigrant waves and by other groups during the fifth *aliyah*. The number of businessmen and industrialists, for example, increased sharply during the 1930s, bringing in turn an influx of financial potential. Previously, businessmen and industrialists had never accounted for more than 20 percent of the total population of Palestine.[6] Other professions felt the impact of German immigration in equally profound ways. In 1931, only 847 physicians lived in Palestine. German immigrants would contribute more than that number during the three years from 1933 to 1935; such an increase was equally dramatic for lawyers, teachers, and public administrators.[7]

Widespread transformation of Palestine's socioeconomic structure resulted from the impact of Central European immigration. Most profoundly affected were the financial, scientific, political, and humanistic sectors and professions. Before the German *aliyah* the economy of Palestine had depended heavily on agriculture. Small industries were present, but their productive capacities were modest. From 1933 to 1939, the number of industrial firms increased from 1,625 to 4,325, which boosted the industrial labor force from 14,000 to 36,500.[8] Industrialization stimulated the growth of the cities, which in turn provided the basis for the cultural activities transferred from the urban Jewish community of Central Europe to Palestine.

Central European cultural organizations quickly sprang up to assist new immigrants in all aspects of adaptation to the new land. The largest organization of German-speaking immigrants, the *Hitachduth Oley Germania* ("Association of Immigrants from Germany"), established a cultural branch in 1934, the *Vereinigung für Kultur und Erziehung* ("Union for Culture and Education").[9] The cultural branch established wide-ranging educational programs, both for nurturing the arts and for encouraging rapid acquaintance with more practical aspects of life in Palestine, for example by offering extensive courses of Hebrew language instruction. The *Vereinigung* thus provided one of the first instances of institutionalized language study for new immigrants. The *Hitachduth Oley Germania* also launched publication programs for both books and periodicals. German publications flourished during the 1930s, setting new standards for the publishing industry in Palestine. In the late 1930s, Salman Schocken moved his publishing house from Berlin to Palestine, thus transferring the major German-Jewish publishing concern to the new land.

Professional integration into Israeli society was not without its problems for many immigrants. Intellectuals, especially writers, found it difficult to adapt to the demands of the new culture and its changing audiences. To parry these problems the ethnic community relied extensively on its organizational resources, that is, its ability to form institutions to support cultural activities.[10] These cultural institutions generally reflected the structure of similar organizations within the pre-immigrant Jewish community; many, in fact, were altered not at all during the transferral to Palestine.

Musical institutions were among those that the new immigrants most effectively reconstituted; not surprisingly, some of the most visible evidence of the Central European community's penchant for organization survives in such organizations. During the 1930s Central European immigrants founded the major orchestras of Israel, the Palestine Orchestra (later the Israel Philharmonic) and the broadcasting orchestra of the radio (also known as the Jerusalem Symphony), which, in turn, largely contained a membership of musicians from that ethnic group. New music academies also came into existence at this time, drawing from the influx of immigrant musicians. These musical institutions depended on more than simply an increase in the population of musicians, for their administrative capacity and financial survival was contingent upon the socioeconomic transformation afforded by Central European immigration. Not only did this transformation provide a large measure of economic security and broadly based audience support for the burgeoning concert life, but it established a bulwark behind which the musical institutions could survive the radical and irreparable severance from their most important resource: the Jewish community of Central Europe.

The Central European ethnic community is not without its detractors. Members of the community have long borne the name "Yekkes" (or "Jeckes"), a label that is at once derogatory and respectful. The exact meaning of Yekke may vary according to social and linguistic background, but those applying the term usually mean to suggest that the German-speaking Jew is out of step with the rest of Israeli society. Eastern European Jews were probably the first to apply the term to German Jews. Pre-immigrant usage suggests origins in the dialect of the region around Cologne, in which the word frequently designated a "clown." Another possible source stems from the era of emancipation, when German Jews abandoned the traditional long frock of orthodoxy for the shorter jacket, or *Jacke,* worn by non-Jews, thus signifying departure from the ghetto and conformity to the customs of the external society. In Israel this variant of the German *Jacke* is also a frequent explanation. There, however, the term further implies that German Jews are so staid that even in the heat of an Israeli summer most will not think to remove a formal coat or suit jacket.

Whatever its origins, Israelis outside the Central European community often invoke the term as an ethnic slur. An entire genre of jokes with the Yekke as its brunt has evolved in Israel; almost always in these jokes the

Yekke appears as an individual not quite assimilated into Israeli society.[11] The widespread use of the term in Israel has caused it to enter into common parlance, and today nearly any Israeli could both characterize a stereotypic Yekke and offer a litany of Yekke jokes. The various images of the Yekke, thus, lend further shape to the Central European ethnic community by sharpening the differences between its presumably naive adherence to pre-immigrant culture and the realities of life in Israel and the Middle East.

If one searches for definitions of the Yekke type, through both general Israeli or sociological literature,[12] a rather surprising image for an ethnic caricature emerges. Heading the list of characteristics is usually exceptional discipline; Yekkes labor with zeal simply because they like to do so. Daily life is characterized by orderliness; the Yekke arrives at a 10:00 A.M. appointment at 10:00 A.M., not simply sometime before lunch.[13] Yekkes emphasize the importance of the arts and humanistic education; many continue to regard *Bildung* as the most valuable measure of one's achievement. Despite this obsessive concern for education, many Yekkes reputedly cannot speak fluent Hebrew, much less passable Yiddish, which is even stranger because of the relation to their own mother tongue of German. The list of ethnic traits differs qualitatively from the motifs in other ethnic jokes in Israel and, for that matter, Jewish humor elsewhere. The Yekke in the joke seems like a fairly upstanding individual. The Yekke remains, however, an anomaly in Israeli society. His or her characteristic behavior is both respected and mocked for its artificiality.

There are other negative sides to the Yekke character in the popular preconception. A failure to master Hebrew is sometimes taken as a lack of fully accepting Israel, especially when that should extend to the religious polity of the modern state. Some see that same failure as the absence of sufficient former orientation to Judaism, which would have provided the Yekke with a foundation for quickly learning modern Hebrew.[14] The Yekke also contrasts dramatically with the *halutz*, who laid the foundations for the modern state in the earliest periods of immigration. Whereas the pioneer endeavored to build from scratch, the Yekke did not willingly discard a European past. Ultimately, the Yekke could be no more than the emigrant from an assimilated society in which Jewish culture had long ago been abandoned; accordingly, the ability of the Yekke to make a commitment to a new Jewish culture was subject to question.

The negative assessments of the Yekke, of course, derive from a stereotyped image, one not shared by all. Others recognize that the term describes a way of acting and responding to a particular environment, rather than a belief system. Thus, a Yekke may be religiously orthodox or may have participated actively in Zionist organizations prior to immigration. There is, furthermore, no real connection between complete assimilation and the Yekke type. By definition, the term applies only to Jews, an implicit recognition of a non-assimilated status; that the Yekke stood out from non-Jewish society can be assumed from the complex of meanings the term has historically conveyed.

Many characteristics of the Yekke are also regarded as generally positive. The economic transformation that took place during the 1930s and 1940s owed much to the attributes of hard work, punctuality, and orderliness that were inseparable from the Central European community. The Yekke's passionate respect for a humanistic education was also indispensable for the nation-building process. Yet even this attribute occasionally yields to the exaggerated juxtaposition of positive and negative traits. It is the faith in Western culture, for example, that made it inconceivable for many Central European immigrants to leave pianos and personal libraries in Europe. Even during the late 1930s, when exit from Germany was most complicated, restricted, and dangerous, the unwieldiness of the family piano—often a grand piano—rarely dissuaded the immigrant from shipping it to Palestine. Although the risk involved might make such decisions seem slightly ludicrous, many immigrants saw an even greater cultural risk in a land bereft of pianos. The piano, so vital to *Hausmusik,* teaching, and the maintenance of a wide variety of other musical traditions, also contributed fundamentally to the building of a new musical culture. Had the Central Europeans not brought family pianos and trunks of musical scores, the musical life of Israel might be very different today.

Few areas in the expressive culture of the Central European community stir as much controversy and produce such conflict as the complex role of the German language. It is hardly surprising that overt hatred should often be expressed toward the language because of its association with the Holocaust. For many in the community, however, the historical associations of the language are quite different. German is a language whose cultural value depends more on great literature and philosophy, on the role played by *Bildung* in the emancipation of Jewish artistic and intellectual life. The conflict centered around German has intensified as a result of the language's failure to drop from currency in the Central European community. Though officially shunned, German has not disappeared from the cultural activities of many immigrants and is even essential to some activities. To both the Central Europeans and other ethnic groups the German language stands as a special case, a language symbolic in ways that none other could be. It is a language that defines the Central European community in ways unique, yet fundamental to its structure.

For the early pioneers settling in Palestine Hebrew was an essential element reestablishing contact with an ancient ancestral culture. In the early decades of the twentieth century Central European communities were also expanding programs of Hebrew language training, which similarly increased community awareness of the language as a symbol of historical and contemporary Jewish culture. When they arrived as settlers in Palestine, however, the Central European immigrants were somewhat slower to abandon their mother tongue and replace it with Hebrew.[15] They preferred to deny a communicative role to neither Hebrew nor German, instead allowing dual roles for the languages in both cultural streams within the community. With the heavy influx of German-speaking immigrants during the 1930s, use of German in Palestine increased substantially, especially when compared to its previously negligible role. Many non-German speakers quite naturally regarded this change with some trepidation and as an affront to the nation-building function they had envisaged for Hebrew.

Nor did German disappear from the ethnic group during the early years of statehood. A 1948 survey of 50,867 individuals who spoke German as a mother tongue (virtually identical with the number of Germans immigrating during the German *aliyah)* indicated that 41 percent spoke only German as an "everyday spoken language." Fourteen percent spoke mainly German, but occasionally took recourse to Hebrew; 45 percent used Hebrew as a first language.[16] These figures represent an extremely low percentage of Hebrew use when compared to many other immigrant groups, especially considering the lag of at least ten years since immigration.

Conducting field research in the early 1960s, Eva Beling discovered that the trend showing only selective use of Hebrew was still characteristic of the Central European community thirty years after the German *aliyah* had begun. Of those interviewed, 51 percent spoke only German within the family, and 47 percent spoke only German with friends; 23 percent spoke a mixture of German and Hebrew within the family, and 18 percent spoke a mixture of the two languages with friends. Only 26 percent spoke Hebrew as a first language within the family, while 35 percent spoke Hebrew as a first language among friends.[17] These statistics further illustrate other contexts of social interaction requisite for a persistent ethnic community. Most of those interviewed lived within close proximity of others who spoke German, thus making everyday use of Hebrew unnecessary.[18] Considered together, the various statistical studies of German-speaking immigrants reveal that they supplanted German with Hebrew very slowly and that the language retained a salient function in defining the ethnic community.

The reasons for Hebrew's slow and rather restricted inroads into the community are again manifold, having both positive and negative facets. Most immigrants from Central Europe had very little exposure to either classical or modern Hebrew prior to immigration. Unlike their coreligionists from Eastern Europe, speakers of German lacked familiarity with the Hebrew alphabet that knowledge of Yiddish provided. When the Central Europeans arrived in Palestine, programs of language instruction, *ulpanim,* were either very primitive or nonexistent in most places. Immigrants who wanted to learn Hebrew, therefore, found it necessary either to hire tutors or learn Hebrew on their own, and more often than not this, too, was not possible.[19]

The professional situation of the German-speaking immigrants also enters into the explanations for the slow acquisition of Hebrew fluency. They did not find or seek those occupations preferred by the earlier settlers, but worked in the more urbanized sectors of the social structure. Those who took positions that depended on the British government—for example, musicians employed at the radio network—actually confronted a far more pressing need to learn English. English was the language of all legal work, so the high percentage of lawyers accompanying the German *aliyah* first studied English in order to meet British licensing requirements. Many of these same lawyers worked with German reparation agencies after World War II, where again their knowledge of German, not Hebrew, was professionally most valuable.

German also became professionally important in the business and residential districts that formed rapidly during the 1930s. In the business district of Tel Aviv, established primarily by German-speaking merchants, there was relatively low demand for languages other than German, and English was equally as important as Hebrew. In Jerusalem, however, the need for a mastery of Hebrew was more pressing. For a Central European academic to teach at the Hebrew University he or she needed to learn Hebrew quickly. Governmental positions in Jerusalem, many of which benefited from Central European administrative experience, nevertheless required fluency in Hebrew when it became the language of state in 1948. Because of Jerusalem's position as a cultural and intellectual center, that city's Central European residents demonstrated more rapid acquisition of Hebrew and adaptation to other areas of Israeli life.[20]

Central Europeans were not the only Jewish community to attach such high cultural symbolism to the German language. During the century prior to the Holocaust, German increasingly came to function as the cultural lingua franca for Jews throughout Europe. The extremely high percentage of German letters in the archives of the World Centre for Jewish Music in Palestine (see Chapter 6) from Jews throughout the world bears witness to this attitude toward German. Knowing German expanded one's cultural base. The frequency with which young musicians came to study in German music academies and the virtual hegemony of German music publishing further intensified the function of the German language (and culture) beyond the borders of the nation itself. Jews from various parts of Europe came to Germany to study and often remained there as performers. Thus, it was quite natural for the rehearsals of the Israel Philharmonic, in spite of the large number of non-Germans, to be conducted in German, that being both the language common to all present and the professional language customary for orchestral rehearsals. German, as a language of the arts, was therefore not limited to the Central European ethnic group in Israel. Its persistent role in musical and intellectual activities associated it directly with the promulgation of Western art music and Central European cultural values. Throughout Israel other institutions and activities that enhance this cultural role for German are not uncommon. Most bookshops in Jerusalem, for example, are owned and managed by Central Europeans. These shops are amply stocked with German literature and a broad range of books devoted to music and the other arts, books recently published in Germany, and those purchased from the estates of immigrants.

Because of the direct association of German with the Holocaust, there are many who respond negatively to any persistence of the language in Israel. Negative attitudes have frequently resulted in the exclusion of German from public cultural activities. University study of German, for example, is almost impossible; even in the 1980s only the Hebrew University offers a few courses, most of them at an extremely advanced level inaccessible to beginning, younger students. Only the Goethe-Institut, through the German Embassy, has begun to make a few successful inroads for the teaching of German in Israel. With such impediments to overcome, disappearance of the language might appear inevitable. Nonetheless, persistence may also be more widespread than popular prejudices might allow one to predict. During the 1960s, 80 percent of all children of German-speaking parents could also speak German, a figure not too surprising when compared with the amount of German still spoken in the home at the time.[21] Among third-generation Central Europeans, however, knowledge of German drops off sharply, largely as a result of the inability to study the language in any systematic way outside the home.

German survives today in Israel as a language linked primarily to specific cultural institutions, rather than one whose currency depends on domestic use. There are some cultural activities in which the dominance of German remains quite unchallenged. Music, more than most cultural areas, continues to bear witness to its support from the immigrant generation. Several of the most important scholarly works concerning music in Israel have appeared only in German, for example Max Brod's *Die Musik Israels* (1951), which was the first comprehensive study of music composed in Israel and remains the most thorough work of this sort. Moreover, when the book was revised and expanded by Yehuda Walter Cohen in 1976, it again appeared only in German.[22] Effectively, this renders the book inaccessible to most young Israeli musicians, even those of Central European heritage.

A few genres of music also depend on audiences and musical institutions in Germany. The most notable of these has been opera, which has had almost no success in Israel. One result of this dependency has been the need to set or translate works composed by Israelis, often based on biblical texts, into German because such works find consistent performance only in Europe. Even though the audiences may not be Israeli or Hebrew-speaking, interaction with musicians elsewhere suggests that musical life will continue to depend on an international musical community in which the German language is not just indispensable: musical life may come to depend on German in ways quite different from those of the immigrant generation.

Although the lingering memories of the Holocaust have caused many Israelis to view Germany with considerable mistrust, many in the Central European community have reestablished contact with the Federal Republic of Germany, especially with the institutions of German culture. The reestablishment of cultural relations has not been without some official sanction — however sheltered that might be from widespread public scrutiny — for Israel has generally benefited from extremely favorable economic and cultural interaction with West Germany.[23] Public reaction to cultural relations with Germany varies greatly, depending for the most part on the degree and direction of official interaction. Thus, even though Israeli musicians have traveled to Germany for study and performance since the late 1940s, German musical groups have been able to perform in Israel only since the late 1960s. It has been, in fact, this period of about one generation that has been necessary for at least superficial healing of the Holocaust's wounds.

Initial reestablishment of cultural relations with Germany has taken place on two levels, the national and the community. At the national level the reparation process was the first major reconciliation, which in turn brought growing numbers of Germans and Israelis into contact with each other. Several of the professions in which Central Europeans predominated were actively involved in reparation negotiations; the best example here was the legal profession, to which the German-speaking Israelis could contribute not only their legal expertise but also their linguistic skills. At the community level contact with German culture came in more indirect ways, often through literature and the other arts. German newspapers, magazines, and fiction are today widely available in Israel and have served to increase Israeli awareness of politics, cultural activities, and other aspects of life in Germany.

Reestablishment of contact with German culture has been fairly widespread among Central Europeans, so much so that it seems to be an attribute of the ethnic community as a whole. During the 1960s, Eva Beling found that about 80 percent of those she interviewed maintained some sort of contact with Germany. Twenty-five percent had already visited Germany at least once since World War II, and 70 percent indicated an interest in visiting Germany in the near future. About 70 percent read newspapers published in Germany (there are also German newspapers published in Israel), and about 45 percent read postwar German literature.[24] Research further correlated this positive response to German culture with the urbanized culture of the Central European community; 78 percent of the city dwellers in the Beling study showed a positive response to postwar West Germany, whereas immigrants living on kibbutzim demonstrated almost no interest.[25] During the 1980s it has become increasingly common for German cities to sponsor reunions of former Jewish residents and their families. Most Central European Israelis with whom I consulted had participated in such return visits, if for no other reason than to visit old neighborhoods and friends. At the same time, these reunions forged new contacts with the contemporary Jewish communities of Germany and increased Israeli interest in and support of such communities.

The reestablishment of cultural relations with Germany has frequently stirred turmoil, at times isolating the Central European community and its musical institutions. After World War II, Israel restricted all of its musical organizations from concertizing in Germany. The first organization that attempted to perform in Germany was the Ramat Gan Chamber Orchestra in 1962. When the public learned of this, a critical uproar quickly followed, and the mayor of Ramat Gan threatened to withdraw public funds from support of the orchestra. The Ministry of Foreign Affairs did approve the tour, but had to cancel it at the last minute because of protests from the "Organization of Holocaust Survivors and Fighters against Nazism." The first "German" musical organization to perform in Israel was the Vienna Symphony in 1968. Following this initial contravention of the cultural impasse, musical relations improved rapidly, and in the 1970s cultural exchange between Israel and West Germany became almost commonplace. Such exchange also succeeded in reintroducing the German language into Israeli musical performances. Prior to this time, large-scale public performances of works such as the Beethoven *Ninth Symphony* or the Mahler *Second Symphony* utilized either Hebrew or English translations of the vocal parts. As cultural interaction with West Germany has escalated, performances in the original German have also become more frequent and generally uneventful.

The urbanized culture of the Central European community has provided a variety of conduits through which contact with German culture has been reestablished since the Holocaust. Music has functioned as one of the most important of these channels, no doubt a result of the ways Israeli and German musical organizations have formed similar institutions and encapsulated similar values. Musical activity further stimulated the reestablishment of new relations in other areas of Israeli society, as well as between the Central Europeans and other ethnic groups. Still, the degree to which the Central European community has actively sought to renew and nurture relations with West Germany unquestionably distinguishes it in certain ways. Not wishing to ignore the sensitive problems still implicit in contemporary German culture, many Central Europeans also chose not to ignore the richness of past cultural interaction and the potential of future rapprochement. At times such activity has isolated the Central European community because of the scorn from other groups in Israeli society; at other times such activity has achieved sanction as another cultural contribution to Israeli society that only the Central European community, as a result of the two cultural streams in its particular heritage, could accomplish.

Central European Jews have articulated a clear sense of ethnic community in both Europe and Israel. In both venues the community depended less on physical boundaries than on the vital inculcation of cultural values in the community's social institutions. These values grew from traditions that were not structurally unique to the community itself—for example, the traditions of Western art music — but nevertheless acquired functions investing them with an intensity that clearly distinguished the Central European Jews from other ethnic groups. These traditions required the involvement and interaction of numerous groups within the community, and their persistence often stimulated the formation of organizations that drew widely from all parts of the community.

Had it not been for such organizations, transferral of Central European cultural traditions to Israel would have been impossible. The immigrants of the 1930s had insufficient time to plan for the orderly transplantation of the community's external structure. That external structure, moreover, would have stood little chance of survival, for it could not have contrasted more with the social framework already established in Palestine. The ethnic group found, instead, that its internal structures, its cultural organizations so well suited to the urban environment, could provide for the establishment of a new community and the maintenance of its traditional ethnic values.

Also distinctive of the German-speaking ethnic community in both Europe and Israel was the role played by fine-art traditions and professions dependent on a faith in the enlightening potential of *Bildung*. This case of ethnicity bound not to folk-music traditions, but to the cultivation of Western art music, thus provides a paradigm for better understanding the continuity linking German-Jewish culture in two different worlds, in two different eras. Above all, the ethnic patterns resulting from special cultivation of Western art music will serve to define the special characteristics of the Central European community, distinguishing it from the larger society in both settings. Each setting throws light on the other; both were cultural streams with a common source. The following chapters will investigate the establishment of a strong, culturally pluralistic foundation for Jewish culture in Central Europe; the nature of that foundation, in turn, was fundamental to the shape and strength of a transformed ethnic community in Israel. This interpretation of Jewish culture in Germany will not portray a community in decline, rather one that had become ethnically distinct by identifying those aspects of German culture that best served the community's infrastructure. Though no longer tied strictly to religious tradition, the Jewish community was healthy in the decades prior to the Holocaust. It was beginning to remold the traditions of its forebears into a flourishing renaissance, for which music would serve as one of the most important voices.

NOTES

The epigraph at the beginning of this chapter is from Schalom Ben-Chorin, *Juden an der Isar* (Gerlingen: Bleicher Verlag, 1980), p. 200. In English, the lines read:

"The two cities in my land with two streams remained Munich
and Jerusalem, but over both shone the words:
Because we have no permanent city here,
we seek instead that of the future."

1. The most complete intellectual history of *Bildung* and its meaning to the Jewish community of Central Europe is George L. Mosse, *German Jews beyond Judaism* (Bloomington and Cincinnati: Indiana University Press and Hebrew Union College Press, 1985). See also H. I. Bach, *The German Jew: A Synthesis of Judaism and Western Civilization, 1730-1930* (New York: Oxford University Press, 1984), passim, but especially pp. 169-243.

2. The modern Hebrew word for immigration to Israel is *aliyah,* literally "coming up," a concept steeped in symbolic and historical meaning. Major periods during the history of modern settlement in Israel are also denoted by the term and the ordinal succession thereof. Within this system of nomenclature, the German *aliyah* is also the *aliyah ḥamishit,* the "Fifth Wave of Immigrants."

3. Individuals were allowed to transfer as much as 12,000 marks, with increased rates for additional family members. F. Wilder-Okladek, "Austrian and German Immigration in Israel," in *Integration and Development in Israel,* ed. S. N. Eisenstadt et al. (New York: Praeger, 1970), p. 391.

4. Eva Beling, *Die gesellschaftliche Eingliederung der deutschen Einwanderer in Israel: Eine soziologische Untersuchung der Einwanderung aus Deutschland zwischen 1933 und 1945* (Frankfurt: Europäische Verlagsanstalt, 1967), p. 31.

5. Wilder-Okladek, "Austrian and German Immigration," p. 394.

6. Beling, *Die gesellschaftliche Eingliederung,* p. 34.

7. Ibid., pp. 37-38.

8. Dorothy Willner, *Nation-Building and Community in Israel* (Princeton: Princeton University Press, 1969), p. 52.

9. Curt D. Wormann, "German Jews in Israel: Their Cultural Situation since 1933," *Year Book: Leo Baeck Institute* 10 (1970): 77. For extensive accounts of the cultural activities supported by the *Hitachduth Oley Germania* see Hitachduth Olej Germania, *Die Deutsche Alijah in Palästina: Bericht der Hitachduth Olej Germania für die Jahre 1936/1937* (Tel Aviv: Hitachduth Olej Germania, 1937), and idem, *Der Weg der deutschen Alijah: Rechenschaft, Leistung, Verantwortung* (Tel Aviv: Hitachduth Olej Germania and Olej Austria, 1939).

10. Writers, for example, formed a *Verband deutschsprachiger Schriftsteller in Israel* ("Association of German-Speaking Writers in Israel"). This organization is still active and sponsors publications in German, such as the recent anthology of its members, Meir M. Faerber, ed., *Stimmen aus Israel: Eine Anthologie deutschsprachiger Literatur in Israel* (Stuttgart: Bleicher Verlag, 1979).

11. Elliott Oring notes that in a standard joke "the *Jecke* is often too refined, too proper, and too civilized"; see his *Israeli Humor: The Content and Structure of the Palmah* (Albany: State University of New York Press, 1981), p. 100.

12. See for example Beling, *Die gesellschaftliche Eingliederung,* p. 51.

13. In Yekke jokes, faulty timepieces usually receive the blame when an event does not begin when it should; Oring, *Israeli Humor,* p. 246.

14. Statistics do, in fact, show that German Jews were not particularly disposed toward conservative forms of Judaism. Prior to immigration fewer than 10 percent

participated in Orthodox religious observances; Beling, *Die gesellschaftliche Eingliederung*, p. 56.

15. Roberto Bachi, "A Statistical Analysis of the Revival of Hebrew in Israel," in *Scripta Hierosalymitana Publications of the Hebrew University* (Jerusalem: The Magnes Press of the Hebrew University, 1956), pp. 178-79.

16. B. Gil and M. Sicron, *Rishum ha-toshavim* ("Registration of Inhabitants") (Jerusalem: Ha-lishkah ha-merkasit le-statistika, 1956), p. 29, Table 16, "Jewish Population by Every Day Spoken Language and Sex" (8 November 1948).

17. Beling, *Die gesellschaftliche Eingliederung*, pp. 192, 237.

18. Ibid.

19. Many older residents of the Central European community offer this defense of their language skills.

20. This is the conclusion of Bachi, "Statistical Analysis," with which Beling, *Die gesellschaftliche Eingliederung*, p. 198, concurs.

21. Beling, *Die gesellschaftliche Eingliederung*, p. 195.

22. Max Brod, *Die Musik Israels* (1951), revised and expanded by Yehuda Walter Cohen (Kassel: Bärenreiter, 1976).

23. An in-depth treatment of this unexpectedly propitious relation is Lily Gardner Feldman, *The Special Relationship between West Germany and Israel* (Boston: Allen and Unwin, 1984). The German Democratic Republic officially defers blame for the Holocaust to the fascist government that predated the founding of East Germany. Political, cultural, and financial relations between East Germany and Israel therefore have been virtually nonexistent. Only in 1988 did the East German Party Secretary, Erich Honecker, announce that his nation would accept some measure of culpability and would consider the possibility of reparation payments.

24. Beling, *Die gesellschaftliche Eingliederung*, p. 185.

25. Ibid., pp. 185-86; it should be kept in mind, however, that German immigrants settled in relatively small numbers on kibbutzim.

2

The Awakening of a Modern Community

THE RELATION of Jews to Germans and German culture forms a history replete with paradox and contradiction. Even though the most incomprehensible of human tragedies terminated this history, there were moments of ecstatic creativity and optimism. In the midst of the history stands the German-Jewish community itself, often the transgressing and culpable party in the eyes of both fellow Jews and non-Jews; at times, it seemed that, wherever the German Jews might turn, their community was surrounded by detractors and critics. The historical paradox lay both inside and outside the community, forming in different ways its two cultural streams.

The contradictions inherent in this history strike at the most basic considerations. Definitions become difficult and almost always demand qualification. The specific populations of both Jewish and non-Jewish societies in nineteenth-century Germany, for example, were in constant flux. It is not altogether obvious what defined a German during this period: language, national boundaries, history, religion? Not only does the constantly shifting geographical landscape of Germany during the century make accurate definitions difficult for modern interpreters, but the endless philosophical and political debates concerning nationalism reveal that the concept was not completely clear even to those creating and manipulating it.

Even more difficult to characterize concisely at this time was the exact nature of Jewish culture and community in Germany. Whereas some emancipated Jews regarded German-Jewish culture as the ultimate and long-awaited release of Jewish creativity, more traditional voices answered that this culture could no longer be considered Jewish at all. While many Germans saw emancipation as the abandonment of Jewish heritage, many Jews saw it as a reformed and renascent manifestation of Jewish heritage. With such rampantly contradictory concepts of both German and Jew in nineteenth-century Germany, it would seem that discussion of German-Jewish history would be greeted more often by caution and tentativeness than by conclusive evidence and irrefutable fact.

Contradictions notwithstanding, German-Jewish history embarked on a radically new course during the nineteenth century, one that shaped a community unlike anything European Jewish culture had experienced prior to that time.[1] The changes that made the emergence of such a community possible were not completely intrinsic to Jewish society, nor were they by any means unique to that community vis-à-vis other minority and ethnic groups in Germany. Rather, they were the result of widespread cultural and socioeconomic progress and modification throughout German society. No other segment of that society, however, felt the impact of the changes as profoundly as the Jewish community. Within a remarkably short period of time, Jews were actively engaged in cultural areas in which their previous contributions had been negligible. Jews had entered into many of the most favored and economically rewarding professions in numbers many times disproportionate to the relative size of their community. To the degree that German culture benefited from the nineteenth century's sweeping socio-economic changes, the Jewish community benefited even more and served to quicken the pace of the changes.

The transformation of Jewish culture from a community gathered about a more traditional, religious order to one manifesting a modern, more secular order took place on two planes. Occupying the first was the community's religious, philosophical, and political life, all three components being largely synonymous before the nineteenth century. The term *emancipation* best describes the transformation on this plane. The other impetus for change was economic and derived from the very sweeping process of modernization. Modernization was a major stimulus for the mass migration of Jews from rural areas to the cities where new occupations were plentiful in a rapidly industrializing society. Closely related was the pervasive urbanization of the Jewish community in the nineteenth century. It was the coupling of emancipation and modernization — the first more influential on the community's internal structure, the second on the external — that invested the community with the capability of transforming so rapidly.

Transformed though it was, the German-Jewish community was none-theless clearly discernible in the early decades of the present century. Some had thought — others, even, had hoped — that the distinguishing characteristics of the community would disappear, that full and total assimilation would be the ultimate transformation of the community. But such was not the case, nor did it seem likely to become the case on the eve of the Holocaust. Although Jews had migrated to the cities, they usually chose to live near other Jews in Jewish neighborhoods. Taking advantage of the more open public education system at the end of the nineteenth century in exceptional numbers, Jews were frequently the predominant group in many schools and classes in the universities. The more traditionally Jewish professions of rural Germany gave way to new professions in urban Germany, these too dominated by Jews. Far from causing the German-Jewish community to disappear, emancipation and modernization redefined it.

One of the richest outgrowths of German and Jewish interaction during the era of emancipation and modernization has been the culture of Central European Jews in Israel. The momentum of cultural change stemming from rapid urbanization spilled over into the immigration of the German *aliyah,* for it was the newer manifestation of the Central European ethnic community—the one that had served the group in so many positive ways in an urbanized Germany—that the immigrants sought to transfer to Palestine. The German *aliyah* transpired at exactly that moment when its potential contribution to the immigrant culture was most in need. Despite the inherent contradictions in German-Jewish history, there is a deep, underlying continuity that links the culture of Jews in nineteenth- and early twentieth-century Germany and the Central European ethnic community in Israel. Had new ethnic values not emerged to replace those of a more traditional era, that continuity would never have been possible.

Comparatively, the changes through which the Jewish community passed during the centuries preceding emancipation seem almost insignificant. Indeed, the very speed of German-Jewish modernization and emancipation may be one of the underlying causes for the community's eventual destruction, for neither Jews nor non-Jews were completely prepared for the former's entrance into Central European society. Throughout most of the emancipation period, both groups experienced a previously unknown flowering of culture. In many cases, the advances of one group benefited also the other; in other cases, the advances were not mutually propitious, but did pursue parallel courses. For German society, the primary outgrowth of these advances was the rich artistic and scientific traditions of the nineteenth and twentieth centuries. These same traditions characterized also the advances of the Jewish community, whose members fully participated in them. More important for the community's history in the present century, however, many of these traditions served as foundations for modern Israeli culture.

Jews had begun to settle in the lands now inhabited by German-speaking nations as early as the Roman times. Accompanying the Roman legions in a number of capacities—from slave to soldier—many remained in Central

Europe, most often settling along the major waterways to become merchants and traders.[2] As early as the ninth and tenth centuries, documentation of Jewish life in Germany appears. These early records portrayed a Jewish society that was to remain relatively unchanged until the eighteenth century.[3] The position of Jews at the edge of Christian society was from time to time endangered. Commonly, they received the blame for other ills, such as periods of pestilence, that befell society. Sometimes, they survived the external threat against their communities; at other times, such as in the fourteenth century when they were largely driven eastward from Germany, thereafter to lay the groundwork for Eastern European Yiddish culture, their existence was considerably more endangered. Most influences from medieval and renaissance Christian society on Jewish neighbors did little to alter the basic shape of the Jewish community. Jews in Europe had successfully created a society based on rabbinical rule of the political, social, and religious life in the community, which further offered the advantage of isolating the community from the outside world. Jewish culture maintained a particularly strong sense of historical continuity with the distant past, one in which law and learning were bound to religion. Interaction with the Christian world usually took place only through trade or the political mediation of the rabbinical administration, thus making traversal of the ethnic boundaries separating individual Jewish communities from non-Jewish society rarely necessary.[4]

In the mid-eighteenth century approximately 175,000 Jews lived in the lands that were to become Germany, constituting less than 1 percent of the entire population of this geographic area. Another 75,000 Jews lived in other areas in which German was the primary tongue, namely Austria, Bohemia, and Moravia.[5] Throughout the period of modernization, the percentage of Jews in German-speaking countries changed little and was still less than 1 percent overall in the 1920s; almost all other aspects of their society — where they lived and how they lived — would, however, change radically.

The first stirring of modern German-Jewish history occurred in Prussia in 1671, when a group of some fifty Jewish families that had been driven from Vienna were extended limited political asylum. This act in effect granted a form of political recognition to a Jewish minority living in Prussia and Brandenburg.[6] During this period of proto-emancipation Jewish communities gradually moved from relative self-government to increasing interaction with the state. Differences between the Jewish polity and Christian government accordingly diminished. The state began to interfere more in community affairs, for example in the election of elders and sometimes through the limitation of family size. More politically significant, all community records had to be kept in German, a change resulting in the rapid encroachment of the state language into community education.[7]

These early changes prepared the Jewish community for the possibility of emancipation without actually bringing it about. That would only follow a movement of some intellectual transition and then political reform. Intellectual reformulation came first from dominant figures in the eighteenth-century *Aufklärung*, the German Enlightenment, most notably Moses Mendelssohn and Gotthold Ephraim Lessing.[8] Politically, emancipation would follow at a considerably slower pace. The first political steps toward emancipation in Central Europe were not German but Austrian. In 1771 and 1772 Emperor Joseph II issued an Edict of Toleration, which effectively liberated the Jews from many repressive laws.[9] Although the Austrian moves toward political recognition brought about important reforms, certain aspects of Jewish status in Austrian society remained the same. Jews were not allowed to acquire land outside their own neighborhoods. Public religious services in Vienna were still forbidden, and population limitations were still imposed. Together, these restrictions continued to confine many Jews to rural areas and limited any embarkation along a path of modernization. Still, the Austrian reforms contained some provisions that augured well for the future. Most important was the granting of family names to the Jews, the first instance of such civil recognition in a European state.[10]

The first German provinces to implement reform of Jewish laws were those that were either controlled directly by the French at the beginning of the nineteenth century or were heavily influenced by the liberalism following upon the heels of the French Revolution. The earliest German provincial governments granting citizenship to Jews were Bonn in 1801, and Frankfurt and Westphalia in 1807.[11] Reform followed in Prussia finally in 1812 with the enactment of the *Edikt betreffend die bürgerlichen Verhältnisse der Juden in dem preußischen Staate* ("Edict concerning the Civil Circumstances of the Jews in the Prussian State"), whose major provision granted Jews the privilege of choosing their own professions. The consequences of this provision were monumental: With the boundaries circumscribing their traditional community finally open, Jews would be able to participate fully in the cultural achievements and modernization of German society.

With the extension of at least limited political recognition to German Jews and their community, the most immutable impediments to emancipation dissolved. Beginning in about 1820, attitudes toward the Jewish community began to change noticeably. Previous descriptions of German Jews held them to be members of a Jewish nation within Germany; but after 1820, quite different descriptions began to appear, such as Germans of "Mosaic persuasion." Many of these de-emphasized any national difference, conceptual or otherwise, between Jew and German.[12] Undoubtedly, the drive toward Jewish emancipation received impetus from the burgeoning consciousness of German national culture in the nineteenth century; to a certain extent, the obverse was also true. The speed with which Jewish emancipation progressed was due in part to the spread of Romanticism in Germany and the impassioned response to the movement by German artists and intellectuals. Jews also wished to contribute to the new movement and quickly endeavored to do so. A people who had always valued education, Jews were quickly able to adapt themselves to the German university system and soon found themselves at the forefront of various German intellectual movements.[13] Their historical involvement with trade and commerce was also of tremendous value to a nation rapidly undergoing industrialization. In short, the first steps toward emancipation came at an opportune moment for both Germans and Jews, and stood potentially to benefit the whole of German culture.

Unquestionably, the de-emphasis of religion in the wake of the French Revolution made emancipation easier for many Jews. Those who so desired could now participate in intellectual activities outside the community without feeling that they had abandoned their own religion in deference to another. For these reasons, the social organizations that were most favorable to the inclusion of Jews, such as the Freemasons, had also deliberately substituted a completely new intellectual and mystical fabric for previously Christian ideologies.[14] Those intellectual figures whose work achieved the greatest significance for Jews — Schiller probably the outstanding example — often aimed to transcend religious dogma altogether.[15] In general, the relative secularization of the arts at the beginning of the nineteenth century rendered them professionally attractive to Jews seeking new cultural inroads into German society.

When new organizations began to appear in the Jewish community, they were often modeled on similar institutions in German society. In some cases, Jewish organizers explicitly copied non-Jewish counterparts in order that the two cultures would appear to be similar. Parallel institutions developed for both secular and religious activities. Jewish *Turnvereine* ("athletic societies"), for example, appeared in many German cities and fostered the same cult of physical well-being that pervaded the ubiquitous non-

Jewish *Turnverein*. The *Blau-Weiß* ("Blue-White") youth movement began as an extension of the German *Wandervogel* ("Wandering Bird") movement, even though the former's association with Zionism increased during the twentieth century. Closer contact with Christian society also brought about the institutionalization of alternative holiday celebrations. Christmas, for example, was celebrated by some Jews as a type of German folk festival, quite devoid of its religious significance. A somewhat less secular response to Christmas was the "Maccabee Ball," given on Christmas Eve by opponents of the folk-culture emphasis who still wanted Jewish children to have something special to do on Christmas Eve, even when Hanukah may have preceded by several weeks.[16]

Despite the considerable achievements of emancipation, there remained an enemy that constantly checked the transition from emancipation to assimilation: anti-Semitism. Public and private invectives against Jews and the Jewish community throughout the period of emancipation continued to distinguish Jews from all other minority groups. Anti-Semitism found advocates not only in more conservative working classes, but also in professions that presumably espoused liberal attitudes toward Germany's national culture.[17] German Jews were a people without a nation in an age of overwhelming nationalism. At the beginning of the era of emancipation, Jews were still regarded as citizens of a dispersed nation. By the mid-nineteenth century that citizenship had become nebulous, but another had not superseded it. This dilemma is evident even in the difficulty with which official and unofficial terminology identified Jews: whether in literature or public documents their citizenship was qualified by a reference to their religious background. The decision to obtain only partial nationality was, in fact, often mutual. Simply to become a German would symbolize a loss that was greater than even many emancipated Jews wished to admit. They preferred to remain, in effect, a nation within a nation, albeit in more direct coexistence with the larger nation.

The benefits and dangers of emancipation were confined largely to an urban setting. Not just a shifting of external attitudes toward the Jewish community, emancipation was a conduit that allowed Jews to participate in the new cultural environment of nineteenth-century German cities. It increasingly became a factor in the transformation of the Jewish community when Jews migrated from rural areas to the cities. Thus emancipation did not pose a threat to traditional Jewish life *in situ,* but only through the decimation of its population, a demographic shift virtually complete by the 1920s.

At the end of the eighteenth century urban Jewish communities had scarcely come into existence. In part this was due to the ability of the rural community to serve the economic and religious needs of its residents. In part it was due to the relatively recent decisions of the urban governments to allow Jewish settlement. Many European cities in which Jewish culture flourished at the beginning of the twentieth century had only a few hundred families at the end of the eighteenth.[18] Most Jews in rural areas pursued professions that had traditionally been associated with Jews for centuries. Trading and commerce were the most common of these, both attributing a role of Jews as mediators between the community and the outside world. Whereas there were a few settlements in which Jews comprised almost the entire population, far more common was the small town in which Jews were an organized subgroup, occupying 10 to 20 percent of the population. Jews generally interacted freely with non-Jews in such towns, but certain steps were taken to ensure the sense of Jewish community in an environment dominated by Christians. Jews often made sure that they had Jewish neighbors on at least one side. Proximity to religious institutions — the synagogue, school, and ritual bath — defined the demographic landscape.[19]

The structure of the rural community offered its residents the stability of tradition. But it also depended on stability, and when stability was undermined by egress to the cities in the nineteenth century, so too did the structure of the rural community disintegrate. The Jewish community could respond rapidly to modernization because it had already demonstrated a procilivity toward urbanization. The rural towns in which Jews lived were never isolated from larger cities and, in fact, often depended economically on the cities for trade. Jews, moreover, rarely engaged in farming or other agricultural occupations, even when residents of agricultural areas.[20] Their migration to the cities was thus a response to opportunities of which they could take advantage more readily than non-Jews.

Migration to the cities demonstrated two general patterns. The first effected a more radical severance from the rural community and usually followed upon Jews' moving to the city to take jobs. Jewish migration of this sort was both quantitatively and qualitatively different from non-Jewish. Not only did Jews enter the urban work force in proportionately greater numbers, but they moved to the cities as entire families, whereas non-Jews tended to move as individuals. Jews then remained in the cities, unlike many non-Jewish urban immigrants, who more frequently moved elsewhere, often back to the rural area when they had acquired a more fortuitous financial situation.[21] A less radical migration resulted when Jews took advantage of the city's educational and cultural offerings. Jewish children, for example, were often sent to the city to attend the *Gymnasium* ("humanistic secondary school"), and many moved on to the universities and to urban professions thereafter. Non-Jews in rural areas were much less likely to send their children to the city for such reasons.[22] Such a pattern diminished the rural Jewish community slowly, but those in the younger generations became fewer and fewer, leaving only the elderly by the early twentieth century.

The economic opportunity that attracted Jews to the cities increased rapidly after the mid-nineteenth century, and so did the pace of Jewish migration. The Jewish population of Berlin, for example, doubled in a two-decade period from 1880 to 1900, reaching almost 100,000. By 1925, the turn-of-the-century population had almost doubled again, increasing to more than 170,000. Population statistics were equally as dramatic for Vienna. Its population of 73,000 Jews in 1880 reached 202,000 in 1923, over 10 percent of the total population.[23] Statistics also reveal that the urbanization of the Jewish community was quickly more extensive than the non-Jewish. Two-thirds of Germany's Jews lived in cities in 1925, compared to only one-fourth of the nation's non-Jewish population. Vienna's population was only about 1 percent Jewish in 1857, but had increased to 13 percent at the turn of the century. By 1934, nearly 93 percent of all Austrian Jews lived in Vienna.[24] The urbanization of Central European Jewry proceeded at an unmitigated pace during the century before the Holocaust, and by the 1920s the city had become virtually the only venue for the Central European Jewish community.

Although the initial motivation for Jewish migration to the cities had been economic, Jews were quick to transform the financial success of their community into a means of paving inroads into the intellectual and cultural life of the cities. The most effective route was the system of public education, the *Gymnasien* and the universities. Throughout Central Europe Jews filled the classes of secondary schools and universities in massively disproportionate numbers. In 1900, when Jews were about 1 percent of Germany's population, they were 9 percent of its university students. They were 30 percent of Vienna's *Gymnasium* students, compared to 8 percent of the population. In Prague's German *Gymnasien* Jews comprised 46 percent of the student enrollment in 1910.[25]

New educational opportunities also meant a new professional place in the urban society, which in turn completely reshaped the Jewish community. In 1925 Prussia's physicians were 16 percent Jewish, its dentists 15 percent Jewish, and its lawyers 25 percent Jewish, even though its population was still less than 1 percent Jewish. In Vienna 45 percent of the university's medical faculty were Jewish, and one quarter of the total faculty was Jewish.[26] In contrast there were few Jews who worked as industrial or manual laborers. When compared to the rest of German society, Jews were involved in professions that created and controlled wealth to a far greater degree than non-Jews. In 1933, 46 percent of all Jews engaged in a profession were "employers," compared to only 17 percent of the non-Jewish population. In contrast, 46 percent of all Germans were laborers, compared to only 9 percent in the Jewish community.[27] As a whole, the Jewish community was professionally and financially very stable.

These statistics tend to suggest on their surface that Jews were assimilating rapidly into Central European society. Closer examination of the urban Jewish community, however, reveals quite a different pattern of change. Considered from almost all perspectives, the Jewish community remained intact and clearly distinct from non-Jewish society. Jews lived in close proximity to other Jews, not because of religious or traditional necessity, but in order to reinforce ethnic ties. Although the *Gymnasien* were public educational institutions, Jews usually sent their children to those with large Jewish enrollment, sometimes because of the location of these schools, but often because they offered the best education. In Vienna's Jewish districts, for example, Jewish enrollment in some *Gymnasien* was as high as 80 percent.[28] The association of Jews with other Jews, thus, did not diminish upon immigration to the city, but often intensified because of the growing population in primarily Jewish neighborhoods.

The formation of new Jewish neighborhoods also spawned a vast network of new Jewish social institutions, again undergirding the sense of community. These institutions functioned in quite different ways, but were always firmly anchored in the community. In her study of Vienna's Jews Marsha Rozenblit identified a total of 324 such institutions.[29] Some fell under the purview of the *Israelitische Kultusgemeinde* (IKG), a sort of officially mandated organization deriving its form and function from community religious organizations. The orthodox and marginally observant were all served by constituent institutions of the IKG. Other institutions had very limited membership and functions, however still restricted to the community. In fact, the complex web of cultural activities and social cohesion fostered by this institutional structure rarely spilled over to the larger society. If an institution needed legal help, it turned to Jewish lawyers; boards of directors contained only Jews; membership did not draw from non-Jewish sectors, where, of course, the residents joined their own organizations. This form of institutional interaction strengthened the Jewish community both by bringing it closer together and keeping it apart from non-Jewish society.

Numerous reminders of the Jewish community's traditional roots and movements advocating a more nationalistic potential also arose as counterforces to emancipation and modernization. These served in part to brake the impetus toward assimilation and in part to shape new values and institutions in the community. In general, such counterforces heightened an awareness of Jewish groups elsewhere and the broader Jewish culture that these constituted. In various ways—most of them not yet apparent to German Jews—this heightened awareness would lay some of the cultural groundwork for the transferral of the Jewish community to Israel.

Accompanying the migration of Jews to German urban centers was also a considerable influx of Eastern European Jews. To some German Jews the culture of the Eastern Europeans was markedly different from their own, and they regarded the Yiddish-speaking Jews as unprogressive and an embarrassment to the Jewish community as a whole. As the number of Eastern Europeans settling in German cities increased throughout the nineteenth century and more traditional settlements appeared alongside urban Jewish neighborhoods, the meaning of traditional Jewish culture became again apparent to those in the urbanized community.[30] Many German Jews began to develop an interest in this culture—at first with almost scientific detachment, but later with fascination and enthusiasm. The *Hochschule für die Wissenschaft des Judentums* was one of the most formal institutions for the scientific study of Jewish culture.[31] Max Grunwald's founding in 1896 of an organization devoted to the study of Jewish folklore, the *Gesellschaft für jüdische Volkskunde,* was another outgrowth of this intellectual tendency in the community.[32] Artists and writers developed the themes of Eastern European culture in their works; Franz Kafka, for example, began to study Hebrew as a direct outgrowth of a Yiddish theater group's visit to Prague in 1911.[33] For the folk-song traditions of Jewish social organizations, the incorporation of Yiddish songs and their particular motifs formed a pivotal transition in the development of these traditions. If nothing else, the more direct confrontation with Eastern European Jewry reminded German Jews that emancipation was not the only possibility for Jewish cultural expression.

In the fifty years prior to World War II, Zionism also emerged as a counterforce to the sweeping influence of emancipation. Zionism was unquestionably a direct rebuttal to assimilation. After all, it was a German-speaking Jew, Theodor Herzl, formerly editor of the feuilleton in Vienna's *Neue Freie Presse,* who assumed the leadership of the Zionist movement in the last decade of the nineteenth century; without question, he was keenly sensitive to the pluralistic admixture of German and Jewish cultures at the time. The various Zionist organizations assumed the leadership of the forces opposing assimilation, thereby uniting and organizing them, at least in a more political sense than before. The Zionists were totally opposed to the abandonment of Jewish heritage in order to enter German society. Their words of warning — sometimes couched as invidious insults — frequently found their way into the Jewish press by the beginning of the twentieth century and shocked many into an awareness that they were sacrificing their ethnic identity by so willingly abandoning traditional values.[34] Gradually, the Zionists became a more influential force in Germany, linking German Jews with those throughout Europe. Zionism provided a rallying point for other Jewish groups and thus extended its influence over expanding cultural terrain. The extent of this incursion into the institutional structure of the Jewish community is clearly evident in the emergence of Zionism as the central motif in the musical traditions of the community's diverse cultural institutions after World War I.

The structure of German society and the pluralistic relation of Jewish culture to it precluded complete assimilation. Germans and Jews held rather contradictory interpretations of assimilation, as well as certain other transformations of the Jewish community that would make entrée to German society more accessible.[35] From their viewpoint, many Jews did not believe that modernization and change necessarily meant they needed to abandon their own cultural and religious background, especially if these did not pose a threat to German society. Nationalistic Germans held just the opposite viewpoint. Assimilation to them meant complete capitulation, complete abnegation of any sense of community. That this failed to happen kept the issue of German and Jewish relations on the public agenda, causing critics to question Jewish willingness to participate in German society. For some in the Jewish community it thus became increasingly apparent that an ultimate German-Jewish rapprochement might never fully transpire.[36]

In the early decades of the twentieth century many in the Central European Jewish community began to express a resurgent interest in the more traditional aspects of Jewish culture. During the final years before the Holocaust this interest often shaped the formation of new cultural institutions, or reshaped the old. The intellectual attitudes and cultural values of these individuals fell into three specific, yet overlapping categories. Those espousing the values in the first category were the traditionalists. The traditionalists were individuals like Martin Buber or Gershom Scholem whose intellectual training was heavily indebted to German educational systems, yet who, even at an early age, were unwilling to abandon a more traditional Jewish heritage. Traditionalists were often more interested in Jewish culture than were their parents. They often drew upon German ideas or philosophical concepts, but always reshaped them so that they would reflect Jewish tradition. The cultural institutions initiated by Buber, for example, often reflected a German model.[37]

The second category embodied an understanding of the community that we might label reform-pluralism. Reform-pluralists wished to break away somewhat from Jewish traditions, but consciously refused to deny or abandon them. Such individuals were generally educated in the German system and were deeply involved with artistic and intellectual activities in German society before they came in contact with, or rediscovered, the richness of Jewish traditions. Such a path of rediscovery was characteristic of many participants in the folk-song movements associated with German-Jewish social organizations. Rediscovery sometimes resulted from accident or from a more conscious search for new sources of inspiration or tradition. This response loomed especially important for German Jews who immigrated to Palestine, for there rediscovery of traditional culture became especially dramatic for many.

The final category contained the liberals, those who turned, seemingly in a subconscious fashion, to the explication of Jewish values throughout their lives, but were not specifically interested in portraying these as quintessentially Jewish. Perhaps the earliest of the liberal German-Jewish intellectuals was Heinrich Heine. One of the last was Walter Benjamin. Almost totally lacking traditional Jewish education, Benjamin never lost sight of the relation of the contemporary Jewish community to ancient and medieval Jewish society.[38] The liberals were perhaps the most tragic figures among the intellectuals of the community, for they lived in an idealistic world of German-Jewish culture that would vanish irrevocably with the rise of Nazism. They remain important, however, because their works stand as outstanding monuments to the positive aspects of an emancipated Jewish community.

Although emancipation and modernization may have loosened the traditional sense of community Jews had earlier known, new processes of change in the early decades of the twentieth century succeeded in reversing that trend, effecting a new sense of community based on entirely different cultural values. New organizations formed to serve the needs of the community. Very often, these needs were not—at least at first—specifically related to the Jewish community. German-Jewish musical organizations prior to about 1920, for example, performed a standard repertory no different from that of non-Jewish musical organizations. Still, cultural organizations with Jewish memberships found themselves turning more toward the specific needs of the Jewish community during the 1920s and 1930s. Most important, the new sense of community depended on a revitalized and renewed social structure within German-Jewish culture in the final decades before the Holocaust. That culture had transcended any simple appropriation of German society, but had, instead, sent out new tendrils, discovering fertile soil of its own.

NOTES

1. For a thorough study of the Jewish community in Central Europe during the century and one half preceding emancipation, see Herman Pollack, *Jewish Folkways in Germanic Lands (1648-1806): Studies in Aspects of Daily Life* (Cambridge: MIT Press, 1971).

2. Alex Bein, "Vorraussetzungen: Ein Wort der Einführung," in *Juden in Preußen: Ein Kapitel deutscher Geschichte,* ed. Roland Klemig (Dortmund: Die bibliophilen Taschenbücher, 1981), p. 19.

3. Walter Grab, "Der preußische Weg der Judenemanzipation," in ibid., p. 24.

4. Jacob Katz, *Out of the Ghetto: The Social Background of Jewish Emancipation, 1770-1870* (1973; New York: Schocken, 1978), pp. 19-20; and Rita Thalmann, "Nationale Identität und kulturelle Spezifität: Die Erfahrungen des deutschen Judentums im liberalen Zeitalter," in *Juden in Deutschland: Zur Geschichte einer Hoffnung,* ed. Peter von der Osten-Sacken (Berlin: Institut Kirche und Judentum, 1980), p. 191.

5. Alfred D. Low, *Jews in the Eyes of the Germans: From the Enlightenment to Imperial Germany* (Philadelphia: Institute for the Study of Human Issues, 1979), p. 13.

6. Reinhard Rürup, "Juden in Preußen: Probleme ihrer Geschichte," in Klemig, *Juden in Preußen,* p. 31.

7. Katz, *Out of the Ghetto,* pp. 31-32.

8. For an excellent series of articles addressing the relation of the German Enlightenment to Jewish emancipation, see Walter Grab, ed., *Deutsche Aufklärung und Judenemanzipation,* Vol. 3: *Jahrbuch des Instituts für deutsche Geschichte* (Ramat-Aviv: Tel Aviv University Press, 1980).

9. Low, *Jews in the Eyes of the Germans,* p. 18.

10. Ibid., p. 19.

11. Ibid., p. 75.

12. Gershom Scholem, "Jews and Germans," in *On Jews and Judaism in Crisis: Selected Essays,* ed. and trans. Werner J. Dannhauser (New York: Schocken, 1976), p. 75.

13. A well-stocked and diverse library was a part of many German-Jewish homes even before emancipation; see Pollack, *Jewish Folkways,* pp. 7-8.

14. Katz, *Out of the Ghetto,* pp. 44-45.

15. Scholem, "Jews and Germans," p. 79; many Jews adopted Schiller as a surname (for example, Salomon Schiller, the Zionist) to symbolize their respect for his ideals.

16. Gershom Scholem, *Von Berlin nach Jerusalem* (Frankfurt: Suhrkamp Verlag, 1977), pp. 42, 52.

17. Peter Gay, "Begegnung mit der Moderne: Deutsche Juden im deutschen Geistesleben," in Klemig, *Juden in Preußen,* p. 43; and Low, *Jews in the Eyes of the Germans,* p. 410.

18. Elfie Labsch-Benz, *Die jüdische Gemeinde Nonnenweier: Jüdisches Leben und Brauchtum in einer badischen Landgemeinde zu Beginn des 20. Jahrhunderts* (Freiburg im Breisgau: Verlag Wolf Mersch, 1981), pp. 36-37; and Calvin Goldscheider and Alan S. Zuckerman, *The Transformation of the Jews* (Chicago: University of Chicago Press, 1984), p. 16.

19. Labsch-Benz, *Die jüdische Gemeinde Nonnenweier,* p. 20.

20. Goldscheider and Zuckerman, *The Transformation of the Jews,* pp. 14-15. Jewish immigration to the cities extensively depleted small-town populations; the southwest German village of Nonnenweier had a Jewish population of 244 in 1855, but only 65 in 1933; Labsch-Benz, *Die jüdische Gemeinde Nonnenweier,* p. 19.

21. Marsha L. Rozenblit, *The Jews of Vienna, 1867-1914: Assimilation and Identity* (Albany: State University of New York Press, 1983), p. 23.

22. Labsch-Benz, *Die jüdische Gemeinde Nonnenweier,* p. 31, note; from the upper class of 1901 in Nonnenweier, two of five Jewish children went to the *Gymnasium,* whereas none of the thirty-five non-Jewish children did.

23. Goldscheider and Zuckerman, *The Transformation of the Jews,* p. 82.

24. Rozenblit, *The Jews of Vienna,* p. 16.

25. Goldscheider and Zuckerman, *The Transformation of the Jews,* p. 85, and Rozenblit, *The Jews of Vienna,* p. 99.

26. Goldscheider and Zuckerman, *The Transformation of the Jews,* p. 82.

27. Beling, *Die gesellschaftliche Eingliederung,* p. 16.

28. Rozenblit, *The Jews of Vienna,* p. 124.

29. Ibid., pp. 199-207 (Appendix II).

30. See Steven E. Aschheim, *Brothers and Strangers: The East European Jew in German and German Jewish Consciousness, 1800-1923* (Madison: University of Wisconsin Press, 1982).

31. Bach, *The German Jew,* pp. 116-21.

32. Christoph Daxelmüller, "Die deutschsprachige Volkskunde und die Juden: Zur Geschichte und den Folgen einer kulturellen Ausklammerung," *Zeitschrift für Volkskunde* 83, no. 1 (1987): 1-20.

33. Frederic V. Grunfeld, *Prophets without Honour: A Background to Freud, Kafka, Einstein and Their World* (New York: McGraw-Hill, 1980), p. 196.

34. Scholem, "Jews and Germans," pp. 83-84; the most complete analysis of the confrontation between Zionist and other Jewish organizations is Jehuda Reinharz, *Fatherland or Promised Land: The Dilemma of the German Jews, 1893-1914* (Ann Arbor: University of Michigan Press, 1975).

35. Low, *Jews in the Eyes of the Germans*, p. 411.

36. Fritz Stern, "Die Bürde des Erfolgs oder die Rolle des Judentums in der deutschen Geschichte," in Klemig, *Juden in Preußen*, p. 42.

37. George L. Mosse, *Germans and Jews: The Right, the Left, and the Search for a "Third Force" in Pre-Nazi Germany* (New York: Howard Fertig, 1970), p. 25.

38. See, for example, his letters; Walter Benjamin, *Briefe*, ed. Theodor W. Adorno and Gershom Scholem (Frankfurt am Main: Suhrkamp Verlag, 1966); see especially the letters exchanged with Scholem that appear in Gershom Scholem, ed., *Walter Benjamin/Gershom Scholem Briefwechsel 1933-1940* (Frankfurt am Main: Suhrkamp Verlag, 1980).

3

Folk Music and Emerging National Consciousness

DURING THE nineteenth century a variety of social organizations began to occupy the German cultural landscape. Some of these organizations were descendants of the guild tradition. Others had formed more recently to provide small groups a measure of individuality that would serve as a bulwark against the geographic and social expansion of the German state. Among those who organized themselves most effectively, especially toward the end of the nineteenth century, were Jews. The ubiquitous social organization, the *Verein,* could serve virtually any group, preserving its special interests while still presenting a front of relative social homogeneity. The *Verein* was thus a vehicle for cultural pluralism in a nation that was striving for unity, at least at a structural level. Early in the nineteenth century German-Jewish groups recognized the possibility of adapting the *Verein* structure to their own particular needs, whereby they fulfilled the two-pronged goal of emancipation and retention of cultural patterns that separated the Jewish community from the rest of German society. Jewish *Vereine* were much like those of other groups: a single organization encompassing students, occupational groups, individuals with similar avocations, or simply residents of a particular area. Hence, whereas the individual *Verein* represented somewhat limited groups of individuals, the multitude and variety of German-Jewish cultural organizations cut across society as a whole.

Music was an essential part of the German social organizations. Most published some form of songbook designed ostensibly for specific use by the individual *Verein.* The songbooks were used during meetings and at musical events sponsored by other groups with similar goals. Individual members used them at home, more as literature than as music, thus symbolizing the extension of *Verein* ideology into the life of the individual. Initially, the songbooks of German-Jewish organizations were intended for functions similar to those of non-Jewish groups; however, as the organizational song, the *Vereinslied,* increased in popularity at the beginning of the twentieth century, new goals and activities developed among Jewish groups. The *Vereinslied* was really not a single type or genre of song, but a diverse range of folk songs unified by the functions they served for the social organization. The new functions in the Jewish community paralleled the changes with which the community was forced to struggle while resisting the vortex of assimilation. The music of the Jewish social organization thus stood as a receptacle of community attitudes and values, a means for the promulgation of new ideas and the casting aside of those deemed ineffective when the Jewish *Verein* found it necessary to respond to external challenge. More historically conscious at the end of the nineteenth century, German-Jewish *Vereinslieder* turned increasingly toward Israel in the early twentieth century.

The songbooks of Central European Jewish social organizations provide unusual insight into community cultural attitudes and the degree to which these penetrated Jewish society for several reasons. First, the songbooks were immensely popular. Virtually every edition sold out quickly, and subsequent editions almost always followed during the years after initial publication. Second, each new edition and songbook included more songs and new genres. Unlike other *Vereine,* Jewish groups had few songbook prototypes within their own community until the final decades of the nineteenth century. Soon after the first important songbook was published in 1894,[1] however, the tradition proliferated rapidly among Jewish groups. Third, several central themes unified the multifarious Jewish songbooks, and these demonstrated a clear, historical continuity, as well as the tangible interrelations that unified the purposes of the different groups.

No single theme was more predominant than that of *Heimat* ("homeland"), a theme that was reified in the 1920s and 1930s when settlement in a Jewish homeland became first a reality and then a necessity. The degree to which the *Vereinslied* penetrated and influenced Jewish society has underscored historical continuity because many who sang from these books succeeded in reaching Palestine in the 1920s and 1930s, and there they continued to use the books in symbolic ways, at least as long as the memory of the organizations they represented survived.

The books of *Vereinslieder* are vital to an examination of the Jewish community in the half century prior to the Holocaust for yet another reason: they are among the few extant documents from the organizations that employed them.[2] Only scant accounts of meetings and group activities survive, and virtually all other written documents generated by the organizations have disappeared or were destroyed. Indeed, the survival of the songbooks against the same odds is perhaps the most convincing testament to a salient role in the transformation of the Central European community.

The emergence of the *Vereinslied* symbolized a general movement in Germany that encouraged the dissemination and practice of folk song at all levels of society, thus strengthening and redirecting the goals espoused by the singing-society movement in Germany, whose genesis dated from the beginning of the nineteenth century. Through the emergent importance of widespread nationalistic song repertories, the musical activities of vastly different organizations became a symbol for German democratic or populist attitudes that followed quickly on the heels of the 1871 centralization of government by Bismarck. A parallel attitude flourished in Jewish groups, but was focused in a somewhat different direction by a rather different nationalism. Whereas the general movement reinforced the notion of what constituted *ein deutsches Lied*, its manifestation among Jewish groups rein-forced — or in some cases created — the concept of *ein jüdisches Lied*.

Like their non-Jewish counterparts, Jewish *Vereine* provided a sense of group identification. In the late nineteenth century, however, the sense of group identification sought by many Jewish organizations began to differ from that of non-Jewish groups. With other groups identifying nationalism with the German state, Jewish *Vereine* began to direct their vision of nationalism toward the future, thus linking it to the potential foundation of a Jewish state. This intensified Jewish nationalism quickly found a voice in the songbooks of Jewish organizations, whose songs came to espouse it openly.

The historical development of the Jewish *Vereinslied* assumed two different directions, referred to here as mainstream and secondary. The songbooks of the first category were produced in significantly greater num-bers than the second. Their editors intended them to reach a far greater and more diverse audience. Whatever goals they served, these mainstream songbooks cut across the wide range of Jewish groups and unquestionably influenced their cultural attitudes.

The secondary songbooks had a more restricted nature. Often they served only a small group; at other times, their scope addressed only modest goals, such as the local celebration of a special event or holiday; sometimes they merely supplemented the mainstream songbooks. Some secondary books became very important when they influenced other secondary books, as well as those of the mainstream. A few of these songbooks acted as catalysts, redirecting historical tendencies. Thus, the secondary songbooks were very important as undercurrents that at times altered the course of mainstream developments.

The historical development of German-Jewish songbooks unfolded quite gradually despite the claims of successive editors and compilers that they were rendering dramatic changes. In the mainstream songbooks there is never a case of wholesale abandonment of previous material; instead, new folk songs entered by gradually replacing ones felt to be less suitable and by simply expanding the contents of the songbook itself. Dramatic changes in the overall historical development occurred only in the secondary books, albeit here often because of the limited scope of most. If the completely new repertory exhibited by some of these songbooks subsequently reached other books, then a form of dramatic change often followed. Still, such alterations as might result in these cases rarely displaced a familiar genre in the mainstream songbooks.

Most songbook editors occupied themselves in some way with identifying the exact characteristics of a Jewish folk song. Understandably, there was little agreement concerning these characteristics, although there were certain traits that most editors accepted and therefore included with some consistency in their anthologies. These characteristics stemmed from both text and melody. The first characteristic named by most editors and, in fact, upon which there was almost universal editorial agreement was the core of sadness present in almost all Jewish music. One editor remarked: "In the modern secular folk song the entire existence of the Jewish people is reflected with exhaustive completeness. The total sadness of the Jewish soul speaks from the mournful melancholy of the song. The song cries forth with sadness; one clearly perceives in it the repressed, unshed tears of undeserved, incessant offenses, the difficult suffering and confrontation that this truly martyred people has endured for centuries."[3] Tragedy was also portrayed as an influence on other aspects of Jewish life and other genres of folk song; it became, for instance, the primary mood underlying the different collections of Jewish *Liebeslieder* ("love songs") that appeared in the 1910s and 1920s, presumably distinguishing even Jewish love songs from those of other ethnic groups.[4]

For virtually every editor Jewish folk song encapsulated a sense of history. This history was not only that of the ancient Jews, but also of more recent eras and the present. It was noted, for instance, "In the content of the song, in its words is mirrored the entire existence of the Jewish people, their customs and traditional feelings, their present situation and their memories of the past. The historical songs are also to a certain extent especially characteristic of the Jewish song."[5] In later collections this tragic motif became one that turned hopefully toward the future and the return to some form of historic homeland.

Another question tackled by songbook editors was the relation of language to culture: Exactly which Jewish communities truly represented Jewish culture? Responses might vary from the urban ghetto and its oppressive labor conditions to the liberating power of nature, which was the true home for Jewish *Wandervogel* groups like the *Blau-Weiß*. At different stages in the historical development the editors supplied different answers to the question. At the middle stage, Eastern European culture and the Yiddish language took the position of true cultural representative; in the late stage, the culture of Palestine and Hebrew assumed this position. At no stage, however, was German considered the proper language for cultural representative. The compilers therefore faced a problem, for their potential audience had only limited knowledge of Yiddish and Hebrew, and preferred — as the songbook prefaces often confessed — to sing in a language in which they were fluent. As a process of historical change in folk song, this was quite an unusual situation. Songbook contents generally reveal the results of compromise, conceding to the German language with the rejoinder that it was not truly the language of Jewish folk song. One means of ameliorating this conflict was to stress the interrelation between Yiddish and German; this approach especially characterized later songbooks, whereas the early prefaces usually suggested that Yiddish culture was strange and faraway, even at odds with German culture.[6]

A canon of Jewish melodic characteristics also emerged during the fifty years prior to the Holocaust. As a primary principle in this canon, Jewish folk songs should usually be in a minor key, or the Aeolian or Dorian mode. Most editors described this modal ascription merely as an outgrowth of the folk song's relation to tragedy and sadness.[7] The canon of melodic characteristics for the German-Jewish organizational song did not contain the modal variety found in Eastern European Jewish folk song, even when a collection was intended to evoke a particularly Eastern European pathos.[8] This somewhat streamlined approach to melody resulted from both the uses and functions of the *Vereinslied*. Of utmost importance, the songs needed a melodic style that amateur singers could learn quickly. It was incumbent on the compilers that they use "well-known melodies," which they often announced on a collection's title page, as well as those primarily utilizing step-wise or triadic melodic motion. The melodic model for such *Vereinslieder* was generally the German folk song; any special Jewish flavor usually resulted from stereotypic embellishments.

Genres whose use was not that different from the organizational songs of non-Jewish groups might well need only slight changes to render them

Jewish. Textual motifs, combined with a slightly different melodic structure, were sufficient to identify them as Jewish. By the 1920s the genres of Jewish *Vereinslieder* had become relatively fixed, forming a substantial corpus from which many editors drew. The following categories summarize the most common genres:

Religiös-mystisches Lied ("the mystical religious song"): These are songs that grow from religious texts, ideas, or traditions, but have come to exhibit a currency like folk song.

Wiegenlied ("lullaby"): This is a genre that several compilers claimed to be both the saddest and the most widely disseminated of Jewish folk songs; like children's songs, lullabies did not occur very often in the organizational songbooks because of the general nature of the Jewish *Verein*.

Kinderlieder ("children's songs"): The genre was limited in number and quality, a claim that some editors related to the Jewish boy's early preoccupation with philosophical questions in the *yeshiva*. Whether acknowledged by all editors or not, most songs of this nature in the anthologies came from German repertories.

Liebeslieder ("love songs"): This is a common genre to which several complete anthologies were devoted; traditionally represented by sad, rather than happy stories.

Hochzeitslieder ("wedding songs"): Despite the general happiness such events brought to the Jewish household, the wedding songs in anthologies rarely lacked a tragic tinge.

Soldatenlieder ("soldiers' songs"): These were not particularly representative, but unusual because of their occasional mixture of Yiddish with Russian.

Allgemeine deutsche Lieder ("common songs in German"): This is a category unto itself in most anthologies, but usually contains at least half of the songs.

Heimatlieder ("homeland songs"): This category bridges all others and is one in which songs from all genres are found.

Songs in Hebrew: These songs are increasingly represented in almost all anthologies during the twentieth century.

The sections organizing the songbooks increasingly identified these genres in overt fashion. Not every anthology used all the genres, rather only three or four. During the final phase of songbook development, however, the categories became considerably less arbitrary and solidified into the systems of organization to which most editors adhered.

The historical development of German-Jewish *Vereinslieder* falls into three fairly distinct stages. The first dates from 1890 to 1910 and represents a period in which the German-Jewish books were based largely on general German folk-song themes. The second dates from approximately 1910 until 1925 and encompasses the major period of transition brought about by World War I and increased awareness of Eastern European Jewish culture; for this reason, I shall refer to the second period as the Yiddish stage. The third stage dates from approximately 1925 until 1938 and bears the imprint of increased contact with Palestine and settlers there, thus making it most appropriate call this period the Israel stage.

On their surface the changes through which German-Jewish songbooks passed were not unlike those characterizing the songbooks of other groups from approximately 1890 to 1938. All songbooks drew more heavily from the general folk-song repertory at the beginning of the period, but relied to a greater extent on songs specifically suited to the individual organization at the end. All exhibited a developing and increasingly intense sense of nationalism throughout the period. The major difference occurred beneath the surface, more in degree than in kind. Whereas nationalism had always been a theme for German-Jewish songbooks, it took the form of very Romantic, if not nebulous, images at the beginning. Toward the end, the focus sharpened because it became apparent that a potential homeland in Palestine did exist. Therefore, during the same period when German organizational songbooks became more intensely fixed on nationalism in Germany, Jewish songbooks for the most part appeared increasingly alienated from that venue.

There were two important turning points for the German-Jewish songbooks. The first occurred when an increased interest in Eastern European Jewish culture emerged in Central Europe. The second came at the same moment a general shift in focus transpired in the songbooks of other groups in Germany, namely during and just after World War I.[9] For the German-Jewish organizations these two turning points occurred at approximately the same moment.

The Early Stage (1890-1910) was seemingly born of greater optimism than the later stages. The prevailing spirit in the songbooks was one of Romanticism, and both Jewish songs and non-specific German songs reflected that spirit. Although the use of organizational songbooks in German society had a long history, perhaps stretching to the Middle Ages, Jewish groups compiled such anthologies for the first time only at the end of the nineteenth century. The earliest Jewish songbooks thus owed a greater debt to non-Jewish prototypes. They also contained many songs composed or adapted by the compiler of the anthology itself or by well-known compilers active at the same time. It was in this way that Heinrich Loewe fashioned the first German-Jewish songbook of major importance, *Lieder-Buch für jüdische Vereine* ("Songbook for Jewish Organizations").[10] The earliest compilers found little conflict between the songs with German contents and those with Jewish themes. The songbook of the second Zionist Congress of 1898 in Basel, *Lieder zum Fest-Commers* ("Songs for the Festive Gathering"), primarily contained German student songs, with a few adapted for use by the Zionist movement.[11] A song entitled "Ein Hoch dem ganzen Judentum" ("A Toast to All of Jewry"), for example, was sung to the melody of "Gaudeamus Igitur," probably the best known of all German student songs.

Somewhat later during the early stage there arose cries for increased quantities of songs with Jewish content; other cries for retention of the German section were equally impassioned. The simple truth remains that the German songs were those best known by most *Verein* members, who were not prepared to abandon them for songs that were relatively unknown. Editors had to weigh the opposing arguments, but in the early stage most opted for the retention of a generous section of German songs.[12]

In the early stage the emphasis on sadness and tragedy was considerably less than in the later stages. Several books consciously attempted to create a greater sense of optimism. One editor, for example, asserted that the plethora of sad songs in Jewish repertories resulted from the limited concentration of earlier collections on the tragic side of Jewish life and history; he, in contrast, advocated that more attention be turned to the joyful side of Jewish life.[13] This more optimistic tone, combined with that attending the wealth of German songs in the anthologies of the early stage, serves to distinguish the contents of the earliest books in a marked way from those of the later stages.

Hebrew occurred only sparingly in the songs of the early stage; Yiddish was used almost not at all. Hebrew songs were usually translations of well-known songs from the German repertory or recently composed songs that were beginning to establish the foundation of a Hebrew song repertory in Central Europe. "Gaudeamus Igitur" was one of the most common examples of the first category, "Ha-Tikva" (now the Israeli national anthem) of the second.

The predominant genre in the songbooks of the early stage was the *Heimatlied.* Homeland songs did not occupy sections of their own; rather, they dominated sections that usually bore titles like "jüdische Lieder" or "Lieder jüdisches Inhalts" ("songs with Jewish content"). A "Jewish song" for the earliest compilers was most often a *Heimatlied.* The "homeland" of these songs was ancient Israel, referred to as Zion. (Figure 1 reproduces the first publication of the most common of these homeland songs, "Nach der Heimat!" ["To the Homeland!"].) The image of Zion was extremely Romantic, and the descriptions of it lacked realism and accuracy. Successive editors incorporated these early *Heimatlieder,* many of them composed specifically for the new songbooks, into each of the following stages of development, where they became the cornerstones of a new tradition. The considerable continuity and the wide dissemination of this tradition identify *Heimatlieder* as a genre of Jewish folk song that grew directly from the Jewish community of nineteenth- and early twentieth-century Germany.

The Yiddish Stage (1910-25) was also characterized by Romanticism, albeit with a somewhat different focus. The focus had shifted from a homeland that was most akin to ancient Israel to one that fitted the Romantic images of the *shtettl* in Eastern Europe. There were probably many reasons for this new fascination with Yiddish culture, not least of which was that it was better described in the literature of the day. Many editors during this stage had grown up in East Prussia, thus on the borders of Eastern European Jewish culture, or in Eastern Europe itself. For the songbooks of German-Jewish groups there were new sources and collections of Yiddish songs being published in Eastern Europe, and these provided the first real font from which the editors could draw.[14]

The Yiddish influence appeared gradually, probably because many potential users were unfamiliar with the Jewish culture of Eastern Europe and may have regarded it as inferior to that of Central Europe. Prefaces introduced Yiddish song by describing the ways in which it differed from German song: more spontaneous; less cultivated and more natural; and a cultural force able to lend unity to the diverse Jewish groups in Eastern Europe.[15]

For the first time the Central European Jewish songbooks contained songs that were, in practice, not readily performable by members of the social organizations. True, "Gaudeamus Igitur" in Hebrew may have been difficult for many, but at least the Latin version and the melody were familiar. Both Yiddish songs and their melodies were strange. When the songs referred to aspects of Eastern European culture that were completely foreign, for example, the *Hassidim,* the situation became even more prob-

Nach der Heimat!

Fern im Osten, unter grünen Bäumen,
Wo die Wiege meiner Väter stand,
Möchte ich auf blüh'nden Feldern träumen,
Möcht' ich weinen an der Tempelwand.

Fig. 1. Music and text for the song "Nach der Heimat!"
("To the Homeland!"), from *Lieder-Buch für jüdische
Vereine,* probably the first Jewish organizational songbook. Source: Heinrich Loewe, ed., *Lieder-Buch für Jüdische Vereine* (Berlin: Hugo Schildberger, 1894).

lematic. It is possible, thus, that the symbolic value of the Yiddish songs was more significant than widespread use by Jewish *Vereine*. Sometimes such songs filled single volumes, further suggesting a primarily symbolic role in which the unity of European Jewry was the central message.

Several other historical factors came to bear on the songbooks during the Yiddish stage. Zionism was more widely recognized as a viable possibility for the solution to the Jewish need for a homeland. Some Jewish *Vereine* were affected by this emergence of Zionism because they allied themselves, at least informally, with Zionist organizations. For many, the concept of Zion did not yet mean a political entity in Palestine, but it did suggest the potential for unity. In the songbooks calls such as "unser Volkslied vereint uns"[16] ("our folk song unites us") were not uncommon. Still, the songs of the Yiddish period retained a certain abstract attitude toward a homeland: in part, it already existed in Eastern Europe; in part, such a homeland was both temporary and inadequate, and must give way to one of more permanence.

During the Yiddish stage several important figures emerged as leaders of an effort to bring about a German-Jewish folk-song revival. The most prominent of these was Arno Nadel (1878-1943), himself born in Eastern Europe (Vilna), but living in Berlin since 1895. Nadel was an amateur musicologist of sorts and engaged in the collection of both Eastern European folk songs and old manuscripts of synagogal music. He published many of these in newspapers and journals, such as the *Berlin Gemeindeblatt* and *Ost und West*, and contributed articles about Jewish music to dictionaries and encyclopedias of Jewish studies. His publication of songbooks dramatically affected the Yiddish stage, and he was frequently asked to revise songbooks so that they might more meaningfully reflect Jewish themes. The sources for Nadel's work were almost exclusively Eastern European, whether intended for secular or religious anthologies. Throughout the second and third stages of the historical development of German-Jewish songbooks, Nadel's activities continued, both close to his home in Berlin, where he was responsible for restoring old traditions of synagogal music, and at great distances from Central Europe, for example through his participation in undertakings of the World Centre for Jewish Music in Palestine.

The growth of new German-Jewish publishing firms acted as a stimulus to the increased interest in the Jewish culture of Eastern Europe. Either well-known Jewish publishing houses or smaller presses owned by Jews published the Jewish songbooks. The absence of such firms before the late nineteenth century points to another reason for the relative lack of Jewish organizational songbooks before 1890. The most important Jewish press of the twentieth century was the Jüdischer Verlag of Berlin, founded in 1901. This house would publish the *Blau-Weiß* songbooks, as well as numerous collections by Arno Nadel and Ludwig Strauss, another of the most active editors from the final period. Other firms that published German-Jewish songbooks were the Weltverlag and Philo Verlag, both of them established in 1919, and Schocken Verlag, which was most active during the 1930s.[17] In some instances, the special publishing interests of a firm became apparent in the songbooks published by it. This was true of the anthologies published by the Jüdischer Verlag, which devoted considerable attention to both Zionist and Yiddish literature.[18]

The Romanticism of the earlier two stages gave way to a more realistic conceptualization in the final stage of development, the *Israel Stage* (1925-38). Again, historical factors partially explain this shift, namely the increasing awareness of Jewish settlement in Palestine and the emergence of a culture and literature using modern Hebrew. Symbolizing these changes was the strengthened posture of Zionism. More Jewish *Vereine* in Central Europe allied themselves with the Zionist movement, and the alliance was increasingly reflected in their songbooks.

What had happened to the ideologies that had dominated the two earlier stages? In a simple answer: their Romantic images became anachronistic in an age when reality belied those images. The view of Zion as a land associated with ancient Israel had not disappeared, and Eastern European Jewish culture still provided the tentative recognition of contemporary unity. But the concepts had been transformed. Yiddish culture was no longer the central focus of songbooks. Instead, larger collections relegated Yiddish songs to special sections. Often, songs in Yiddish appeared only in German translation or in Germanized Yiddish. Discussion and glorification of the culture of Eastern European Jews gradually disappeared from the prefaces. Replacing the emphasis on Yiddish was greater emphasis on songs in Hebrew. Not only did more religious songs appear in the anthologies, but songs from Palestine were included. More songs also incorporated Hebrew translations. For the first time many *Verein* members probably knew enough Hebrew to sing in that language with relative ease. Many Hebrew songs also had ostensibly didactic ends, namely to instruct the members of Jewish groups in Hebrew.

Other traditions from Palestine also appeared in the songbooks of the final stage. Textless sections, usually entitled "Horra-Melodien" ("hora melodies") or "Niggunim" (instrumental melodies, usually sung without text), often appeared with explanations that the tunes came from Palestine or were sent by a pioneer now living there. In the 1930s the activities of various *Vereine* were united under the auspices of the *jüdischer Kulturbund* ("Jewish Cultural Federation"), a cultural organization forced upon Jewish communities by the Nazis, but one which served the cultural development of many communities in positive ways by strengthening the sense of community. Because of the increased and coordinated activities of Jewish *Vereine*, songbooks had a broader distribution and could disseminate cultural unity more effectively. Indeed, the period during which the cultural activities of German-Jewish groups were most widespread was also the final one before the Holocaust.

The five songbooks that I discern as the components of the songbook tradition's mainstream attest to the continuity of the tradition from 1890 to 1938. Not only did these books successively utilize one another for prototypes, but many of the lesser known songbooks were also based on them. They provided a gradual transition for the tradition, and, in some ways, their editors may actually have been responsible for determining the course of the tradition.

The preface to the first important Central European Jewish songbook, *Lieder-Buch für jüdische Vereine* (Heinrich Loewe, editor, 1894), expressed two very definite ideologies (fig. 2). The first was a reaction to assimilation, which the editor saw as ultimately destructive of Jewish life in Central Europe. Loewe believed that many Jews, especially intellectuals, had for too long approached Judaism from an objective and scientific standpoint and had thus failed to experience it in an emotional and immediate way. Loewe was himself an intellectual, being a librarian and later a professor at the University of Berlin, but he was also an ardent Zionist from an early age. In 1892, he founded "Jung Israel" ("Young Israel"), the first German Zionist student group. Later, he was among the founders of the "Vereinigung jüdisches Studierenden" ("Association of Jewish Students"), from which grew the "Kartell jüdischer Verbindungen" ("Cartel of Jewish Associations"), the parent organization for Zionist student groups in Germany.[19] It is hardly surprising to discover that such an organizer should also edit the first major songbook for Jewish cultural organizations. His preface was relatively short, but Loewe expressed very clearly his goal of making the songbook a part of the more immediate and emotional quality inherent in Judaism; this immediacy, he further claimed, would give rise to a second goal for the songbook, the emergence of a sense of Jewish nationalism.[20]

The contents of the volume comprised three sections plus an appendix.

Fig. 2. Title page for Loewe, *Lieder-Buch für Jüdische Vereine*. Source:
Heinrich Loewe, ed., *Lieder-Buch für Jüdische Vereine* (Berlin: Hugo
Schildberger, 1894).

Actually, a more appropriate subdivision might have been two parts, one with songs of Jewish content and the other with songs from the German folk-song repertory. The songs of Jewish content were predominantly *Heimatlieder*, many of which were composed especially for the songbook. Even the poems in the third section, "Jüdische Gedichte zum Vortrage" ("Jewish Poems for Public Reading"), were primarily devoted to subjects relative to the homeland. Loewe had himself contributed much to the volume, both to the songs in the way of texts and to the poetry section. Loewe's interest in Zionism expressed itself throughout the songbook, as borne out by the multitude of titles such as "Heimkehr" ("Returning Home") and "Die Rückkehr in's Vaterland" ("The Return to the Fatherland"). Significantly, however, Loewe relied heavily on standard German folk-song repertories to flesh out the book, reflecting the lack of Jewish *Vereinslieder* from which to draw. The appendix contained only two songs in Hebrew, the first a "Chanukahhymne" ("Ḥanukah Hymn") and the second, "Gaudeamus Igitur" in Hebrew. The *Lieder-Buch für jüdische Vereine* influenced scores of songbooks that followed. Subsequent editors incorporated many individual songs by Loewe into other anthologies, and in doing so they amended the lacunae in the German-Jewish *Vereinslieder* repertory.

The *Vereinsliederbuch für Jung-Juda* (Turnverein "Bar Kochba," Berlin, Max Zirker, ed., 1905), the songbook of the *Bar Kochba* athletic society of Berlin, was the most popular book from the first period (fig. 3). It quickly sold out and was widely distributed among Central European Jewish groups. The book clearly represented the first stage of development, although themes from the Yiddish stage — especially in the second edition (ca. 1909) — were also evident in its pages.

The main part of the songbook had three sections: (1) traditional German folk songs; (2) songs in Hebrew with Zionist texts; and (3) songs in German with Zionist or Jewish themes. Again, traditional German songs predominated. The editor did, however, take steps to increase the Jewish content, and songs in Hebrew increased in number. Although there was some editing of German songs with Jewish contents — apparently because they caused some misunderstanding and were of questionable authenticity — this book included a few songs with Yiddish texts in an appendix; in his preface Zirker expressed his belief that the *Vereinsliederbuch für Jung-Juda* was the first German-Jewish songbook to do this. Zirker called attention to a new movement toward Jewish national consciousness, but he stopped short of linking it to Eastern Europe, preferring, instead, to relate it to Jewish culture in Germany: "With the new stirring of the Jewish soul, the Jewish-

Fig. 3. Title page for Zirker, *Vereinsliederbuch für Jung-Juda.* Source: Max Zirker, ed., *Vereinsliederbuch für Jung-Juda* (Berlin: Jüdischer Buch- und Kunstverlag, [1905]).

German is also awakened to new life."[21] Zirker had reached a critical point in his attempt to maintain the tradition established by Heinrich Loewe. He drew heavily from Loewe's work and cited it as his model in the preface to the second edition, but he realized that new sources had to be found. He began to turn his search eastward for those sources, but it was not until the second stage that the richest sources were unveiled and incorporated into the songbooks.

The anthology *Blau-Weiß Liederbuch* (first edition, Karl Glaser, ed., 1914) was the first Jewish songbook to address itself to *Wandervogel* groups. The *Wandervögel* were not specifically Jewish groups, but the Jewish branch, *Blau-Weiß*, became immensely popular during the 1910s and 1920s, and laid the groundwork for several youth immigrations to Palestine during that period. Most of the people I interviewed in Israel who had immigrated prior to 1933 had been members of the *Blau-Weiß* and claimed it as a major stimulus in their decision to immigrate. Felix Sulman of Jerusalem acknowledged this complex interrelation among folk songs, the *Blau-Weiß*, and emerging nationalism, and the role it played in his youth with the following thoughts: "One thing is clear: my whole education was based on a Romantic approach to music and all the music which a hiking person would like to hear. . . . I was then a conductor of the Youth Movement. We had a choir of the whole unit together. We normally had a program of German folk songs, and here and there embellished by Hebrew national songs."[22] Many of these same informants made similar claims for the persuasive power of the *Blau-Weiß* songbook, which many of them continued to use years later in Israel.

The songs of the first edition evoked a sense of unity in the *Blau-Weiß*. Editors exhorted young singers to rejoice in singing and to regard it as the purest emotional outlet: "Feeling is everything. One can only sing correctly when one knows how to be sensitive to that which lives in every soul, in the springlike jubilation of the wandering comrade, as in the defiant song of our hopeful people."[23] The first edition portrayed Jewish content in the songs in much the same way as the *Vereinsliederbuch für Jung-Juda* and relied primarily on songs with German texts. The *Blau-Weiß* first edition did not include a Hebrew section, although there were a few songs in Hebrew. There was a substantial number of songs in Yiddish, but the Yiddish had been somewhat Germanized for easier performance; the image of Eastern European culture, while present to a greater degree than in the *Bar Kochba* songbook, was very stylized, retaining a sense of foreignness. It was through the abandonment of that sense by the second edition that the major transition in the songbooks of the mainstream occurred during the Yiddish stage.

The songbook contained a single section devoted exclusively to *Heimatlieder*, the first such section in the mainstream books. The nine songs in the section, entitled *Freiheitslieder* ("freedom songs"), were set to well-known melodies, only two of which were printed, "Ha-Tikva" and "Dort, wo die Zeder" ("There, Where the Cedar"). The other songs were to use tunes from other common folk songs or those that appeared in the repertories of well-known Jewish *Vereine*. The presence of this section reveals that a corpus of *Heimatlieder* had evolved by 1914, so much so that an editor merely needed to cite their familiar melodies from other books.

Even though the songbook was intended specifically for *Blau-Weiß* groups, its appeal reached many Jewish organizations because of the successful way in which it gathered popular songs, but arranged them in order that they might broaden the sense of Jewish organizational camaraderie. In large part the editor was able to achieve this goal because the currency, circulation, and performance of such songs had increased during the previous twenty-five years to a point at which a Jewish folk-song repertory was extensive enough to obviate dependence on the standard German repertory.

Immediate success greeted the first edition of the *Blau-Weiß Liederbuch* (first edition, 1914 [fig. 4]; second edition, 1918), for it sold out in less than two months. One would naturally have expected that such a success would be followed quickly by additional printings, if not new editions. This probably would have been so had World War I not intervened, thereby bringing cultural activities of this sort to a standstill. Because the *Blau-Weiß* songbook did not immediately pass into new editions, the editors had the time necessary to examine the first edition and to consider carefully if it really did fulfill the needs of the *Blau-Weiß* groups. The editors concluded that the book fell somewhat short of these needs and that it would be necessary to reconceptualize the book's contents in order to bring the second edition into line with the changing philosophy of the *Blau-Weiß*.

There were probably several factors precipitating this dramatic reassessment of contents: the prevailing cultural attitude created by the war; and increased awareness of Eastern European culture, if not some concern that the German army was at war with Jews living in Eastern Europe. Arno Nadel, the new editor, set about to revise the *Blau-Weiß* songbook by expanding its Jewish contents, a task he planned to achieve by turning directly to Yiddish culture. The potential meaning of this culture for Central European Jews was announced in the preface almost as if it were a revelation, a radical departure from the more Romantic images of the first edition:

The fundamental contrast with the first edition is found in the

Fig. 4. Title page for first edition of the *Blau-Weiß Liederbuch*. Source: "Leadership of the Jewish Wanderbund," ed., *Blau-Weiß Liederbuch*, 1st edition (Berlin: Jüdischer Verlag, 1914).

greatly expanded treasures of Hebrew and Yiddish songs. It is almost four years since the first songbook appeared and in that time our relation to the songs of our people has become different, more intimate than it was. What was in the first edition only an experiment of timid Romanticism, a tentative striving for the resuscitation of the Jewish folk song for western Jewry, has today become an expression of our spiritual essence. It is not an exaggeration when we notice that the Yiddish and Hebrew songs have achieved more than broadening our understanding: they have won a place in our heart.[24]

To what degree Arno Nadel influenced the new edition is not immediately obvious. The title page of the first edition actually proclaims that it was the "leadership *of the Blau-Weiß* ("die Führerschaft des Jüdischen Wanderbundes"), that edited the book. The second edition, however, makes individual editorship clear, suggesting a shift from group consensus to the decisions of a single individual acting on behalf of the entire *Blau-Weiß.* It is highly probable, thus, that Nadel, drawing on his extensive experience with Eastern European Jewish music, took responsibility for altering the Jewish sections of the songbook. Supporting this argument is the fact that the changes in these sections were more alterations of kind than of sheer number. In other words, the new Yiddish songs were quite different from the Yiddish songs of the first edition, perhaps revealing the influence of a native speaker of Yiddish, but they were not present in a relatively greater quantity. The Yiddish used in the songs was not as Germanized as in the first edition, a change emphasized by a new orthography. The dramatic changes claimed by Nadel were not, therefore, quite as dramatic as he stated. The most important change was in the attitude expressed toward these songs: for the first time, we witness the full assertion that these songs from Eastern Europe were the true representatives of a united Jewish cultural spirit. With the second edition of the *Blau-Weiß* songbook the Yiddish stage of songbook development was in full swing.

The songbook had three main sections. The first was undesignated, but contained standard German songs, as well as some songs in German that evidenced various influences from Yiddish culture; this section contained 114 songs, by far the largest number in any section. The second section contained 23 Hebrew songs, quite a significant increase when compared to previous songbooks of the mainstream. The third section, containing 17 Yiddish songs, seems surprisingly small when weighed against the editor's assertions. Again, Nadel's assertions were less dramatic than he claimed.

Ignoring for a moment the sectional boundaries used by Nadel, one might divide the songs into five different categories. The dominant category would contain songs akin to the standard German *Vereinslied,* many of them well-known German folk songs. Others would be songs common to *Wandervogel* groups; some of these seem at odds with the philosophy of a Jewish group, for example "Je höher der Kirchturm" ("Ever Higher the Church Tower"). In the second category would fall songs that were a sort of hybrid of Yiddish and wandering songs. The focus remained on wandering, but the songs clearly came from Yiddish sources (for example, "Fun Spanien trog ich" ["I've Traveled from Spain"] or "Gee ich mir spazieren" ["I'm Going for a Stroll"]). The third category would contain seasonal and children's songs in Hebrew and Yiddish; these would probably tend only to reinforce Jewish song repertories already known rather than introduce new repertories from Eastern Europe or Palestine. Religious songs would constitute a fourth category; in Hebrew and Yiddish these songs were probably new for many Central European users. The fifth category would in many ways be the most interesting, for it represented the major innovation of the songbook. These songs straightforwardly addressed the search for a homeland, but were only in Hebrew or Yiddish. German songs of this type, that is *Heimatlieder,* were absent. Nadel had thus completely transformed this genre from "allgemeine deutsche Lieder" to a repertory using languages specifically associated with Judaism. By so doing, he has rendered a dramatic change in the genre lying at the core of the mainstream songbooks.

The final mainstream songbook, *Jüdisches Liederbuch — "Makkabi"* (Nathan Kaminski, ed., 1935 [1930], [fig. 5]), represented both culmination and innovation. On the one hand, it summarized and codified the developments of its predecessors; on the other, it clearly crystallized the changes characterizing the final stage of development. The contents of the Makkabi songbook pushed to the extremes the new directions evident in the second edition of the *Blau-Weiß* songbook. There were both considerably more Hebrew songs and considerably more German songs. The songs of the German section seem chosen more because of popularity than for reasons of cultural similarity to Jewish songs; thus, the German section was replete with the same types of songs found in the earliest German-Jewish songbooks, such as "Gaudeamus Igitur" and "C-A-F-F-E-E," rather than those used in the books of the middle period. Kaminski noted in his preface that the *Blau-Weiß* second edition was the model for his songbook, citing further each of the other books of the mainstream as influential. Strongly steeped in consciously Jewish heritage, the book also brought about several major changes that grew directly from contact with Palestine and the Jewish

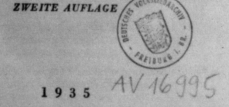

Fig. 5. Title page for Kaminski, the "Makkabi" *Jüdisches Liederbuch.*
Source: Nathan Kaminski, ed., *Jüdisches Liederbuch—"Makkabi,"*
2nd edition (Berlin: Jüdischer Verlag, 1935 [1930]).

settlements established there.[25] In his description of the Hebrew songs and dances in the Makkabi songbook, Kaminski also noted that they were collected and sent by several pioneer settlers in Palestine. He did not hesitate to designate Hebrew as the only true language of Judaism, other languages representing only the intervening centuries of wandering since expulsion from ancient Israel. The dawn of a new movement of Hebrew song emanating from Palestine would be but the logical culmination of Jewish history. Kaminski wrote: "The Hebrew song has undergone a dynamic transformation in recent years. The harp silenced more than 2,000 years ago on the shores of the Euphrates again sounds anew. Our Hebrew songs are the first harbingers of a new epoch of Jewish history. Through them the newly arisen Eretz-Israel illuminates Judaism throughout the world with the glow of its passion. The songs have passed from mouth to mouth in the Diaspora. Groups and organizations have taken them as their own. The need for a new collection of these songs is therefore obvious."[26]

The organization of the Makkabi songbook was more carefully conceived than that of its predecessors. The "Lieder jüdischen Inhalts," for example, was a section with particular genres rather than a potpourri of whatever Jewish songs the editor could find. Thus, this section utilized the same organization found in many songbooks for German *Vereine*. The focus of most of these songs was again the search for a homeland, a focus that rendered the entire section quite consistent with other sections in the book. Indeed, the motif of *Heimat* appeared throughout the book and manifested itself in diverse ways in all the sections.

Although the mainstream songbooks bore witness to a progressive unfolding of the musical traditions of Jewish cultural organizations, they often did not offer the clearest reflection of the influences coming to bear on the organizations. The mainstream books were, for example, sometimes conservative in their absorption of trends that had arisen elsewhere in Jewish society several years earlier. Some of the songbooks outside the mainstream reflected these changes more rapidly. Produced in smaller numbers, these books focused more specifically on single aspects of Jewish culture, for it was usually unnecessary that they reach a large audience. They did, however, influence the mainstream songbooks, sometimes indirectly, sometimes directly through their editors who were on occasion also involved with the publication of mainstream books.

The most consistent influence channeled by the books outside the mainstream was Eastern European Jewish culture. Although this influence was not reflected in the mainstream songbooks of the early period, it did appear in specialized songbooks from the period. Morris Rosenfeld's *Lieder des Ghetto* (fig. 6) was one of the most elaborate publications of "song" texts from the ghetto of Eastern Europe.[27] Clearly, the book was intended for a literate and cultivated readership, and was probably not used as an organizational songbook as such, an inference further suggested by its format, which was larger than that of most songbooks. The song texts appeared on pages that had elegant art nouveau borders. Most texts were in German, albeit with frequent recourse to Hebrew and Yiddish words. The spirit of the book was clearly German post-Romantic, heightening the emphasis on tragedy and suffering found throughout the book. Books such as *Lieder des Ghetto* did influence Jewish organizational songbooks during the early stage, not because they stood squarely within the tradition, rather because they confronted the reader directly with a portrayal of Jewish life in Eastern Europe. Such books utilized a literary style more familiar to the Central European than reflective of the culture being described, which probably intensified the effectiveness of the books. Eastern European Jewish culture, fomerly a mysterious realm separated from Germany by time and distance, was thereby brought closer to home.

During the second period of development numerous books devoted specifically to Yiddish folk music appeared. One of the most influential editors of these books was Ahron (Alexander) Eliasberg. In general his songbooks reflected an extremely high level of musicological source study, and he never failed to cite the many Yiddish collections that he had plumbed. Eliasberg's *Ostjüdische Volkslieder* (fig. 7)[28] appeared in 1918, the same year as the second edition of the *Blau-Weiß Liederbuch.* Although the book had the same format as most songbooks, it, like the *Lieder des Ghetto,* was probably intended as much for private use as for organizational singing. In a somewhat different tone from other editors Eliasberg did not make claims about the ways in which Yiddish songs represented the true spirit of Jewish nationalism. Instead, he recognized that dispersion throughout the world also bore with it a sense of homeland intrinsic to Jewish history.[29]

Eliasberg printed some of his songs in numerous versions, carefully annotating his sources and presenting variants in Polish and Lithuanian dialects of Yiddish as well as German. A scholarly aura pervaded the collection and served as its own means of convincing the reader that a strong tradition of Eastern European Jewish song did exist. The linguistic treatment of the texts was meticulous, and the orthography in the voluminous notes was a valuable didactic aid for those not knowing Yiddish. *Ostjüdische Volkslieder* acted as a counterpart to most German-Jewish songbooks from

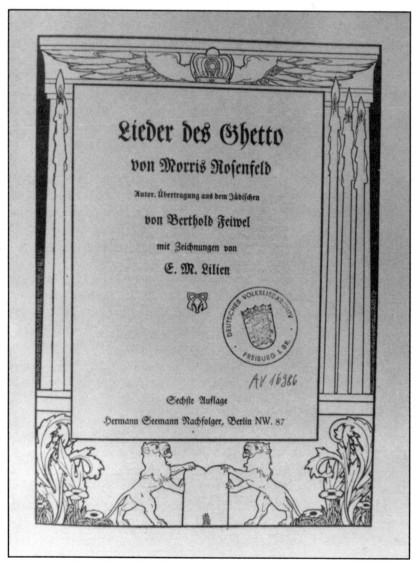

Fig. 6. Title page for Rosenfeld, *Lieder des Ghetto*. Source: Morris Rosenfeld, *Lieder des Ghetto*, 6th edition (Berlin: Hermann Seemann, 1902?).

the middle stage, for it made its case in musicological terms rather than in an emotionally polemic appeal. For subsequent editors, moreover, it provided a major source study for the Yiddish sections of their books. Its service to the tradition was, therefore, one of defining an already existing repertory and providing the guidelines with which that could be employed in future songbooks.

By the third stage the Eastern European influence had become very stylized. Its impact continued to be felt, for most songbooks devoted at least a few pages to songs in Yiddish. A few songbooks still concentrated on Yiddish song in particular. Most of these, however, served a function completely different from the songbooks of the middle stage. Gone now was any assertion that Yiddish songs could provide a core for a larger repertory of Jewish folk songs. Replacing this belief was a museum-like conceptualization of Yiddish songs. For the most part Yiddish songs were published in German translations, and the life they portrayed was considered quaint and archaic, equally foreign as that pictured in the first stage.

Ludwig Strauss's *Jüdische Volkslieder*[30] exemplified this conceptualization common to the third stage. Even though all the folk songs in the volume were taken from Yiddish sources, they were translated into German. Strauss made a certain scholarly bow by citing the sources from which he had taken the songs, but there was no attempt to clarify the various references in the songs. The collection was, therefore, a distillation of the Eastern European tradition, not intended for extensive use by German social organizations. If Strauss presented these songs as Jewish songs, he also depicted them as anachronistic folk songs, no longer participants in a vital, persistent tradition.

The census of Hebrew-language songs increased sharply in the final stage of songbook development, not only because of the influence from Palestine, but also because of the appearance of collections of religious music utilizing the format of the organizational songbooks. The songs of these books were not, of course, new introductions to the musical repertories of Jewish communities, but the books including them suggest a new function for the songs similar to that of other organizational songbooks. Hebrew literacy was rising in German-Jewish communities, often as the result of a special school, the *Lehrhaus*, established under the auspices of the local community for religious and secular instruction. Thus, it is not surprising to find that Jewish publishing houses, such as Schocken, were turning to editors like Arno Nadel to compile anthologies of religious songs in Hebrew.

A number of different types of songbook reinforced the Hebrew lan-

Oſtjüdiſche Volkslieder

ausgewählt

übertragen und mit Anmerkungen verſehen

von

Alexander Eliasberg

1 9 1 8

München bei Georg Müller

Fig. 7. Title page for Eliasberg, *Ostjüdische Volkslieder.* Source: Alexander Elias-berg, ed., *Ostjüdische Volkslieder* (Munich: Georg Müller, 1918).

guage as a symbol for nationalism during the final stage. The songbooks represented and encouraged the expansion of Hebrew literacy and consciousness of the expressive force Hebrew was acquiring in Palestine. As such, one can claim that the songbooks joined other community transformations at the forefront of a newly emerging tradition of Jewish cultural attitudes, rather than simply standing as the final stage of a fifty-year development. At the very least, the tradition of fifty years was thriving as never before.

The transformation of German-Jewish organizational songbooks exhibited the qualities of a traditional folk music within an ethnic community for several reasons. First, musical changes were widespread, touching not just Zionist groups, but Jewish social organizations of all sorts. Second, they were continuous throughout the half century prior to the Holocaust and reflected many of the ideologies and cultural attitudes that prevailed among German Jews during that period. Third, the songbooks succeeded in stimulating a new attitude toward the Jewish homeland, which is borne out by the attitudes of immigrants encouraged by such ideologies to settle in Israel. Finally, the organizational songbooks formed a tradition of Jewish music: created by German Jews, the tradition spread through Jewish communities using the cultural means and organizations available in those communities.

The songbook tradition challenges several widely held attitudes concerning Central European culture. The evidence of the tradition and its strength during the 1920s and 1930s refutes the interpretation that the German *aliyah* was no more than a response to untenable conditions in Germany, causing German Jews to flee because of the specter of Nazi persecution. The songbook tradition reflects a continually growing awareness of an emergent Jewish homeland. Enthusiasm for that homeland was increasingly realistic during the final stage of songbook development. The songbooks functioned in conjunction with other activities of Jewish groups to prepare for settlement in the new homeland; again, this was most apparent during the final stage when learning the Hebrew language assumed a position of great importance for Jewish groups. The tradition of canon singing, for example, long practiced by German singing groups, was reshaped in Palestine into a Hebrew version by the Austrian immigrant, Max Lampel, and P. (or F. or Ph.) Greenspoon (see fig. 8).

The songs and songbooks of the *Vereinslied* tradition functioned later in Israel in various ways. Some immigrants continued to use the books more or less privately in the home; others attempted to form new groups

50 קנונים

לשירה ולנגינה

חוברו ולוקטו

ע״י

פ. גרינשפון

מ. ל מ פ ל

ע״ש עמנואל קיפר ודוד נשרי

הוצאות המכון לשעורי נגינה ותזמורת מרכזית בבתי־הספר העירוניים בתל־אביב

Fig. 8. Title page for Greenspoon and Lampel, *50 Kanonim le-shirah ve-le-neginah*. Source: P. (or F. or Ph.) Greenspoon and Max Lampel, eds., *50 Kanonim le-shirah ve-le-neginah* ("50 Canons for Singing and Playing") (Tel Aviv: Maḥon le-shuri neginah ve-tismoret merkasit, n.d.).

שירי ארץ ישראל

מטעם

הסתדרות המכבי בגרמניה
והסתדרות החלוץ בגרמניה

לוקטו והוצאו ע"י

דר' יעקב שנכרג

1947

הוצאה עברית בע"מ, ירושלים

Fig. 9. Title page for Schönberg, *Shireh Eretz Yisrael.* Source: Jakob Schönberg, *Shireh Eretz Yisrael* ("Songs of Eretz Yisrael") (Jerusalem: Hotza'ah ivrit, 1947).

in which the songbooks functioned exactly as they had in Germany. Just as German immigrants were responsible for bringing other genres of music to Israel, their songbooks were a valuable contribution to musical life in Palestine during the 1930s and 1940s. Folk-song books for the instruction of children were in demand during these critical decades, and musicians and music teachers from all ethnic backgrounds found the German song-books to be ideal teaching aids. For the most part, texts were unimportant for such educational goals because solfège or Hebrew translations supplanted the German texts. Some of the best-known songbooks even relied on plates produced in Germany prior to World War II and imported to Palestine, where Israeli imprints incorporated them for several decades thereafter (see fig. 9).

Most important, the *Vereinslied* tradition challenges the assertion that Central European Jews were completely assimilated. Most songbooks openly impugned the notion of assimilation by addressing it in the preface or with individual songs. The very existence of groups espousing the philosophies found in the organizational songbooks further belied assimilation. Never was the homeland so often mentioned as in the various kinds of German *Heimatlied.* As the movement progressed, that homeland was increasingly indistinguishable from the physical reality and political potential of Palestine. The songbooks' popularity serving as the strongest challenge to the notion of complete assimilation, they and the groups using them were far more numerous at the end of their half-century history than at its beginning.

NOTES

1. Heinrich Loewe, ed., *Lieder-Buch für jüdische Vereine* (Berlin: Hugo Schild-berger, 1894).

2. The vast majority of songbooks examined in this chapter are housed in the archives and libraries of the Deutsches Volksliedarchiv, Freiburg im Breisgau, and the Jewish National and University Library, Jerusalem. Several of the sources are also in the Leo Baeck Institute, New York City.

3. Ahron Eliasberg, ed., *Die jüdische Gemeinschaft* (Berlin: Jüdischer Verlag, 1913), p. 7.

4. Arno Nadel, ed., *Jüdische Liebeslieder* (Berlin and Vienna: Verlag Benjamin Harz, 1923), p. 87.

5. Eliasberg, *Die jüdische Gemeinschaft,* p. 8.

6. Ludwig Strauss, ed., *Jüdische Volkslieder* (Berlin: Schocken Verlag, 1935), p. 9.

7. Emil Breslauer, *Sind original Synagogen- und Volks-Melodien bei den Juden geschichtlich nachweisbar?* (Leipzig: Breitkopf und Härtel, 1898), pp. 5-6.

8. For discussions of Eastern European Jewish modal forms in different contexts see Moshe Beregovski, "The Altered Dorian Scale in Jewish Folk Music (On the Question of the Semantic Characteristics of Scales)," in *Old Jewish Folk Music: The Collections and Writings of Moshe Beregovski*, ed. and trans. Mark Slobin (Philadelphia: University of Pennsylvania Press, 1982), pp. 549-67; and Mark Slobin, *Tenement Songs: The Popular Music of the Jewish Immigrants* (Urbana: University of Illinois Press, 1982), pp. 182-97.

9. Heinrich W. Schwab, "Das Vereinslied des 19. Jahrhunderts," in *Handbuch des Volksliedes*, ed. Rolf Wilhelm Brednich et al., Vol. 1: *Die Gattungen des Volksliedes* (Munich: Wilhelm Fink Verlag, 1973), p. 866.

10. Loewe, *Lieder-Buch für jüdische Vereine*, op. cit.

11. Verein "Jung Zion," comp., *Lieder zum Fest-Commers des II. Zionisten-Kongresses* (Basel: Verein "Jung Zion," 1898). Clearly, the six songs in this small book most explicitly addressed the experiences of German students: "Zions-Lied"; "Stosst an!"; "Alt Heidelberg"; "Ein Hoch dem ganzen Judentum!"; "Ergo Bibamus"; and "O alte Burschenherrlichkeit!"

12. See, for example, the editor's preface in Max Zirker, ed., *Vereinsliederbuch für Jung-Juda* (Berlin: Jüdischer Turnverein "Bar Kochba," 1905), p. 3.

13. Ibid.

14. The most frequently cited of these was S. M. Ginsburg and P. S. Marek, *Evreiskie narodnye pesni v Rossii* (St. Petersburg: Voskhod, 1901).

15. See, for example, the preface to Nadel, *Jüdische Liebeslieder*.

16. Eliasberg, *Die jüdische Gemeinschaft*, p. 22.

17. "Publishing," *Encyclopaedia Judaica*, 2nd ed., 1971, vol. 13, column 1373.

18. Getzel Kressel, "Jüdischer Verlag," *Encyclopaedia Judaica*, 2nd ed., vol. 10, columns 463-64.

19. "Loewe, Heinrich," *Encyclopaedia Judaica*, 2nd ed., vol. 10, columns 446-47.

20. Loewe, *Lieder-Buch für jüdische Vereine*, p. 8.

21. Zirker, *Vereinsliederbuch für Jung-Juda*, p. 4.

22. Interview with Felix Sulman, 30 April 1981, Jerusalem.

23. Karl Glaser, ed., *Blau-Weiß Liederbuch*, 1st ed. (Berlin: Jüdischer Verlag, 1914), p. 4.

24. Arno Nadel, ed., *Blau-Weiß Liederbuch*, 2nd ed. (Berlin: Jüdischer Verlag, 1918), pp. iii-iv.

25. Nathan Kaminski, ed., *Jüdisches Liederbuch—"Makkabi"* (Berlin: Jüdischer Verlag, 1935), p. 6.

26. Ibid., p. 5.

27. Morris Rosenfeld, *Lieder des Ghetto*, 6th ed. (Berlin: Hermann Seemann, 1902?).

28. Alexander Eliasberg, ed., *Ostjüdische Volkslieder* (Munich: Georg Müller, 1918).

29. Ibid., p. 7.

30. Ludwig Strauss, ed., *Jüdische Volkslieder* (Berlin: Schocken Verlag, 1935).

4

Mannheim on the Eve of
World War II

We had been left for dead, but were not dead! We had again awakened
to life, but could still not proclaim: This, now, is life. Feeling, faith,
patience, and a tenacity seldom granted are essential if we are to sustain
ourselves. Art is already a means to weather such times. He who has
devoted himself to art knows precisely that!

HUGO ADLER

THE RENASCENT Jewish culture symbolized by the *Vereinslieder* tradition
penetrated virtually the entire Jewish community during the early twentieth
century. New attitudes toward Jewish culture arose in the home, in the
synagogue, and in the sundry social organizations that touched ever more
aspects of community activity, hence strengthening the community's very
concept of itself. Musical life, too, responded directly to the new concept
of community. In its musical activities the community recognized a cultural
realm in which its members had long been extremely successful. Music
clearly had the potential to serve as a shaping force for the representation
of new values, and for this reason it quickly became one of the central
focal points for the resurgence of Jewish culture after World War I.

Just as the sense of community assumed new vigor, so too was there
a consolidation of Jewish traditions. Many barriers separating religious and
secular life disappeared; the ranks of Jewish cultural groups swelled; those
who had previously taken little interest in Jewish life became intensively
involved in community affairs. This consolidation resulted in part from
the increasing urbanization of Jewish life in Central Europe, and it thus
followed that the structure of the Jewish community should undergo processes of urbanization and modernization. Accordingly, Jewish cultural life
became increasingly centralized, thus rendering the community more dependent upon itself, much as it had been in the centuries prior to emancipation.

The Jewish community of Mannheim responded to the transformations
through which Central European Jewish society was passing in ways that

conformed to general historical patterns, as well as with a particularity reflective of its own unique musical organizations and personalities. Jews were actively involved in the cultural and intellectual life of Mannheim far in excess of their relative numbers. They had enjoyed a considerable degree of emancipation during the nineteenth century and participated fully in every sector of city life. The Jewish community in Mannheim, however, had not witnessed the same oppression and anti-Semitism that characterized many other German urban centers. Even if their rights were not always equal to those of the Christian population, Mannheim's Jews did enjoy peaceful coexistence throughout their history until the Nazi era. Although the cultural transformation of Mannheim's Jewish community was gradual, it increasingly bore witness to intensified awareness of Jewish settlement in Palestine by the early decades of the twentieth century. Contacts with Palestine were most frequent and extensive at the height of Mannheim's renaissance, for community musical leaders were contributing directly to musical activities in Palestine. The cultural transformations in Mannheim, therefore, served as one of the links to the musical culture taking root simultaneously in Palestine. Indeed, the renascent Jewish culture in German urban centers such as Mannheim presaged in many ways later developments in Palestine during the German *aliyah*.

The relations between Mannheim and its Jewish community differ in some important ways from those of other German cities. First, Mannheim was historically a liberal and progressive city, and as such attracted and encouraged Jewish settlement. This is dramatically illustrated by eighteenth-century population figures showing that the several hundred Jewish families in the city during this period constituted approximately one-eighth of the total population.[1] Second, founded only at the beginning of the seventeenth century, Mannheim exhibited a carefully planned grid of streets and neighborhoods. Typical patterns of ethnic segregation did not develop, and no Jewish ghetto formed; there were no Jewish streets or gates announcing a quarter housing Jewish homes and institutions.[2] Third, the city expanded as an economic power during the nineteenth century, a period coeval with Jewish political and social emancipation. Throughout Mannheim's history Jews enjoyed relatively favorable integration into the cultural life of the city.

The Jewish community comprised roughly two groups, the liberals and the orthodox. The majority considered themselves members of the liberal segment, but the orthodox congregation was nevertheless quite visible and powerful. The activities of the two were separate and independent, although financial affairs and certain institutions sometimes overlapped. The community's newspaper, for example, covered events sponsored by both groups and contained articles by proponents of opposing religious views. Protest sometimes emanated from the orthodox congregation if community funds were used inappropriately, for example to purchase an organ for the liberal synagogue in the mid-nineteenth century, but quarrels and conflicts never led to deteriorating coexistence.[3]

Little in the history of the Jewish community suggests that the cultural renaissance of the early twentieth century was a specific response to anti-Semitic pressures. In fact, anti-Semitism had never played an important role in the city, even during those periods when it was particularly troublesome elsewhere in Germany.[4] Official acts of government, which in many instances treated the Jewish community as a third group alongside the Catholics and Protestants, encouraged the favorable position of Jews. By 1802 Mannheim *Gymnasien* admitted Jewish students, who quickly took advantage of the educational opportunities afforded them by the city and constituted a percentage of the schoolchildren far in excess of their numbers, for example 28.3 percent in 1875.[5]

Mannheim's many Jewish intellectuals and professionals again show it to be typical of Central European Jewish urban culture, yet somewhat atypical with regard to degree.[6] This exceptional degree further supports a hypothesis that a cultural renaissance was underway in the early twentieth century because of—not in spite of—the general transformation of the Jewish community. The immense success of Jews in virtually every sector of Mannheim's cultural and financial life did not stunt cultural change within the Jewish community. Quite the contrary, numerous changes seem to have resulted directly from the community's healthy coexistence in all aspects of city life. For the community's musical life, however, change gradually shifted to and increasingly concentrated itself within community structures.

During the period of cultural renaissance many prominent musicians resided in Mannheim's Jewish community. Some, for example Ernst Toch, who first began teaching composition and piano in Mannheim in 1913, came from the outside; many others received their musical training in Mannheim itself. Indeed, there was a noticeable increase in Jewish musicians during the early decades of the twentieth century as musical life in general became more active. Accordingly, the boundaries between the musical institutions of the Jewish community and those of the non-Jewish gradually dissolved and in some cases disappeared completely. The breakdown of institutional boundaries, moreover, caused several musical organizations to flourish and additionally led to the creation of new institutions, which, in turn, stimulated more community members to express their interests in music.

Musical organizations formed from the Jewish and non-Jewish communities in different ways, ranging from strictly observant to completely secular. The orthodox Klaus Synagogue maintained conservative musical traditions, allowing only a male chorus. The larger liberal synagogue also supported traditions with specifically religious functions, but its members often preferred to embellish these traditions with instrumental ensembles or their large organ. The synagogue traditions, in their different ways, constituted one end of the spectrum of musical organizations. Slightly removed from that end were groups with totally Jewish membership, but with activities not substantially different from non-Jewish groups. The best example of such a musical group was the *Liederkranz* ("Wreath of Songs"), a Jewish *Männerchor* ("men's chorus") that grew out of the chorus in the liberal synagogue, but adopted the traditions of a German men's singing society. Moving a bit further from the religious traditions, one finds groups with disproportionately large Jewish memberships; several amateur orchestras in the city exemplified this type. Finally, at the other end of the spectrum were musical organizations, such as the orchestra of the *Nationaltheater*, with no overt relation to the Jewish community, but drawing extensively from the abundance of Jewish musicians.

One measure of the Jewish cultural renaissance in Mannheim was the expanded involvement of Jewish musicians in their community. During the early twentieth century these musicians increasingly founded new musical organizations, many of them loosely connected to the official purview of the community. We know of many of these groups and their activities because announcements of their rehearsals appeared quite regularly in the community newspaper during the 1920s and 1930s: the mixed synagogue chorus; the Orthodox men's chorus; the chorus for Friday services (*Freitagschor*); the *Liederkranz*; the youth orchestra; the youth chorus; the speaking chorus (*Sprechchor*); the *jüdisches Mandolinen-Orchester* ("Jewish Mandolin Orchestra"); choruses for both opera and oratorio productions; the *Stamitz-Gemeinde* orchestra; various chamber ensembles; and ensembles associated with special groups, such as Zionist organizations. The activities of these groups were so numerous that the community built a new rehearsal facility and auditorium in the early 1930s. Organizational musical activities were remarkably diverse and interwoven into the complex community structure. Two ensembles, however, exerted the most wide-ranging and profound impact on the Mannheim Jewish community: the *Liederkranz* and the *Stamitz-Gemeinde*.

Large-scale choral activities in the liberal synagogue began during the 1850s at approximately the same time the community built its new and larger synagogue. The first synagogue chorus came to life in 1854 under the name "Israelitischer Singverein," suggesting the prototype of a *Gesangverein* ("singing society"). The repertories of a *Gesangverein* were usually general and secular, and by no means confined to religious organizations. The first director of the synagogue chorus was, in fact, a non-Jew, one Eberhard Kuhn, who had already achieved considerable local fame conducting other choral societies.[7] In 1855, when the synagogue chorus began accepting women and performing with the accompaniment of the main synagogue's new organ, protest arose from the orthodox sector of the community. Perhaps in response to the ensuing controversy, Kuhn formed a *Männerquartett* ("male quartet"), which several years later changed its name to *Männergesangverein Liederkranz*.[8] The members of the early *Liederkranz* were also obliged to attend all rehearsals of the synagogue chorus, and the early repertory still included Jewish religious music. Both synagogue chorus and *Liederkranz* were sizable ensembles from the start, the former claiming a membership of eighty-four (forty-nine women and thirty-five men) and the latter thirty-three in 1858, further demonstrating the interdependence of the choruses, for all but two male members served in both.[9]

Though originally rooted in the synagogue chorus, the *Liederkranz* followed quite a different path of development. It soon discontinued performance of Jewish religious music, turning instead to a wide variety of other genres. Already in 1864 the society staged its first operetta, and its concerts until World War I attracted soloists from throughout Europe. Like other German choral societies the *Liederkranz* performed classical and semi-classical music in addition to its core of German folk song. Absent from accounts of the *Liederkranz* repertory from the 1860s until World War I is any evidence that the society contained only Jewish members, depended on direct contacts with the main synagogue, or performed any Jewish religious or folk music (see, for example, figs. 10 and 11, from the program of the fiftieth-anniversary celebration). It is important to remember, however, that the audience for the *Liederkranz* extended beyond the Jewish community, thus making it unnecessary to perform a repertory anchored in Jewish traditions. Performances of religious music would only duplicate the synagogue chorus.

Fig. 10. Announcement of concert and visiting soloists in the booklet for the 1906 Jubiläums-Fest-Konzert of the Mannheim Liederkranz. Source: Gustav Hecht, *Zum 50jährigen Jubiläum!* (Mannheim: Handelsdruckerei Katz, 1906). Photo: Stadtarchiv-Mannheim, reprinted with permission.

Vortragsfolge.

1. **Vorspiel** zu „Die Meistersinger von
   Nürnberg" . . . . *Richard Wagner*
2. **Prolog,** gedichtet von Hermann Waldeck.
   (Gesprochen von Toni Wittels.)
3. **Festhymne** für Männerchor, Sopran-
   Solo und Orgel . . . . . *Julius Lorenz.*
   (Sopran-Solo: Frl. Hilda Schoene.)
4. **Arie** aus der Oper „Armida" . . *Christoph Gluck.*
   (Frl. Lucienne Bréval.)
5. **Violin-Konzert** G-moll · . . *Max Bruch.*
   (Herr Eugen Ysaye.)
6. **Der Tod des Sardanapal,** für
   Männerchor und Bariton-Solo . *Lothar Kempter.*
   (Manuscript) unter persönlicher Leitung des Komponisten.
   (Bariton-Solo: Joachim Kromer.)
7. **Lieder** mit Klavierbegleitung.
   a) La Chevelure . . . . . *Debussy.*
   b) Noël Païen . . . . . . *Massenet.*
   (Frl. Lucienne Bréval.)
8. **An das Vaterland,** Männerchor . *Max Gulbins.*
9. **Violin-Konzert** G-dur Nr. 3 . . *W. A. Mozart.*
   (Herr Eugen Ysaye.)

Fig. 11. Program in the booklet for the 1906 Jubiläums-Fest-Konzert of the Mannheim Liederkranz. Source: Gustav Hecht, *Zum 50jährigen Jubiläum!* (Mannheim: Handelsdruckerei Katz, 1906). Photo: Stadtarchiv-Mannheim, reprinted with permission.

By the early twentieth century the society was frequently performing with other musical organizations in Mannheim. During the second decade of the century the *Liederkranz* occasionally combined forces with the orchestra of the *Nationaltheater,* whose conductor at the time was Wilhelm Furtwängler. From outward appearance the society functioned exactly like any other German choral society. Most programs praised the German fatherland and German culture; even works espousing a strictly Christian viewpoint were performed.[10] The involvement of the *Liederkranz* outside the Jewish community reached its zenith during the second decade of the twentieth century. When World War I began, this involvement was fully evident from accounts of the society's many patriotic concerts and the military service of two-thirds of its membership.[11]

Immediately after the war the *Liederkranz* took on a new role. The war had necessitated considerable restructuring of Mannheim's musical organizations, bringing about many changes, several of which caused Jewish musicians to assume more active roles. The number of Jewish musical organizations also multiplied.[12] Among these organizations the *Liederkranz* assumed an increasingly central position. Evidence of the *Liederkranz's* changing role appeared most noticeably in its new repertory. Gradually, works that contained an explicitly Jewish content entered the programs and rehearsal schedules of the chorus. These changes were largely in keeping with those attending the Jewish *Vereinslieder* tradition, but they began somewhat later in the *Liederkranz* and transpired with greater speed. Programs and newspaper accounts from the 1920s reveal that the audience for *Liederkranz* performances was gradually shifting from the general public to the Jewish community. During this decade the chorus still served both audiences, albeit now with quite different music. Increased service to the Jewish community — especially at specific events in the community — was itself a major reason for adopting a new repertory. Not only did the works of nineteenth-century Jewish choral composers enjoy more frequent performances, but many concerts emphasized the "Old Testament" works of composers better known to the general public.[13] As the role of the *Liederkranz* changed, so too did certain aspects of its structure: early in the 1930s women began to enter its ranks. The *Liederkranz* thereby assumed some of the religious functions that the mixed synagogue chorus, with which its membership was now virtually interchangeable, had alone performed. The acceptance of women was symbolic of other changes as well: the *Liederkranz* had become, in short, the musical core of the community.

The centralization of the *Liederkranz* in about 1930 had accompanied a decade of change. New concepts of the community's cultural life, especially those promulgated by several figures assuming musical leadership, had precipitated many of the musical changes. The *Liederkranz* therefore reached its core position before the pressures from the Nazis could have forced such a position on it. The musical leaders envisioned the chorus functioning as a catalyst in the further transformation of musical life within the entire community, and the groundwork for expanding the *Liederkranz's* service quickly took shape. The community made plans to build a new home for the *Liederkranz*, which was completed in August of 1936. The three-story building contained an auditorium on the ground floor, offices on the second, and rehearsal halls on the third.[14] This facility became a musical center for the entire Jewish community and enabled musical activities to continue at least until the *Kristallnacht* in 1938, after which no evidence of large-scale musical activity in the community survives. The new home for the *Liederkranz* symbolized a consolidation that allowed many different musical organizations to strengthen each other through interdependence. Just as the *Liederkranz* played a more central role for vocal music, so did the orchestra of the *Stamitz-Gemeinde* assume a position of central importance for the performance of instrumental music.

Jewish patronage of the arts was essential to the cultural advancement of Mannheim during the century prior to World War II. This patronage often assumed the form of financial undergirding for the city's artistic institutions, but it also took the less obvious form of supporting amateur musical endeavors. Jewish homes often sponsored *Hauskonzerte*, making them as accessible to the general public as professional concerts.[15] It is from this tradition of amateur music-making that the *Stamitz-Gemeinde* emerged in the 1920s to provide a core of instrumental musicians for the changing musical demands of the Jewish community.

The history of amateur orchestral societies in Mannheim followed a course rarely very distant from the *Liederkranz*. It was relatively common, for example, that these organizations shared conductors. The earliest forerunner of the *Stamitz-Gemeinde*, a chamber orchestra called the *Dilettanten-Verein*, was founded in 1858 by Ferdinand Langer (1839-1905). During his tenure as conductor of the *Dilettanten-Verein* ("Society of Amateur Musicians") Langer also assumed the directorship of the *Liederkranz*, holding that post from 1871 until 1905.[16] The *Dilettanten-Verein* disbanded in 1876, but its members formed another amateur orchestra, the *Philharmonischer Verein*, which survived until World War I, when it dissolved because of wartime demands on its membership. In 1921 its former members reconstituted themselves as the *Stamitz-Gemeinde* (see fig. 12), calling upon Max Sinzheimer, who had been at the helm of the *Liederkranz* since 1919, to serve as conductor. As with previous amateur orchestras, there appears to have been no design to make the orchestra either Jewish or non-Jewish, but because the conductor was a member of and musically active within the Jewish community, many Jewish musicians felt welcome in the orchestra.

Like the *Liederkranz,* the *Stamitz-Gemeinde* acted as a cultural bridge between different religious communities. Repertory did not relate directly to the religious activities of the Jewish community, but the orchestra functioned as a core for the broad range of amateur musical activity so important to the community. Financial support came from several sources: the musicians themselves; the underwriting of special needs by Mannheim banking families, many of them Jewish; and by the late 1920s even from public coffers in the city.[17]

In 1933, the new government attempted to terminate the *Stamitz-Gemeinde,* claiming it had effectively become inactive in previous years; the claim had no validity whatsoever, for the ensemble had actually stepped up its performances and had even assumed some trappings of a professional orchestra. To avert dissolution, Sinzheimer turned directly to the Jewish community, forming a new orchestra under the auspices of the *Liederkranz.* In its new role the *Stamitz-Gemeinde,* called also the *Instrumentalgemeinschaft* ("instrumental society"), began both to perform more Jewish music and to expand its repertory into new areas not specifically Jewish. The orchestra now frequently served opera and oratorio performances offered by the community. (Figure 13 is a caricature of rehearsals for a performance by community ensembles of Cimarosa's *Il matrimonio segreto* in 1938.)

This expansion of activity also resulted from the general consolidation of resources accompanying the community's cultural renaissance. The ingathering of musical ensembles now provided more possibilities for the general performance of all types of music, both sacred and secular. Thus, even toward the end of the 1930s, every few months witnessed the production of a new opera, which drew upon the many musical groups serving the community. Musicians from the community banded together to make their services known to all, and newspaper advertisements (see fig. 14) were relatively commonplace. The complete absorption of the *Stamitz-Gemeinde* by the Jewish community during the 1930s yet again demonstrated that the political forces seeking to stem the community's cultural renaissance instead solidified community concern and support.[18]

Fig. 12. Group photo of Stamitz-Gemeinde, 1922. Source: Wilhelm Herrmann, *Musizieren um des Musizierens Willen: 125 Jahre Mannheimer Liebhaber-Orchester* (Mannheim: Kessler Verlag, 1954?). Photo reprinted with the permission of the Mannheim Stamitz-Gemeinde, Dr. Dieter S. Heck, Chairman. Although we cannot identify all of the orchestra members in 1922, Hermann's book reveals that in 1931 the group included:

First Violin: Lene Hesse, Fritz Krayer, Olga Staadecker, Margot Dreyfuß Friedrich Salomon, Hermann Sachse, Dr. Fritz Lux, Prof. Dr. Rehfeld, Käte Dreyfuß, Dr. Walter Raymond, Robert Bühler, Gretel Strauß, Erwin Händel, Kläre Schmidt-Eisener, Jakob Fuchs, Josef Lindner

Second Violin: Käte Back, Eduard Eppelsheim, Frau Dr. Graff, Else Reis, Herbert Sohn, Rudolf Keller, Ilse Kauffmann, Albert Fischel, Georg Zoller, Kurt Hoyer, Robert Buß, Anneliese Gäbert, Berta Fleck, Erich Kallenheim, Gertrud Grasmück, Hans Knecht, Walter Böhr

Viola: Dr. Otto Weiß, Ludwig Metzger, Hansi Krauskopf, Heinrich Kulpe, Dr. Karl Schacherer, Josef Schwarzmann, Karl Prantner

Cello: David Altyzer, Kläre Beierlein, Max Keller, Dr. Paul Gmelin, Erich Eßlinger, Willi Oppenheimer

Double bass: Ferdinand Wilhelm, Hermann Brand

Flute, Oboe: Hans Mayer, August Beck, Richard Eberhardt

Harpsichord: Hellmut Feist, Ernst Hartmann

Fig. 13. Caricature of a rehearsal for the 1938 production of Cimarosa's *Il matrimonio segreto*. Source: Supplement to the *Israelitisches Gemeindeblatt*, early winter, 1937-38. Photo: Stadtarchiv-Mannheim, reprinted with permission.

The Mannheim Jewish community benefited tremendously from its abundance of talented musicians. Among these, more than a few were to leave their mark on the musical activities of the cultural renaissance before fleeing Europe prior to World War II. Some were quite active in the community itself, whereas others made more peripheral contributions. However, even peripheral contributions should not be ignored. The composer and organist Ernst Toch, for example, played an active role in the community only occasionally, usually serving as organist for special concerts given in the main synagogue.[19] But he also taught many other musicians who would serve the community more directly. It was the compositional style that Hugo Adler acquired from Toch that would serve as a model for Adler's concept of "new Jewish music." Another young musician participating in many community activities was Jean Berger, then named Arthur Schloßberg, whose frequent discussion of musical matters in the community newspaper articulated many issues vital to the changing aesthetic of music.

Although the intense musical activities by necessity required broad support from many musicians, two were dominant forces during the 1920s and 1930s: Max Sinzheimer and Hugo Adler. Their careers differed markedly, for Sinzheimer was active primarily outside the realm of Jewish music and only gradually increased his involvement in the Jewish community, whereas Adler, educated as a cantor, contributed explicitly to religious Jewish traditions. In many ways, it was the combination of these very different musical backgrounds that eventually led to such sweeping musical changes.

Max Sinzheimer was born in Frankfurt in 1894 and studied to be a conductor during his student days. By 1917 he had become associate conductor of the orchestra of the Mannheim *Nationaltheater* under Wilhelm Furtwängler.[20] One year after assuming the directorship of the *Liederkranz*, Sinzheimer left the *Nationaltheater* and began laying the groundwork for the establishment of the *Stamitz-Gemeinde*, which came into being in 1921. Sinzheimer was also a skilled pianist and violinist, and his talents were much in demand, especially in the Jewish community, where he and his wife, a violinist, frequently performed chamber music. During the 1920s he did not restrict his musical activities to the Jewish community, but served also in such posts as choral director of the Mannheim Christ Church and of a new ensemble that he founded in 1925, the Mannheim Chamber Chorus.[21]

By the mid-1920s accounts of Max Sinzheimer's musical activity appeared with growing frequency in the newspaper of the Jewish community (the *Israelitisches Gemeindeblatt*), first because of the more active partici-

Musiklehrkräfte
und ausübende Musiker

Toni Auerbach,
Mannheim, B 7, 7, Telefon 206 83.   **Violincello**

Isa Awstreich, staatl. geor. Lehrerin für Klavierspiel.
Mannheim, Holzbauerstr. 3, Tel. 507 06.   Klavier. Theorieunterricht

Lene Diefenbronner, staatl. gepr.
Mannheim, Lameystr. 22, Tel. 445 94.   **Klavier, Theor e**

Lene Hesse-Sinzheimer, Mannheim,
Nietzschestr. 8, Telefon 437 10.   **Violine, Kammermusik**

Max Sinzheimer, Mannheim, Nietzschestr. 8,
Telefon 437 10.   **Klavier, Theorie, Partienstudium**

Mathilde Lazarus,
Mannheim, F 1, 11.   **Gesang und Klavier**

Albert Levi,
Mannheim, Waldhofstr. 7 (bei Groß).   **Violine, Viola**

Jos. Levi, Mannheim, Friedrichsring 36, Tel. 27040 Staatl.
gepr. Lehrer für Klavier, Oberstufe, Gesang, Orgel, Theorie

Jlse Lion, Mannheim, P 7, 17,
Tel. 308 88.   Staatl. gepr. **Klavierpädagogin (Oberstufe)**

Dr. Emmy Lußheimer-Joseph,
Mannheim, Friedrich-Karl-Straße 12, Telefon 434 00.
Konzert, Oratorien, Gesangunterricht, Ensemblestunden

E. Mimi Marx, Mannheim, Charlottenstr. 4,
Telefon 446 79.   **Klavier, Blockflöte, Gehörbildung**

Martha Oppenheim, Mannheim, N 5, 1,
Telefon 306 86.   **Klavier, Gesang, Gehörbildung**

Pauline Rothschild,
Weinheim, Hauptstr. 90. Tel. 23 39.   **Klavierlehrerin**

Erna Stern, Mannheim, B 6, 21, Tel. 262 97.
     Staatl. gepr. **Klavierpädagogin**

Helene Süß, Mannheim, L 13, 17,
Telefon 320 71.   **Klavier, Gehörbildung, Kammermusik**

Alice Wallenstein, Mannheim,
Luisenring 56, Tel 320 44.   **Klavier und Theorie**

Fig. 14. List of Jewish musicians and music teachers, with their
addresses and telephone numbers, in the newspaper of the Mannheim
Jewish community, March 1935. Source: *Israelitisches Gemeindeblatt*
13/6 (20 March 1935), p. 10. Photo: Stadtarchiv-Mannheim, reprinted
with permission.

pation of the *Liederkranz* in the community, but soon because Sinzheimer himself took a more active community role, for example as organist in the main synagogue. Around 1930, Sinzheimer began to contribute articles concerning the role of music in Jewish life to the *Israelitisches Gemeindeblatt,* these in turn reflecting a transition that was personal and religious as well as musical. Indeed, the total absorption of Max Sinzheimer into the Jewish musical life followed an orderly course of events, rather than some form of banishment from non-Jewish organizations.

The Mannheim Jewish community had cultivated its religious music with an intensity no less than its secular musical organizations had enjoyed. The synagogue chorus and the *Liederkranz* were, after all, sister organizations. Religious ensembles performed not only during services at the synagogue, but in public concerts and on tours elsewhere in Germany. There were even times when conservative criticism protested the extent to which the synagogue chorus was undertaking more than its calling might suggest, necessitating an ameliorating response from one of the cantors.[22]

During the period of cultural renaissance Hugo Adler (1894-1955) was the primary force behind religious musical activities. Born in Antwerp, Adler came to Mannheim just after World War I, when the cultural renaissance was achieving its greatest momentum. He was initially associate cantor in the main synagogue, but his musical activities soon branched into many new directions. He began composition study with Ernst Toch early in his Mannheim tenure. His own compositional approach bearing evidence of Toch's musical style, Adler composed primarily for the musical organizations of the Jewish community. His compositions very often combined both choral and orchestral forces, with oratorios based on liturgical and biblical texts among the works most frequently performed. Adler's compositions received performances not only in Mannheim, but from Jewish choruses and orchestras throughout Germany during the 1930s.

In addition to his activities as cantor, conductor, and in-house composer for the Jewish community, Adler was also the didactician. His frequent articles in the newspaper openly called for new directions in Jewish music. He sought to exemplify these directions in his compositions and often explained very precisely the techniques new works employed. He also organized many aspects of the consolidation of performing forces that transpired in the late 1920s and early 1930s. As the leader of community religious musical activities (he became chief cantor in 1933), Adler promulgated an aesthetic of Jewish music with liturgical traditions at its core. His models for this aesthetic were not only the cantorial traditions of the nineteenth century, such as those espoused by Louis Lewandowski and Salomon Sulzer, but also the polyphonic traditions of the Renaissance Jewish composer, Salomone Rossi. Through the polyphonic treatment of liturgical melody Adler sought his link to contemporary European compositional techniques.

Hugo Adler equated the forging of new directions for Jewish music with the blossoming of a new musical culture in Palestine. He symbolizes, in this sense, a connection between the changing musical aesthetic in Central European communities and the emergence of new musical approaches in the immigrant culture of Palestine. Adler, more than any other European Jewish composer, attempted to implant his musical ideas through the activities of the World Centre for Jewish Music in Palestine. Through letters to that organization he hoped to stimulate interest in his compositions, and he expressed his belief that the new direction emerging in Mannheim would find fertile soil in Palestine.[23]

The World Centre for Jewish Music in Palestine responded positively to Adler's efforts and chose as its first major performance his *Balak und Bilam,* an oratorio that had already won considerable acclaim in Jewish communities in Germany during the mid-1930s. Contact between musicians in Palestine and Mannheim was fairly regular and influenced performances in both locations. Max Sinzheimer was a close friend of Karl Salomon, the first musical director of the Palestine Broadcasting Service and formerly a conductor in nearby Heidelberg and Baden-Baden. Sinzheimer turned to Salomon for arrangements of oratorios that had been translated into Hebrew for concerts in Palestine.[24] Mannheim organizations could therefore perform choral works in Hebrew, whose texts were originally German or English, for example, oratorios by Mozart, Handel, or Mendelssohn. Thus, the cultural renaissance in Mannheim grew closer to, and to some extent depended on, the settlement and development of Palestine.

Although Jews had enjoyed relatively favorable conditions in Mannheim since the mid-seventeenth century, the changes that foreshadowed the cultural renaissance did not occur until approximately 1850, when the general structure of the Jewish community underwent dramatic change, giving birth to those musical organizations that were to serve the community for the next ninety years. In the mid-nineteenth century, reform within German-Jewish communities radically transformed attitudes toward tradition and music. In Mannheim, the reform movement was quickly adopted by a new rabbi, Moses Präger, immediately stimulating new attitudes and activity.[25] For the first time the religious service and the music of the synagogue incorporated the German language. New ensembles quickly formed, and both organ and instrumental groups were heard frequently in the newly constructed main synagogue. Community participation in the new musical organizations was swift and abundant. A new community music director, Josef Eschborn, who composed new works for the plethora of new ensembles, even established a precedent for subsequent musical leaders by creating compositions for specific community needs.

The organizational structure of the Jewish community became increasingly complicated between the mid-nineteenth century and World War I, with most organizations roughly paralleling those outside the community. Not all functions of the Christian community were duplicated, however, and by the beginning of the twentieth century Jewish organizations with functions specific to their own community were increasing in number. Educational organizations offering Hebrew instruction multiplied at this time, as did the number of Mannheimers immigrating to Palestine.

The major transition bringing about the Jewish renaissance in Mannheim began just before World War I, when growing interest in Zionism and immigration to Palestine were noticeably more visible.[26] Little further evidence is available from the war years, but immediately thereafter signs of rapid cultural change are again manifest in the records of community activity. In the community's musical life the most obvious of these was Max Sinzheimer's assumption of the *Liederkranz* directorship. As the 1920s began, the Jewish community underwent another surge of organization, and it was not long before it assumed the semblance of a community within a community.

The new musical activities of the Mannheim Jewish community reflected and were supported by the broader organizational changes. Not only were youth more active in the new organizations, but they swelled the ranks of the musical ensembles. The express purpose of many new organizations was to embrace as many members as possible, thus preventing the need to turn outside the community structure. This philosophy of total community involvement was also adopted by the musical leaders and was embodied in a new aesthetic they were attempting to inculcate in the community. They even coined a term, *musizierende Gemeinschaft* ("music-making community"), to describe this new pattern of involvement. The crux of this concept clearly aimed to breach all barriers between those performing and those listening to music: "The word, 'community,' has increasingly appeared in the musical life of the past 20 years — and not without considerable reason. This concept can be identified as a symbol for a fundamental transformation of our place in musical attitudes, for a new concept of 'listening to music' and 'making music,' and from there follows a renewal of the relations between musician and public. We Jews, moreover, have cause at this time to recognize the meaning of such a concept and to render its fruitfulness useful to our more tightly knit community."[27]

The most ambitious project to involve the entire community in musical activities was an "instructional cantata," Licht und Volk ("Light and the People"), for Ḥanukah celebrations in 1930. The text of the cantata came from the biblical Maccabee story, which was not only appropriate to the season, but was also symbolic of a goal to encourage the community to focus more intently on its own history. Hugo Adler composed the musical score, making it theoretically accessible to every member of the community, musically trained or untrained. The work was structurally quite complex, with seven movements and parts written for adult and children's choruses, the speaking chorus, soloists, string orchestra, and, of course, the remaining community members. Licht und Volk was intended to bring the community to a more intimate understanding of the interrelation of ancient Jewish culture and the Mannheim community. This express purpose was a clear statement by the work's creators that they were indeed in the midst of a Jewish cultural renaissance, and they fully intended to bring this message to the entire community.[28] (Figure 15 is a photograph of the performers for the premiere of Licht und Volk.)

When immigrant musicians departed from Central Europe during the German aliyah, they left a world in which new modes of expression for Jewish music had arisen. Many of these musicians had participated in the new institutions of Jewish music prior to emigration and were accordingly imbued with the same spirit of creativity spreading widely through other Central European communities. It is not surprising, therefore, that the immigrant musicians should turn to musicians remaining in Central Europe for new ideas and models for the musical culture they were molding in Palestine.

The exchange of ideas between Central Europe and Palestine was easier because of the general consolidation of musical organizations in both venues. Thus, the consolidation that enabled the new approach to Jewish music espoused by the Mannheim musical hierarchy found resonance in an immigrant institution like the World Centre for Jewish Music in Palestine. By the early 1930s, the consolidation within the Mannheim community — and others similar to it — was actually responsible for a spirit of optimism; many immigrant musicians bore this same spirit to Palestine. Many of the immigrant institutions depended to a great degree on the maintenance of

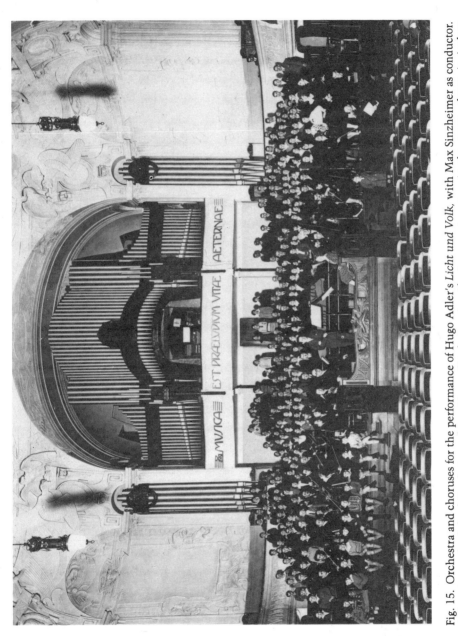

Fig. 15. Orchestra and choruses for the performance of Hugo Adler's *Licht und Volk*, with Max Sinzheimer as conductor. Adler sits to the left of Sinzheimer. Lene Hesse, Sinzheimer's wife, is concertmaster. At the organ, above, is Arthur Schloßberg (later Jean Berger). Photo: Courtesy Samuel Adler, Eastman School of Music, Rochester, New York.

connections with communities and individuals that had fostered them in Central Europe. For many reasons the connections between the two worlds were extremely tenuous, and they eventually collapsed early in 1939. Yet for almost a decade during the 1930s, the musical cultures of Jews in Central Europe and German-speaking immigrants in Palestine seemed to draw more closely together, for they had found a means of investing cultural, religious, and ethnic values in a music whose symbolic meaning they had come to share: the traditions of Western art music.

NOTES

The epigraph is from Hugo Adler, "Die neue Einstellung zur musikalischen Kunst in den Gemeinden," *Israelitisches Gemeindeblatt* 11/7 (28 July 1933), 5.

1. Karl Otto Watzinger, "Die Jüdische Gemeinde Mannheims in der Weimarer Republik," *Mannheimer Hefte* (1980, 1): 70; and idem, *Geschichte der Juden in Mannheim 1650-1945* (Stuttgart: Verlag W. Kohlhammer, 1984), pp. 22-23.

2. Pollack, *Jewish Folkways*, p. 2; several other German cities, such as Koblenz and Trier, the latter dating from Roman times, also did not designate Jewish neighborhoods with special gates.

3. Hugo Adler, "Die Entwicklung des synagogalen Gesanges in Mannheim, II," *Israelitisches Gemeindeblatt* 2/4 (16 April 1924), 6-7.

4. Watzinger, "Die Jüdische Gemeinde Mannheims in der Weimarer Republik," p. 76; see also Hans-Joachim Fliedner, *Die Judenverfolgung in Mannheim, 1933-1945*, Vol I: *Darstellung* (Stuttgart: Verlag W. Kohlhammer, 1971), p. 76.

5. Watzinger, *Geschichte der Juden in Mannheim*, pp. 37-38.

6. Watzinger, "Die Jüdische Gemeinde Mannheims in der Weimarer Republik," p. 71.

7. Hugo Adler, "Die Entwicklung des synagogalen Gesanges in Mannheim, I," *Israelitisches Gemeindeblatt* 2/2 (27 February 1924), 6.

8. Hugo Adler, "Die Entwicklung des synagogalen Gesanges in Mannheim, III," *Israelitisches Gemeindeblatt* 2/5 (21 May 1924), 6.

9. Gustav Hecht, *Zum 50jährigen Jubiläum!* (Mannheim: Handelsdruckerei Katz, 1906), p. 33.

10. Fliedner, *Die Judenverfolgung*, p. 43.

11. *Badischer Sängerbote* 42/2 (April, 1916): 22-23.

12. Cf. similar developments in Munich during this period described in Jehoash Hirshberg, "Heinrich Schalit and Paul Ben-Haim in Munich," *Yuval* 4 (1982): 142.

13. Hugo Adler, "Unsere Gemeinde im 'Liederkranz,'" *Israelitisches Gemeindeblatt* 9/2 (16 February 1931), 9.

14. Arthur Lehmann, "Das neue Heim des 'Liederkranz e. V.' (Jüdischer Kulturbund), Q 2, 16," *Israelitisches Gemeindeblatt* 14/15 (14 August 1936), 7; "Q 2, 16" was the building's address.

15. Karl Otto Watzinger, "Die Jüdische Gemeinde Mannheims in der

Großherzoglichen Zeit (1803-1918)," *Mannheimer Hefte* (1981, 2): 97; see also idem, *Geschichte der Juden in Mannheim*, p. 43.

16. Wilhelm Herrmann, *Musizieren um des Musizierens Willen: 125 Jahre Mannheimer Liebhaber-Orchester* (Mannheim: Kessler Verlag, 1954?), pp. 20-21.

17. Ibid., pp. 35-36.

18. Kurt Düwell examines several reasons for the growing support of cultural activity in the German-Jewish community in "Jewish Cultural Centers," pp. 294-316.

19. Erich Hermann Müller von Asow, "Ernst Toch in Mannheim: Zum 75. Geburtstage," *Mannheimer Hefte* (1962): 19; see also *Israelitisches Gemeindeblatt* 2/2 (18 June 1924), 9.

20. Herbert Meyer, "Max Sinzheimer: Ein Beitrag zur Mannheimer Musikgeschichte," *Mannheimer Hefte* (1979, 1): 14.

21. Herrmann, *Musizieren*, p. 37; see also Watzinger, *Geschichte der Juden in Mannheim*, pp. 135-36.

22. Hugo Adler, "Arbeit im Synagogenchor," *Israelitisches Gemeindeblatt* 1/3 (17 November 1922), 5.

23. See Philip V. Bohlman, "The Archives of the World Centre for Jewish Music in Palestine, 1936-1940, at the Jewish National and University Library, Jerusalem," *Yuval* 5 (1986): 241, 260.

24. "Lokales aus Mannheim," *Israelitisches Gemeindeblatt* 14/6 (19 March 1937), 5.

25. Watzinger, *Geschichte der Juden in Mannheim*, p. 33.

26. "Die Jüdische Gemeinde Mannheims in der Großherzoglichen Zeit," p. 98.

27. Max Sinzheimer, "Musizierende Gemeinschaft," *Israelitisches Gemeindeblatt* 13/17 (4 September 1935), 4.

28. Max Grünewald, "Licht und Volk: Text," *Israelitisches Gemeindeblatt* 8/12 (9 December 1930), 3.

5

Ethnicity and Western Art Music

THE MOST PERVASIVE ethnic music in the Central European Jewish community is Western art music. In part, the ethnicity of the community grew from traditions of art music both before and after immigration to Israel. Central to community musical values was a repertory of music encompassing approximately a century and one half, from about the mid-eighteenth to the early twentieth century. Somewhat less central, but nevertheless highly valued by the community, were more recent endeavors of twentieth-century composers — a disproportionate number of them Central European Jews — to forge an avant-garde for Western art music. Even the historical and systematic science of music, musicology, had captured the imagination of many intellectuals in the ethnic community, winning for that field the same devotion accorded other humanistic undertakings in the community and situating the study of music squarely within the framework of *Bildung.* By the turn of the present century these attitudes toward Western art music had crystallized as a system of cultural values that unified the community and undergirded many facets of its ethnicity.

The values accruing to these traditions of art music had developed continually during the century prior to the Holocaust and the emigration of many in the ethnic community from Central Europe, hence during an historical period that saw widespread transformation of the community. The beginning of this period had marked the intensive migration of Jews to large cities. Accompanying this migration was the remarkably rapid urbanization of the traditional culture of the Jews. Professional choices and folkways within the community changed radically; so also did the means whereby community members could interact with the world outside the community, that is, with other ethnic groups and value systems that differed completely from those sheltered for much of the past millennium in the rural and small-town traditions at the heart of European Jewish society.

Jews quickly established a special place for themselves in the Central European city, special not because it stood distinctly apart from the larger non-Jewish society, but because proximity actually aided the absorption of traditions by the ethnic community, where they came quickly to articulate the ethnicity of the community. Jews excelled in many of the most respected professions in non-Jewish society: law, medicine, academia, journalism, music. They quickly established themselves as successful businessmen, bankers, and industrialists, often effecting widespread financial reform and industrialization in Germany's cities.

Within the urbanized culture that attracted so many in the Jewish community, musical life had intensified and changed throughout the twentieth century. Patrons no longer solely occupied positions in the aristocracy and the church, but came from the middle class and the professional class into whose ranks Jews were entering in unprecedented numbers. As a symbol of this entrance into a rapidly urbanizing society, Jews quickly became patrons and supporters of the arts. When restricted from activities and organizations in non-Jewish society, they remained undaunted and formed their own organizations. More often than not these differed in external structure very little from non-Jewish counterparts; internally, however, they often functioned very differently. Their audience and membership were specific: the Jewish community. They could freely respond to the special needs of that community, especially as these related to religious tradition. Such organizations were so successful in redefining the Jewish community that they proliferated during the half century prior to the Holocaust. Unquestionably, they could do so because they reflected the growing urbanization of the Jewish community. The social structure of which they were a part bore little resemblance to the rural German-Jewish neighborhood or small town of a century earlier. New traditions were now central to the community structure, new cultural values had superseded the old. But the community was nonetheless Jewish and distinct from the rest of society.

When Jews emigrated from Central Europe to Palestine in the 1930s, it was this urbanized community structure that they sought to transfer. Recreating this type of community structure offered them many advantages. First, the Central European immigrants stood to undertake the urbanization of Palestine, thus immediately carving out an essential niche in the new country for the community. Second, implicit in this community structure was the preservation and nurturing of the group's cultural values. Third, all communities in Palestine might gain from the speed with which the cultural organizations of Central Europe would quickly reappear. In short, the new immigrants strove not to begin their lives anew as if confronting a *tabula rasa;* rather, they searched for ways to rebuild the organizational structure that had done so much to transform their community in the previous century.

The history of the Central European community appears at first glance not so very different from that of other ethnic and immigrant groups. After all, the Central Europeans formed an immigrant group seeking to preserve some aspects of its musical values. But there was a difference. The musical values of the ethnic group were not qualities of its folk music, or at least not a folk music circulating by oral tradition; nor were they steeped with religious meaning. These values were, instead, inseparable from the traditions of Western art music.

From the ethnomusicological perspective the study of ethnic music in the Central European community of Israel entails the examination of the ways in which Western art music functions in the community. Who are its practitioners, the musicians? What and where are the venues for its performance? What sources for financial support keep alive a tradition whose professionalism places a substantial economic burden on the community? If the traditions of Western art music differ from folk music, how can they function also as emblems of ethnicity?

To answer such questions we must first examine the patterns of ethnicity appropriate to the context of Central European Jewish culture. These patterns, both before and after immigration to Israel, bear many similarities to those of other ethnic groups, especially those of other Jewish communities or those who emigrated from Europe during the modern era. Although specific traditions may differ, the way in which they interact to yield community ethnicity do not differ in fundamental ways. The constituent parts of individual traditions — the specific genres of music and the individuals responsible for their transmission — do contrast and thus distinguish the Central European ethnic community. For Western art music to become the community's traditional music, it must function in certain ways like folk music. One can say, therefore, that Western art music becomes communally shared, and its traditions lend themselves to various patterns of re-creation as reasons for and responses to change.

The distinctive difference in the ethnic traditions of the Central European Jewish community vis-à-vis the musical cultures of many other ethnic groups lies in the community's ability to form cultural institutions on the basis of specialization and professionalism. Such institutions centralized and then nurtured traditional culture, becoming extensions of the family, kinship, and the religious polity of the community. These institutions often possessed a structure sufficiently flexible to withstand the disruptive forces of immigration. For survival, however, they depended on considerable urbanization to maintain a role of buttressing the immigrant community's ethnicity.

In my investigation of the musical traditions of the Central European ethnic community, I have searched for ways in which the community's ethnicity has changed and manifested itself in various ways in modern Israeli society. My treatment of Western art music therefore requires a reconsideration of some expressions of musical tradition and its relation to ethnicity. This reconsideration should, then, extend and sharpen the eth-nomusicological perspective, turning it also toward the ethnic *terra incognita* of Western art music, which therefore emerges as a new source for the more complete interpretation of musical change and the cultural roles of music in any contemporary urban society.

Although the modern Central European Jewish community can claim a history of not much more than a century and one half, confrontation with external groups and pressures has been almost continuous throughout that history. In some cases, confrontation has been fairly benign; in others, its destructive potential has been all too real. It seems almost remarkable, then, that the community has survived at all and perhaps even baffling that the cultivation of its musical values has only occasionally yielded to the external forces of change. Parrying these external forces, however, was the institutional structure of the community itself. Extremely important in this confrontation with external society was the ability of most cultural institutions to change and yet to protect the identity of the ethnic group itself. That change has not overwhelmed the group and caused it to capitulate through total assimilation has been a factor of the community's reliance on the concerted actions of its members and the institutionalization of its culture.

The history of the urban Central European ethnic community has also been one of almost constant migration, first from rural areas of Europe and then to the Middle East and elsewhere. Population flux of this nature, with individuals frequently moving to and departing from a community, benefits directly from the stability of institutions serving as the community's infrastructure. Structurally, the institution is a mediator between the individual and the entire ethnic group. It acts as a sort of catalyst, altering the particular needs of individuals so that they conform to the general good of the community. Each institution serves as a means of organizing some individuals, but rarely does a single institution touch all members of the community. Thus the religion of the group is not an institution *per se*, but certain aspects of it, for example the role of liturgical music traditions, may become institutionalized. The mediating function of the institution provides a means of better understanding both the larger organization of the ethnic community itself and the many motivations of individual members.

The formation of institutions in a community tends to follow conscious patterns established by the ethnic group; stated differently, institutions may achieve the goals of the group, whether or not these goals conform to the structure of the larger society. It is usually necessary, however, to draw upon structures already existing in the external society, transforming them in such a way that they fit in both societies.[1] Such flexibility has been especially valuable to the Central European community, for the larger societies with which it has coexisted have been both supportive of and hostile toward interaction.

Elements of both change and stability usually characterize the institutions of the ethnic community. On the one hand, the members must be constantly aware of the need for change and acculturation; on the other, change must also achieve a degree of routineness in daily activities, thus articulating the structure of the institution. Indeed, it is the emergence of the institution itself that allows for both change and stability in the ethnic community. Stability is necessary for the ethnic community, for its absence would effect the eventual disappearance or even destruction of the community. Stability, in this sense, becomes a corollary of organization.[2]

The institutions of an ethnic community form in different ways and assume different shapes. They do not fall only into categories such as occupational groups or religious sects, though these could be examples of them. An institution should include the activities of more individuals than the family, either nuclear or extended. It need not include participants from all sectors of the immigrant culture, but it should include participants from several sectors. A social group that is organized for the fulfillment of a specific goal would be one form of institution. One example of this type of institution would be a Jewish *Turnverein*, whose specific goal was the encouragement of physical well-being, though numerous other social functions were intrinsic to its role in European Jewish society. In the musical culture of the Central European community, especially when reestablished in Israel, the performance of chamber music has come to demonstrate an institutional structure. Though the individuals involved with this tradition may be relatively few in number when compared to the entire ethnic community, they do nevertheless come from many different sectors.

The institutions within many ethnic communities may stand in hierarchical relation one to another. This is especially true of highly urbanized communities, such as that of Central European Jews, where the multitude of traditions requires that many be maintained by specialists. One might discover in such cases a structure analogous to the cultural division of labor. An institution with similar functions, though located elsewhere in the hierarchy, may have more specific goals. There are, for example, many different types of chamber music tradition in the Central European com-munity, ranging from those anchored by a single individual to professional ensembles performing primarily on public stages. Both maintain traditions historically associated with the ethnic community but are able to articulate those traditions in unique ways. Many concert-goers in Israel expect that it is the responsibility of public performers to pay at least occasional homage to the works of Israeli composers. In more personalized chamber music traditions such music is almost never performed, and the core repertory of Central European composers is performed almost exclusively. The two in-stitutions, public and relatively private, do stand in hierarchical relation with each other because there is frequent movement of performers and audience members between them. The two institutions thus function in similar ways even though the latitude of their specific undertakings varies greatly.

The way in which individuals may participate in different institutions is flexible and constantly changing, not infrequently giving way to new institutions. In a stable community this interrelation among institutions and membership usually manifests equilibrium. A more skewed shifting of institutional structure within the community may become a primary vehicle for change and acculturation. Were the shifting not present, the community's rigid infrastructure would be less capable of withstanding conflict with the external society.

The hierarchy of institutional structure further illustrates the ways in which institutions serve as conduits between the ethnic subsociety and the host society. Not every type of institution allows movement across the boundaries of the ethnic subsociety.[3] Some institutions, for example, might depend instead on the use of the ethnic group's mother tongue, hence effectively excluding non-members. Another institution standing in close proximity in the hierarchy might serve a similar function without de-pending heavily on a single language. This institution would not be exclusive and would allow participation by members of another ethnic group. In Jerusalem there are several chamber-concert evenings yearly during which only German *Lieder* are performed and German poetry recited, very often by visiting artists and professors from Germany. Such evenings attract almost no one from non-German-speaking communities; in fact, until recent years such programs could not have taken place without being veiled from the general public because of the protest that would have followed. In contrast, there are many other concerts of art song that are not exclusive and thus draw widely from the general public, largely because their programs place no particular emphasis on a single ethnic tradition with linguistic exclusiveness.

The institutional hierarchy in Israel offers many conduits for exchange between ethnic communities and the larger society because of the nation's particular conceptualization of Jewish immigration as a return to a homeland. The legal institutionalization of this interrelation between immigrant and nation of settlement occurred in July 1950 with the passage by the First Knesset of the Law of Return. This law and its many ramifications afforded a wide range of provisions that seemingly furnished the new immigrant with the power to participate fully and immediately in the cultural life of the State. First of all, the new immigrant received certain economic advantages, most of which were not available to those born in Israel or Palestine. These included considerable reductions on the purchase of a new apartment, large appliances, and an automobile, as well as tax reductions during the first years after immigration. Second, cultural conduits derived directly from the institutions associated with the Law of Return, if even by implication. One institution of this type is the Hebrew *ulpan*, the language program through which almost all new immigrants gain basic fluency in Hebrew and with that become — at least theoretically — participants in the culture of modern Israel. Third, the Law of Return inculcates a concept of nationalism that extends also to the pre-immigrant culture through the assertion that all Jews, regardless of their current residence, are at least proto-citizens of Israel. Through the institutional structures appended to the Law of Return, the positive role of pluralism in Israeli society is reaffirmed. These structures permit a system that first accepts cultural differences and then channels them in such ways that they are neither isolated nor placed in direct conflict with the larger Israeli society. From an idealistic standpoint the differences become links between both a past and a future Jewish culture.

At the core of a society's institutional structure are the actions of individual members. The functioning institution is no more nor less than the composite of these actions. Thus the individual stands at the end of a social spectrum, the other end of which is occupied by the external society.

S. N. Eisenstadt interprets the process of institutionalization as the interaction of these two ends. "It may be basically postulated that the extent and scope of such institutionalization is a function of the compatibility of two factors: the immigrants' aspirations (role-aspirations), and the possibility of their normative realization in the absorbing society (conditions of absorption)."[4] The interaction of individuals to form a system of values is a necessary precursor to the formation of institutions, which then serve to protect those values. This quality of the institution as an expression of a "personality system" symbolizes many of the cultural traits and aspirations that individuals hope to maintain in spite of interaction with the larger society.[5]

If the institutions of the ethnic community are not to conflict with the larger society, they should to some degree be parallel with the institutions of that larger society. When the institutions are roughly parallel, generally the value systems do not differ markedly. At times, the institutions of the ethnic community may function within the larger society where they might eventually contribute to it a new institution, which in turn is parallel to the ethnic community. This was the situation in Israel during the 1930s when the influx of Germans institutionalized many patterns of concert attendance, the lack of which had prevented the firm rooting of Western art music in Palestine prior to that time. Not only did these German immigrants supply audiences and performances for their fellow immigrants, but they provided a concert life in which the members of other ethnic groups could participate, in fact had to participate to ensure financial viability. The result of this process was that attending concerts became a traditional value throughout Israeli society, and today support for large subscription concerts comes from virtually all segments. But because there are still concert settings within the Central European community for which there are special types of audiences, the institution has parallel forms inside and outside the ethnic group.[6]

If an immigrant group can organize itself in such a way as to encourage the emergence of a distinct ethnic community, it must undertake the formation of institutions. The greater the ease with which the immigrant group fashions these from the pre-immigrant society, the more rapidly the ethnic community forms. The institutions will inject both structure and flexibility into the ethnic community, hence permitting both preservation and change. Central European Israelis were especially adept at the formation of institutions within their community, partly because of the complex pluralism that pervaded Israeli society and partly because of the degree to which the Jewish community in Central Europe had been highly institutionalized prior to immigration. The immigrants of the 1930s, thus, had long been accustomed to existing as an ethnic community within a larger society and articulating their traditional values through diverse institutions. One of the most clearly articulated sets of cultural values was community musical life.

Although this book consistently addresses Central European Jewish communities both in Europe before the 1930s and in Israel thereafter, those two communities differ in several essential ways. The ethnic community in the immigrant culture, while built upon many of the same traditional values as the urban European community, is clearly distinguishable from it on every social level. Hence, I argue for the existence and importance of an historical link between Central European Israelis and German-speaking Jews of Europe, but I characterize that link as one reflective of change, not unaltered similarity. To clarify further the nature of this link between the two communities, I shall look briefly at the critical moments and processes necessary for reformulating ethnic communities in the wake of immigration.

Despite the divergent patterns and rates of change marking the processes of immigration, certain characteristics define it as a unique type of culture contact. Before immigration is undertaken by a community, it is probable that there has been some continuity, some consciousness of historical tradition. Immigration thus involves the movement of a group of people who share a sense of history. They must conceive of themselves as a people who have coexisted in a society with some sense of unified internal polity intrinsic to their shared history. Their sociopolitical structures may be either tight or loose, recognized or abstract; for example, Zionism served as a means of Jewish sociopolitical organization in Europe and later for Jewish immigration to Palestine and Israel in the late nineteenth and early twentieth centuries.

After the immigrant group has resettled, three broad directions for cultural change are possible; these, in turn, clearly relate to the general pattern that pluralism will assume in the new social setting. In the first, the culture of the immigrant group becomes more like that found in the surrounding cultural environment. The second direction permits the maintenance and preservation of the immigrant group, although the resulting stasis is less likely to yield a social framework for subsequent generations. With the third direction, the immigrant group and the culture of the host environment both change so that a third cultural pattern will evolve and become a component of the larger society. It is this third direction that signals the emergence of a long-term ethnic community and that has characterized the Central European ethnic community in Israel.

One of the most striking ways in which an immigrant group differs from its pre-immigrant community is the composition of the group itself. Rarely, if indeed ever, are there instances of entire communities' moving *en masse* to a new nation and reestablishing themselves exactly as before. Quite the opposite is usually the case. An immigrant group comprises individuals who come to form the community only after resettlement. The Central European immigrants in Israel provide a clear example of this process of re-formation and consolidation. Before immigration they inhabited different nations—Germany, Austria, Czechoslovakia, and some areas of present-day Poland and the Soviet Union. They created a new immigrant culture in Israel based not on the nations from which they came, but shaped from a cultural fabric shared by the former nations and their Jewish populations. The German language and a central repertory of Western art music are examples of the consistent elements of culture shared by these communities in otherwise different settings.

Although change would seem to dominate the processes of acculturation, preservation also comes into play in the emergence of an immigrant culture. Preservation, however, is not just a process restricted to the ways in which culture fails to change. It may also be a much more abstract process and in this way may be a more important determinant of ethnicity. Preservation is most important for the reestablishment of shared values that unite the ethnic group. Thus in this book I observe preservation more often as the symbolic role of ethnic identity for maintaining the community. The cultivation of chamber music in the ethnic community exemplifies this more flexible concept of preservation. More than any other genre chamber music is a cultural setting of focal activity for the Central European community in Israel. Prior to immigration, the genre was an important vehicle for the introduction of new music—of contemporary repertories, the avant-garde—and groups with significant Jewish participation were among the most active supporters of this function.[7] Chamber music, therefore, served as a means of infusing change. Since immigration, new music is rarely included in the repertory of chamber music commonly performed in the Central European community. Quite the contrary, the repertory in most *Hausmusik* traditions comes from the late eighteenth and early nineteenth centuries. The tradition now functions in a very conservative way, completely unlike the European setting. Both before and after immigration Central European chamber music expressed certain aspects of Jewish ethnicity; the immigrant culture has clearly preserved this symbolic value. The contents, nonetheless, have not been preserved *in toto* and have accordingly come to symbolize something quite different.

One of the most important processes allowing ethnicity to persist through several generations is the maintenance of boundaries demarcating the community and its values. These boundaries assume multifarious forms and by necessity must allow flexibility in order to facilitate interaction with the society outside the ethnic group. For the Central European community flexibility has been remarkably extensive and effective. Conflict with those segments of Israeli society that might regard remnants of German culture in Israel with uneasiness has therefore been minimal.

Ethnic boundaries further encourage the process of cultural pluralism, the coexistence of multiple communities in a multiethnic society. The persistence of ethnic boundaries circumscribing the Central European community has expedited this pluralism and has itself been encouraged by the widespread patterns of pluralism found throughout Israel.[8] The Central European ethnic group is but one of many ethnic communities that have formed in Israeli society. Central European immigrants have consistently existed in a pluralistic relation with these other segments of Israeli society. While interacting with each other, these communities show no signs of imminent disappearance in a melting pot.

An ethnic community's pluralism also provides a means for examination of its musical institutions. If an immigrant group passes very rapidly through pluralistic stages and becomes assimilated into the larger society, musical assimilation may pass along similar, if not parallel, paths. Contrastingly, if acculturation produces a stable ethnic community, it may also strengthen the existence and maintenance of musical institutions in both the ethnic subsociety and the larger society. The more an ethnic community tends toward pluralism, the more musical change tends to originate within the community, rather than being precipitated from the outside. The degree to which the community implants institutions in order to retain ethnic identity will cause a collateral restructuring of musical awareness and energy. Pluralism serves as a means of strengthening community musical identity; correlatively, adjustments that facilitate the establishment of musical identity strengthen pluralism.[9]

The institutionalization inherent in the pluralistic structure of an immigrant culture results from the pervasive consolidation of resources available to that culture. The music of an immigrant culture undergoes similar patterns of consolidation. For German-speaking immigrants to Israel consolidation was the natural continuation of cultural change that had distinguished their ethnic community in Europe since the mid-nineteenth century. Their ability to consolidate allowed the immigrants to transfer the institutions stimulated by a Jewish cultural renaissance in Central Europe during the early twentieth century. Indeed, one can understand the renaissance itself as a consolidation of past and present. This process then continued in Israel, still defining the ethnic community. By examining the process of consolidation in both Europe and Israel, I mean to suggest that the musical change occurring in the immigrant culture was well underway long before immigration and had become a fundamental and meaningful symbol in the reestablished ethnic community.

Consolidation encourages both preservation and change, and for this fundamental reason it is so often associated with immigrant cultures. The ethnic community must preserve certain facets of the pre-immigrant culture, yet change them to adapt to the new environment. In this sense, consolidation as a theoretical framework allows one to couple both quantitative and qualitative approaches to ethnicity. Consolidation necessarily accompanies a major wave of immigration when groups from different geographic areas form a neighborhood because of cultural similarities. The same process may influence musical repertories. Consolidation of musical repertories may entail the inclusion of certain types of music in a performance only because of the ethnic relation of the pieces. Anthologies of ethnic music are examples of a consolidated repertory. During the early decades of the twentieth century when Jewish *Gesangvereine* began to offer programs of "Jewish music," they included repertories ranging from Hebrew versions of biblical cantatas to newly composed works by local Jewish composers. The consolidation not only preserved the tradition of the singing society but it served to increase the attention given to the Hebrew language, the music of community composers, and even the interpretation of biblical texts with music, which in turn fostered more community-wide attention to and appreciation of religious music.

Consolidation, therefore, does not necessarily lead to musical loss when certain pieces are abandoned through the process; instead, it more properly describes the restructuring of cultural institutions in such ways that music is able to survive with somewhat different functions. A change in function may also stimulate increased musical activity and the creation of entirely new styles. Often this change in function brings about also a pattern of exaggeration.[10] Exaggeration is a process of change that results when techniques or devices thought to be "ethnic" occur in such abundance that they may no more represent the tradition than does their absence. The introduction of an "Eastern Mediterranean" musical vocabulary into essentially Central European music by immigrant composers in Palestine during the

1930s and 1940s illustrates a form of exaggeration, further suggesting that it in fact preserved very little of the Middle Eastern traditions from which it drew.

Changing the functions of certain types of music may also result in the classicization of tradition.[11] Most commonly, classicization describes the transferral of oral traditions to written means of preservation. Accordingly, music must have related institutions of music education or transmission that support the appropriate forms of musical literacy. The program of music education may be rigid, as one established in a school might be, or loose, as one used by a highly urbanized choral society to learn folk music might be. The activities of Jewish cultural groups in Germany during the 1920s and 1930s, for which "Jewish music" became an important subject of evening academies, was an expression of classicization prevalent in the ethnic community prior to immigration. The predominant influence of Central Europeans on the development of music education and the formation of music academies in Israel are different, but related, means of establishing classicization in the immigrant culture.

The growing impact of urbanization during the past century has rendered consolidation even more significant in modern immigrant movements. By its nature, urbanization brings together diverse groups within a geographically restricted environment. The history of German-Jewish immigration to Israel bears particular witness to urbanization because, as mentioned earlier, Jews lived primarily in an urban culture in Germany during the era of emancipation, having largely abandoned rural settlements during the nineteenth century. The impact of urbanization on their community was so powerful that they endeavored to transpose its benefits to Palestine in the 1930s. In so doing, they transformed a previously agricultural economy to one dependent on rapidly expanding cities. Urbanization and consolidation therefore became interdependent, if not synonymous, in the immigrant culture.

The importance of urbanization and consolidation in the ethnic communities in both Germany and Israel underscores an essential issue: although the external societies encompassing these two communities were different, the internal processes of change were very closely related. It is my task here to determine how those processes of change influenced—and were influenced by—the musical activities of both European and Israeli ethnic communities. The complex social structure ensuing from the diverse processes of musical change reveal that it was the constantly changing sense and expression of ethnicity, however subjected to stress in both worlds, that also linked the musical cultures of German-speaking Jews in Europe and Israel.[12]

There are many musical events in Israel at which Central European ethnicity is expressed, some public, others private. Many take place near the Central European neighborhoods in the urban centers, others in mixed-ethnic areas of the city. The repertory for some conforms to the ethnic community's preferred core of works from the mid-eighteenth to the early twentieth century; for others the program has been determined completely on the basis of decisions with no ethnic bearing. The musicians at some have come primarily from the ethnic community, at others from diverse ethnic groups. Although the particular involvement of the ethnic community at a given concert of Western art music may vary, evidence of the community is rarely absent. The concert is the musical institution around which the community's ethnicity most frequently and most translucently crystallizes.

At no other type of musical event is the community's ethnicity more in evidence than at an evening of chamber music. Here institutionalization is at its most extreme. Attendance, though not restricted, is carefully regulated. Repertory and programming, again not truly restricted, rarely depart from firmly entrenched patterns. The performers are largely specialists in this genre of music. Specialization pervades all the individual and group roles that constitute the evening of chamber music. It is not surprising, therefore, that chamber music has become the most highly valued form of musical expression for the community.

Farthest removed from the private performance of chamber music is the concert of orchestral music. Overt attempts to invest such concerts with specific ethnic meaning would be inappropriate to the national and international scope of the orchestra's responsibilities. Not only does the concert itself draw from all ethnic groups, but broadcasts of all performances by the two major orchestras potentially reach every Israeli household. The Central European community, nevertheless, is not hidden from those who are sensitive to the expression of its values. Conversations in German buzz in the foyer during intermission. Visitors from Germany are shepherded about by residents of a Central European neighborhood and are interrogated about the concert season in Berlin or Vienna. Those cognizant of the orchestra's history know the extent to which its early implantation in Israel depended on the Central European community; if this history is sometimes forgotten, the presence of former players and long-time subscription holders at every concert serves as a poignant reminder. No longer highly institutionalized for the Central European ethnic group, orchestral concerts are nonetheless still an inseparable part of the community's musical life.

From the ethnomusicological perspective the ethnicity of the Central European community in Israel persists. Unlike the ethnicity of many other immigrant groups, that of the Central European community depends—and has depended for a century and one half—on a highly urbanized society. Within that society neighborhoods have formed, and social organizations have served as a buffer against external ethnic conflict. The potential for frequent and intensive interaction with other ethnic groups and social organizations has also been prevalent in the urban environment. The musical life of the ethnic community has continually benefited from the flexibility that this social structure permitted. Specialization, professionalism, passionate cultivation of European intellectual traditions, all these have contributed to and benefited from the urbanization of the Central European ethnic community. But throughout the community's history few forms of cultural activity have expressed its characteristic ethnicity as clearly and pervasively as nurturing the traditions of Western art music.

NOTES

1. Daniel Lerner, "The Transformation of Institutions," in *The Transferral of Institutions,* ed. William B. Hamilton (Durham: Duke University Press, 1964), p. 3.

2. S. N. Eisenstadt, "Institutionalization of Immigrant Behavior," *Human Relations* 5/4 (1952): 374-75.

3. The concepts of ethnic-group boundary used in this study largely come from Fredrik Barth, ed., *Ethnic Groups and Boundaries: The Social Organization of Ethnic Groups* (Boston: Little, Brown, 1969) and Anya Peterson Royce, *Ethnic Identity: Strategies of Diversity* (Bloomington: Indiana University Press, 1982).

4. Eisenstadt, "Institutionalization," p. 375.

5. Talcott Parsons, *The System of Modern Societies* (Englewood Cliffs, N.J.: Prentice-Hall, 1971), p. 5.

6. Eisenstadt, "Institutionalization," p. 392.

7. The "Verein für musikalische Privataufführungen" in Vienna during the early decades of the twentieth century is perhaps the best-known example of such a group.

8. For a study of the complex nature of cultural pluralism in Israel see Sammy Smooha, *Israel: Pluralism and Conflict* (London: Routledge and Kegan Paul, 1978); for different perspectives on the role of music as a cultural component in the pluralistic communities of Israel, see the essays in Philip V. Bohlman and Mark Slobin, eds., *Music in the Ethnic Communities of Israel,* Special issue of *Asian Music* 17/2 (Spring/Summer 1986).

9. Margaret Kartomi has proposed the use of the term "musical pluralism" to describe this relation between musical and other institutions in a pluralistic society; see her "The Processes and Results of Musical Culture Contact: A Discussion of Terminology and Concepts," *Ethnomusicology* 25/2 (May 1981): 227-49.

10. Bruno Nettl, "Some Aspects of the History of World Music in the Twentieth Century: Questions, Problems, and Concepts," *Ethnomusicology* 22/1 (January 1978): 132-33.

11. Ibid., pp. 131-32.

12. The reader will find the readings in the "Ethnicity, Immigration, and Musical Change" section of the "Selected Bibliography" helpful for further investigation of the concepts discussed in this chapter.

6

The World Centre for Jewish Music in Palestine

THE RENASCENT Jewish culture of Central Europe intensified the relations between many German-Jewish organizations and Palestine. Zionism, both directly and indirectly, heightened the awareness of new possibilities for Jewish settlement. Even those who were not members of Zionist groups sang *Vereinslieder* with texts about Palestine or studied modern Hebrew in the community *Lehrhaus*. Many Jewish organizations were conceived explicitly as prototypes that would also thrive when transplanted to Palestine.

Intensified organizational activity proved to be an important channel for ideological continuity during the German *aliyah*. Although the Nazi seizure of power in 1933 prodded along the immigration process for many already engaged in preparations, the political changes did not completely catch unawares those less predisposed toward leaving Germany. For some the prospects of immigration might only have been idealistic, but such prospects too contained a psychological impetus toward preparation. For others the social changes predicated by the Nazis merely confirmed a realization that Jewish life in Germany was becoming unfeasible. By this, I do not mean to imply that, as a community, German Jews were fully prepared to immigrate to Palestine or elsewhere in the 1930s; rather there were individual groups within the community that had taken steps to prepare before the actual need arose.

Immigration afforded some German Jews the long-awaited opportunity to coax into fruition ideas engendered in Jewish social organizations. The heavy concentration of German immigrants allowed and even encouraged the complete transplantation of many institutions. Inflexibility was the corollary of such transplantation, often making adaptation difficult when reality bore little resemblance to idealistic imagery. Virtually no organization was fully prepared for the hardship it would have to endure from 1939 until 1945, when contact with Central Europe was impossible. Hence, many institutions could survive no more than a few years in Palestine, and many individual musicians found it necessary to leave Palestine to seek more favorable conditions elsewhere.

The World Centre for Jewish Music in Palestine (WCJMP) exemplifies well the process of institutional transplantation with its concomitant inflexibility. More than any other musical organization in the early years of the German *aliyah*, the WCJMP attempted to bridge the musical cultures of the contrasting worlds of Central Europe and Palestine. But it failed to effect full cooperation with other institutions, which in turn might have made its protracted survival possible, especially during the difficult years of World War II. The WCJMP's history from 1936 to 1940 illustrates the struggle between continuity and disruption that inevitably characterizes the first generation of all immigrant cultures; that struggle, nevertheless, proves vital to the shaping of new musical attitudes and activities.

Founded and organized by German and Austrian immigrants, the World Centre for Jewish Music in Palestine appeared at an historical moment both auspicious for its goals as a broadly based musical institution and portentous of its eventual decline and failure. The center aimed to provide a place where Jewish music of all kinds could be collected, studied, performed, and nurtured. The center's directors articulated this goal as no less than a Jewish musical renaissance empowered to focus the creative energies of the Diaspora. For many Jewish musicians facing the looming specter of Nazism, the WCJMP offered a glimmer of hope, for it provided a new cultural focus in a world rapidly losing perspective. The response to the center's call for a Jewish musical renaissance was, therefore, widespread and rapid, emanating from the highest echelons of Jewish cultural life. Despite isolation in a still sparsely settled land, inadequate personnel, and sometimes devastating opposition to its efforts, the WCJMP began to thrive soon after it was founded in 1936, sponsoring concerts, public lectures, and a journal, *Musica Hebraica*. Unfortunately, the efforts of the center came too late; at the time of its first major successes, World War II began, hence severing many of the center's external ties and, even more destructive, ravaging the creative force in Central Europe upon which the WCJMP depended most.

The WCJMP was initially conceived and organized by Salli Levi (1894-1951). A dental surgeon by profession, Levi participated actively in Frankfurt Zionist groups before emigrating in 1935 (fig. 16). His musical contributions to the Jewish community were considerable. As a member of Frankfurt's *jüdischer Kulturbund*, he organized choral activities, served frequently as a choral director, and occasionally tried his hand at composition. Levi was in many ways typical of the musicians most active in the renascent Jewish

Fig. 16. Salli Levi in Jerusalem, late 1930s. Photo: Courtesy
Else Levi-Mühsam.

musical culture. His musical activities centered around the organizations of the Jewish community. It seems, moreover, that his musical education was largely the product of community teachers and musical organizations. Levi was an amateur musician, and his musical aspirations included only service to the Jewish community, not the building of a career extending beyond its borders.

Levi's devotion to Jewish cultural activities led him quite naturally to a decision to emigrate. His vision of a musical organization that could link Central Europe and Palestine was conceived already in the 1920s. Writing in later years about his early musical activities, Levi reminisced that his first contact with "Jewish music" took place in 1927, when troupes from Tel Aviv's Habimah Theater and the Moscow Jewish Academy Theater toured Germany.[1] This mode of exposure to Jewish music—namely with musical groups from Eastern Europe and Palestine, rather than the traditional music of the synagogue—was increasingly characteristic of many Central European Jewish musicians. In 1929 Levi first articulated his thoughts on potential new directions for Jewish music in an essay entitled "Das Judentum in der Musik," which he circulated privately to Jewish cultural groups.[2] Already in this essay, Levi imputes to Jewish music an essential orientation to Palestine. The essay, nevertheless, remained more theoretical than practical, more enthusiastic than realistic in its claim that new interest in Jewish music was arising throughout the world.[3]

In the 1930s Levi turned toward more practical goals, organizing concert series in Frankfurt and calling them "Palästina in Ton und Bild." Levi's vision of a worldwide network of Jewish musical life now assumed a more distinct shape. Situated in Palestine, a "world center" could maintain contact with all Jewish musicians and cultural institutions throughout the world. An organizational framework in Palestine would serve two general functions: music education and the support of struggling musical groups. Levi's design paralleled the pattern of consolidation that had characterized Jewish musical organizations and ensembles in Europe during the 1920s and 1930s.

Levi preferred not to enter into long-standing debates over the precise nature of Jewish music, defining it instead as the product of Jewish musicians, who instinctively drew upon a shared Jewish heritage. This formulation was significant for several reasons. First, it was broad in scope, including even musicians who had not consciously brought Jewish elements into their works. Second, it allowed Levi to relate his vision more closely with existing concepts of cultural Zionism, which emphasized inclusivity over exclusivity. This broad conceptualization served Levi well when he later sought official sanction and financial support for his undertakings.

Convinced that the moment was right for the institution of a worldwide organization of Jewish music, Levi immigrated to Palestine and there redesigned and implemented his plans. Though plagued by ill health during his first eighteen months after immigration, Levi used this period to acquaint himself with the country's musical life and previous organizational endeavors. He also made contacts with many leading musicians in Palestine, especially former colleagues from the Frankfurt *jüdischer Kulturbund.* His plans generally met with support, and he remained optimistic despite troubled health. The entry period benefited Levi's plans in yet another way, by affording him the time necessary to establish a dental profession in Tel Aviv, thus providing a financial basis for the World Centre in its first stage.

Levi's organizational activities began roughly in mid-1936, when he initiated discussions with Alice Jacob-Loewenson, a music critic and music cataloguer at the Hebrew University, and together they published a memorandum elucidating the goals of a Jewish musical center.[4] The memorandum enabled Levi to approach leading musicians in Tel Aviv and Jerusalem, although the boldness of the plan first resulted in considerable skepticism. Many, however, were acquainted with Levi's activities in the Frankfurt *Kulturbund* and with his pamphlet, "Das Judentum in der Musik," and thus were quickly persuaded by his capability and sincerity. Among the most important early allies were the journalist Hermann Swet, the conductor Fordhaus ben Tsissy, the choral conductor and organist Max Lampel, and Karl Salomon of the Palestine Broadcasting Service.

Organizational activity proceeded only tentatively at first because of conflicting personalities on the initiative committee. Several, most notably Jacob-Loewenson, chose to act independently, at times even in conflict with Levi. When the conflicts multiplied late in 1936, Jacob-Loewenson and other internal opponents resigned, and Levi placed in their stead members who were both more cooperative and amenable to Levi's concept; the reorganization was to prove auspicious, for Hermann Swet, subsequently the editor of *Musica Hebraica,* was among those agreeing to devote their energies to the WCJMP. In 1938 Levi and Swet were joined by the Austrian-Russian composer and cellist Joachim Stutschewsky, who had been working in Europe on behalf of the WCJMP for about a year. Stutschewsky's arrival cemented the triumvirate that would direct the center during its final and most successful years.

The initiative committee of the WCJMP also received support from other organizations. Most significant was the cooperation of Karl Salomon, who rallied the radio and its musicians behind the World Centre throughout its existence. Max Lampel also proved to be a conduit for outside support because of his connections with the *Va'ad Le'umi*, a national cultural organization that would later assume partial protectorship of the WCJMP. Because of the support from the Palestine Broadcasting Service and the *Va'ad Le'umi*, Jerusalem began to function as the primary operational locus for the WCJMP, thus removing it from immediate proximity with that organization Levi thought would serve as an essential cornerstone, namely the Palestine Orchestra, which never offered more than token support to the World Centre. Nonetheless, the WCJMP found allies throughout Palestine, and musicians from all sectors came forth with encouragement and direct assistance. From the kibbutzim, for example, Hanan Eisenstädt and Yehudah Shertok assisted in the implementation of WCJMP activities. By the beginning of 1937, the World Centre was firmly established in Palestine.

With the assurance of cooperation from a broad group of associates, Levi could set in motion the center's projects. By July 1937 the WCJMP had circulated to musicians and musical organizations throughout the world a three-page report specifying the following seven goals:

1. Identification and collection of all Jewish works written until the present, including those works still unpublished;
2. Creation of a means to unify all Jewish composers throughout the world;
3. Founding of a central Jewish music publishing house;
4. Establishment of a journal for Jewish music;
5. Unification of all activities in the musical life of *Eretz Israel*;
6. Creation of "Committees for the Cultivation and Promotion of Jewish Music" in all important music centers throughout the world;
7. Sponsorship of regular congresses and music festivals.[5]

Despite the ambitious nature of the goals, several were successfully realized; others, however, fell victim to the era in which they were conceived and stood no chance of reification.

Circulation of the documents in which these goals were articulated was a first step designed to gain widespread recognition. Committee members in Palestine also appealed personally to their friends and colleagues elsewhere to act on behalf of the WCJMP and to disseminate information whenever and wherever possible. Yet another avenue of appeal was the mailing of letters directly to musicians and Jewish notables without the intervention of friends and colleagues. The response to these appeals was remarkably positive and assumed many forms. Many people immediately sent inquiries seeking to learn how they could be of assistance. Some correspondents expressed great enthusiasm, even if the practical means by which they could assist were limited (see, for example, the letters from Albert Einstein and Béla Bartók, figs. 17 and 18). Others were in the midst of uprooting their lives and work from Europe, hence making involvement with the center impossible despite their best intentions. Many Germans responded with a mixture of enthusiasm and desperation. The Germans, however, were most prone to undertake the organization of European projects and committees for the WCJMP, a task made considerably easier by the degree to which the German Jews were already forced into separate cultural organizations. Several such organizations enthusiastically adopted this new cause as their own. Some German-Jewish leaders, such as Oskar Guttmann in Berlin, even endeavored to implant committees for the WCJMP in the German-speaking Jewish communities of Eastern Europe.

Among those whose enthusiastic responses were also marked by concrete assistance were Ernest Bloch and Darius Milhaud. Both corresponded regularly with the WCJMP, contributed short articles to *Musica Hebraica*, supported performances of their music in Palestine, and agreed to undertake organizational tasks in Europe; neither, however, apparently achieved much success in this last respect. Most important for the WCJMP was the voice of support from them and other well-known composers. Letters like Milhaud's (fig. 19) proved to be persuasive tools when the center turned to organizations both within and outside Palestine for support.

By early 1938 advisory committees had been established in many European nations, the United States, and several areas of the Middle East, all in all reflecting considerable success after a single year of activity. With this show of support from individual musicians, the WCJMP sought to gain some form of official recognition. Prior attempts to gain sanction and protectorship in Palestine had yielded only limited success. Some organizations, such as the Hebrew University, were themselves too young to extend support to the fledgling center; moreover, the primary goal of the center was not itself explicitly academic, or even scholarly. Prolonged debate and internal quarrels in other organizations, such as the *Va'ad Le'umi*, were yet other impediments to official support. Armed with multifarious statements of support, the initiative committee decided that the best forum for its cause was the Twentieth Zionist Congress, which was to convene in Zurich, 3-16 August 1937. Joachim Stutschewsky, still in Europe at the time, was enjoined to publicize the WCJMP prior to the congress; Karl Salomon, who attended the congress, lobbied also for the cause of the center. This preparation served the cause well, for the congress drafted and accepted a resolution placing the WCJMP under its official aegis.

den 9.Juni 1937

Herrn Dr.S.Levi
King George Ave.
House Halbreich
Jerusalem

Sehr geehrter Herr:

   Lieblich ist ja,was Sie tun,

   Doch Ihr Vorbild sei das Huhn:

   Brav legt es zuerst sein Ei,

   Dann erst folget das Geschrei.

       Mit ausgezeichneter Hochachtung

        A. Einstein.

Fig. 17. Letter from Albert Einstein to the World Centre for Jewish Music in Palestine. Source: Jewish Music Research Centre, the Jewish National and University Library, Jerusalem (Mus. 33 I — Einstein, Albert — 9.VI.37).

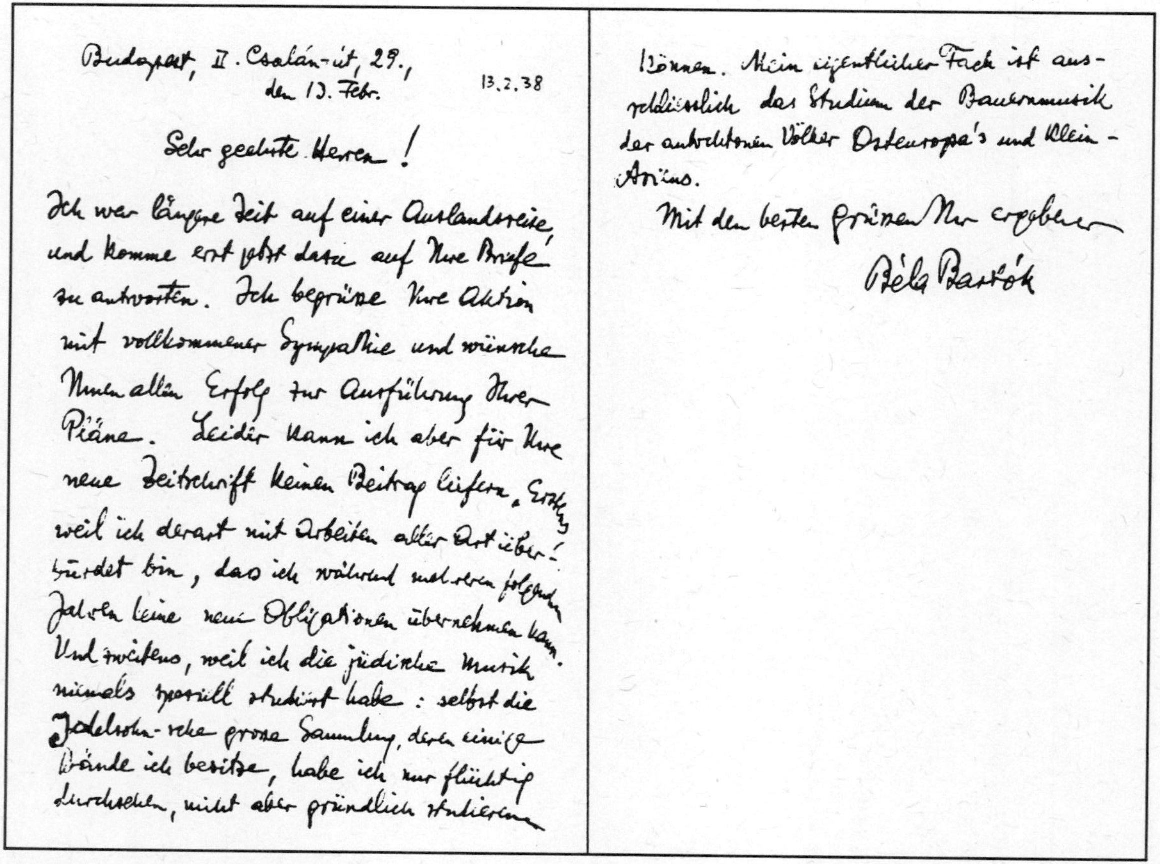

Budapest, II. Csalán-út, 29.,
den 13. Febr. 13.2.38

Sehr geehrte Herren!

Ich war längere Zeit auf einer Auslandsreise und komme erst jetzt dazu auf Ihre Briefe zu antworten. Ich begrüsse Ihre Aktion mit vollkommener Sympathie und wünsche Ihnen allen Erfolg zur Ausführung Ihrer Pläne. Leider kann ich aber für Ihre neue Zeitschrift keinen Beitrag liefern. Erstens weil ich derart mit Arbeiten aller Art überbürdet bin, dass ich während mehreren folgenden Jahren keine neue Obligationen übernehmen kann. Und zweitens, weil ich die jüdische Musik niemals speziell studiert habe: selbst die Idelsohn-sche grosse Sammlung, deren einige Bände ich besitze, habe ich nur flüchtig durchsehen, nicht aber gründlich studieren können. Mein eigentlicher Fach ist ausschliesslich das Studium der Bauernmusik der autochtonen Völker Osteuropa's und Klein-Asiens.

Mit den besten Grüssen Ihr ergebener

Béla Bartók

Fig. 18. Letter from Béla Bartók to the World Centre for Jewish Music in Palestine. Source: Jewish Music Research Centre, the Jewish National and University Library, Jerusalem (Mus. 33 I – Bartók, Béla – 13.II.38). Reproduced with permission of Peter Bartók.

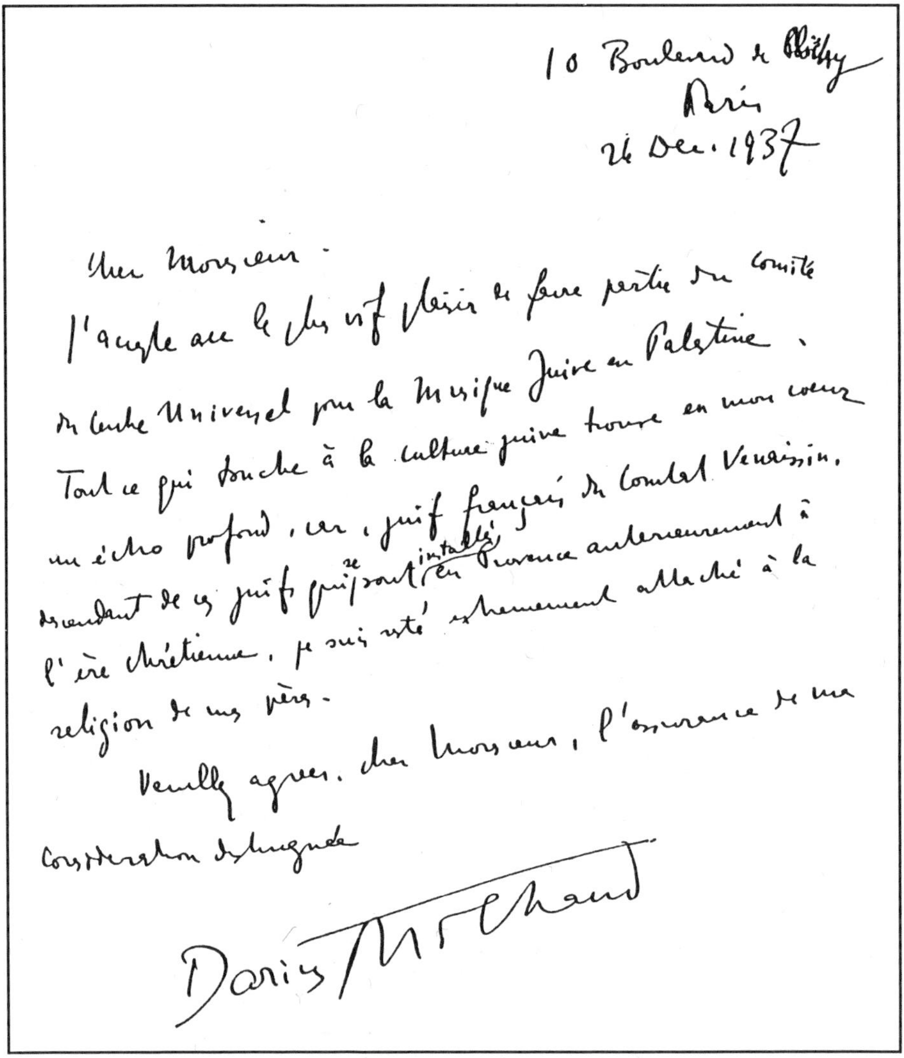

10 Boulevard de Clichy
Paris
26 Dec. 1937

Cher Monsieur.

J'accepte avec le plus vif plaisir de faire partie du Comité du Centre Universel pour la Musique Juive en Palestine.

Tout ce qui touche à la culture juive trouve en mon coeur un écho profond, car, juif français du Comtat Venaissin, descendant de ces juifs qui se sont installés en Provence antérieurement à l'ère chrétienne, je suis resté extrêmement attaché à la religion de mes pères.

Veuillez agréer, cher Monsieur, l'assurance de ma considération distinguée

Darius Milhaud

Fig. 19. Letter from Darius Milhaud to the World Centre for Jewish Music in Palestine. Source: Jewish Music Research Centre, the Jewish National and University Library, Jerusalem (Mus. 33 I — Milhaud, Darius — 26.XII.37).

With the support of the Twentieth Zionist Congress, the WCJMP found its path suddenly cleared of many previous obstacles. Support was now forthcoming from organizations previously offering little encouragement; individual opponents now asked to be counted among the center's members. The *Va'ad Le'umi* now transformed its previously restrained interest into official protectorship, which brought with it a series of affiliations with other organizations in Palestine, thereby broadening the internal base of support for the WCJMP.

After almost two years of organizational struggle within Palestine, the World Centre for Jewish Music held its constituent assembly on 1 March 1938 in the large hall of the Jewish Agency in Jerusalem. In attendance were representatives from most cultural organizations in the country, several of whom delivered addresses of endorsement; the speakers also read messages from an impressive list of supporters abroad. The constituent assembly provided a forum for the public recognition of the activities, goals, and philosophies of the WCJMP. It succeeded furthermore in mustering—perhaps for the first time—musicians, musicologists, music critics, and music educators from all parts of Palestine, thereby engendering potential cooperation among them with the WCJMP as a unifying force.[6]

The year following the constituent assembly was one of success and activity. A large private donation and the inclusion of advertisements enabled the publication of the first two numbers (appearing in a single volume) of *Musica Hebraica.* The journal appeared soon after the constituent assembly, and its international dissemination clearly signaled to all supporters that the WCJMP's activities were well organized and bearing fruit. Materials now arrived at the center at a rate greater than its triumvirate of leaders could process. Before the publication of *Musica Hebraica* 1-2, there were more articles for the third number than it could possibly include. Many composers who had previously sent verbal support now sent scores, some of them still in manuscript. Of the music sent to the WCJMP, almost none remains in the archives, for most was turned over to Karl Salomon at the Palestine Broadcasting Service, which then premiered much of it in Palestine. Correspondence was also most active at this time; the exchange of ideas between Palestine and Central Europe reveals that the WCJMP had begun to exhibit a profound impact in some circles, especially among Jewish cultural organizations in Germany. Indeed, had success continued as in 1938, the WCJMP would have thrived for many years.

One reason for success in Palestine was Levi's solicitation of participation from diverse segments of the country's cultural life. In large part, he appears to have accomplished this so ably because of his organizational skill. Evidence from the archives indicates that many contacted by Levi willingly and quickly devoted their time and talents to WCJMP projects; moreover, there is no evidence of payment for services, thus bespeaking the degree to which the center relied on volunteer energies. Levi was apparently content to remain as the WCJMP's organizer, for he was only tangentially associated with its editorial or musical activities, which he directed to Swet and Stutschewsky respectively. Levi carefully chose committees that comprised representatives from diverse cultural and professional activities. Representing the music academies were such figures as Emil Hauser, Thelma Yellin, and Stefan Wolpe. Lawyers, doctors, educators, and businessmen were also among the members of various committees. Levi's persuasive power was perhaps most effective because he was not himself a professional musician and therefore did not threaten the musical community already in Palestine, and because he often dealt with Central European immigrants well acquainted with his involvement in the Frankfurt *Kulturbund*.

Even greater than his ability to organize within Palestine was Levi's skill at forming committees in the Diaspora. The wealth of correspondence from committee members, moreover, shows a range of support that was quite loyal and far-reaching. Some committees were only loose conglomerations of individuals rarely in contact with one another; others were effectively organized to achieve explicit goals. In Germany the organizational council utilized an already existing infrastructure. In the United States and England, whose Jewish populations were expanding rapidly with the influx of Central European émigrés, the councils succeeded remarkably well in locating potential participants. The undertakings of organizational councils ranged from the symbolic to the pragmatic, for example supervision of *Musica Hebraica* sales.

The success or failure of WCJMP organizational efforts was both directly and indirectly related to the Central European background of Salli Levi and his associates. On the one hand, this background provided a common link to the many recent emigrants of the German *aliyah*. The institutional conception of the WCJMP was thus familiar to those coming from Central European Jewish communities; moreover, German quickly came to function as a lingua franca for the WCJMP. On the other hand, the Central European background sometimes inhibited effectiveness. Levi never succeeded in organizing committees in several nations with considerable Jewish populations, for example the Netherlands and the Soviet Union. Lacking personal contacts in such cases, he was forced to organize from afar or through intermediaries.

Even the sale of *Musica Hebraica* reflected the Central European roots of the WCJMP: the German *jüdischer Kulturbund* alone placed an initial order for a thousand copies, whereas there is no evidence of any sales in many countries.

Financial limitations also restricted Levi's ability to organize both in Palestine and elsewhere. All committees consisted of volunteers despite the considerable expenditure of time by many members. Financial limitations also frustrated the long-term goals of the WCJMP, for implicit in the center's design was the eventual channeling of Jewish musicians to Palestine, a goal inseparable from Levi's intensely Zionist vision. Letters from many European committee members spoke of their desire to emigrate the moment financial means became available, but rarely did letters from the WCJMP reveal that such means might be forthcoming.

Levi hoped that WCJMP performances of works by living Jewish composers would be a stimulus and a vehicle for immigration. In his letters to composers he constantly urges the efficacy of traveling to Palestine to conduct their works in person. Replies to such invitations were usually enthusiastic, though rare was the composer or musician who could make such a journey without financial support and the appropriate visa. Among the most enthusiastic to respond was Ernest Bloch, who hoped that a festival of his compositions would somehow bring him to Palestine (fig. 20).

A major goal of the WCJMP was to sponsor a World Congress of Jewish Music in 1939 or 1940. Indeed, all WCJMP projects prior to the congress were intended merely to serve as a prelude. The congress would provide indisputable proof that the center of Jewish musical life was in Palestine by cultural and historical necessity, which in turn would convince the musicians in attendance that Palestine had become the only possible venue in which to pursue their art. Unfortunately, events in Europe were about to validate this claim in a different, more devastating manner, and the congress stood no chance of materializing.

The most tangible witness to the early successes of the WCJMP is, unquestionably, *Musica Hebraica*. The journal's articles represented diverse styles of musical writing and scholarship with different national perspectives (fig. 21). The journal did not limit itself solely to musicological writing, but aimed its appeal at a wide cross section of readers and musical practitioners, a goal articulated by Hermann Swet in his introduction: " 'Musica Hebraica' is intended to be a forum offering the musicologist the possibility of obtaining wider publicity for the results of his researches; here, through the medium of our columns, the composer will be given the opportunity

Dr Salli Lévi
Jerusalem

Paris
(16ᵐᵉ)

8, rue Georges Ville

March 14ᵗ 1937

My dear Dr Levi,

I thank you for your very kind letter of the 10ᵗ inst. A few days ago, my friend, Mᵐᵉ Tibaldi- Chiesa, had sent me copies of the letter and documents you had addressed her.

I was extremely interested in your lofty plans and I hope sincerely that they will materialize.

In what concerns "Avodath hakodesh" ... the last performance, here, at the great Temple, under my direction, produced a very deep impression; what would it be, then, if this work could be produced in Erз Israël? You may realize what it would mean to

Fig. 20. Letter from Ernest Bloch to the World Centre for Jewish Music in Palestine. Source: Jewish Music Research Centre, the Jewish National and University Library, Jerusalem (Mus. 33 I — Bloch, Ernest — 14.III.37). Reproduced with permission of Lucienne Bloch Dimitroff.

me... and how glad I should be to conduct it myself.

Unfortunately, for _this_ year, it would not be possible, as I have to return to the United States next Fall — after about _seven_ years spent in Europe — and, until my departure all my time will be filled with intensive creative work, which cannot be interrupted —

But could not this be arranged for next year? It would even give more time to organize and prepare carefully everything. At the same time it would be interesting to connect with this event other performances of my "Jewish works" — one or two orchestral concerts, for instance, in which I could conduct my _three Psalms_, _the Three Jewish Poems_, _Schelomo_, my Symphony _Israel_; "Voice in the

2

Wilderness" — which, I think, are not yet known in Palestine — and possibly a few chamber music concerts of my works ... I think that if such a "Festival" could materialize, I should find no difficulties in absenting myself from America — It would certainly be a great joy for me, a great event, to be able to present myself, the "work of my life", in such surroundings as yours ...

Thanking you for your interest and with cordial regards, I am

Yours sincerely

Ernest Bloch

I am leaving Paris, end of March — and my address will then be:

Châtel, Haute Savoie

France

MUSICA HEBRAICA

Publisher: Dr. Salli Levi • Editor: Hermann Swet

CONTENTS
INHALT

"World Centre for Jewish Music" —   „Weltzentrum für jüdische Musik"
Illustrations and Examples   —   Bilder und Notenbeispiele

Price per single copy, in Palestine 2/–, abroad 3/–.
Proprietor: MUSICA HEBRAICA LTD.
43, King George's Avenue, Jerusalem, Palestine.

Fig. 21. Title page from *Musica Hebraica* 1-2 (1938).

of making his work known, whilst the practising musician will be able in 'Musica Hebraica' to give free vent to his views on programme construction, on the problems of musical culture and musical education."[7] Amplifying the breadth of the journal was its polyglot format: most articles appeared in German, English, and Hebrew, a few also in French. The editors intended eventually to include translations into still other languages, such as Yiddish and Russian. After publication, however, the multilingual text drew criticism because the translations, most of them from original German articles, varied in quality. The incorporation of different languages also created an additional financial burden because of translators' fees and increased printing expenses.

Each issue of *Musica Hebraica* was to focus on several themes, usually including music in the Diaspora, music in Palestine, music of a living Jewish composer, and religious music. The editors hoped to provide a forum from which many philosophies of Jewish music could be presented and argued, thus providing a range of approaches appealing to all readers. In the first two numbers the unifying leitmotif was the necessity of a homeland in whose cultural soil Jewish music could be nurtured. To the authors addressing this question, a Jewish homeland was inseparable from the cultural tradition of the Jewish composer and its implicit connection to an ancient homeland.[8] Some authors asserted that Jewish music in the Diaspora was interwoven with Jewish folk music;[9] others believed that only religious music could truly sustain the tradition.[10]

Why *Musica Hebraica* 3 never went to press is probably impossible to determine. Funds were surely tight, but this seems not to have restricted initial preparation of the text. It is evident from the archives that the articles were already translated and edited, and additional articles by authors like Alfred Einstein and David Ewen were ready for the fourth number. But the major funding source for which Levi had been hoping, a consortium of sponsors in England and the United States, did not appear to be materializing. Nor did the national committees seem able to distribute the journal or collect subscription fees.[11] The historical moment was simply not fortuitous for a journal with an international readership; it was no doubt even less so because that readership was largely Jewish. Still, the wide array of articles written for *Musica Hebraica* provides yet another means of evaluating the immense breadth of the WCJMP's eventual design. Ideas taking embryonic shape in early correspondence emerged later in full form on the pages of *Musica Hebraica,* achieving thereby a transferral from the musical culture of Central Europe to that of Palestine.

The archives of the WCJMP contain many sources, heretofore untapped, for the interpretation of musical and cultural life during the 1930s in Palestine. Salli Levi and his associates hoped that the WCJMP would be able to sponsor many concerts, especially those featuring the works of Jewish composers. The WCJMP conceived of its role as an alternative to the larger musical organizations, such as the Palestine Orchestra, which was frequently criticized for programming largely from the standard European repertory, with only token representation of works by living Jewish composers. In its attempt to spawn a new level in the national concert life, the WCJMP had numerous allies, the most active being Karl Salomon, who assisted in the production of several concerts and succeeded in gaining radio performances.

The first major concert was the performance on 21 June 1938 of Hugo Adler's *Balak und Bilam*. The Palestine premiere of a biblical oratorio by a German-Jewish composer was consistent with other WCJMP undertakings and the continued reliance on Jewish musicians from Central Europe. At the time, the Central European style of large-scale religious music was not well known in Palestine, nor was it that well known outside of Germany. Containing a musical style created in the mid-nineteenth century and developed during the renaissance of Jewish culture in Central Europe, the biblical oratorio with Hebrew text was most familiar to the German immigrants in the audience. Among the performers were Karl Salomon, who sang the baritone solos, and Max Lampel, who directed the "Shem" Chorus of the *Va'ad Le'umi* and the Palestine Broadcasting Service Orchestra. As the initial performance sponsored by the WCJMP, *Balak und Bilam* was an immense success. The concert had decisively succeeded in directing public attention to the center, and it affirmed the already close relations between the WCJMP and the Palestine Broadcasting Service.

The WCJMP also sponsored educational programs and chamber music. Most notable of its educational outreaches was its festival to honor the "30th Anniversary of the St. Petersburg Society for Jewish Music," held on 26 May 1939 at the Teachers Seminary in Tel Aviv. The festival focused on Eastern European musicians and folk-music collectors and accorded the honor of plenary speaker to Solomon Rosowsky, a founder of the St. Petersburg Society who had become an active participant in the WCJMP. Chamber music was usually organized by Joachim Stutschewsky, who with his wife, Regina, also a cellist, performed frequently on the programs. Such concerts often introduced new compositions, or works not previously performed in Palestine. Accordingly, the WCJMP hoped to stimulate public awareness of the diverse new directions in Jewish music.

The performance best documented in the archives of the WCJMP is the 1940 production of Ernest Bloch's *Avodat Hakodesh* (1930-33). Negotiations for a performance of works by Bloch began in 1937 and were immediately greeted by a positive response from the composer. The WCJMP invested a great deal of time and effort in performing a work by one of its honorary presidents. Delays, however, plagued the preparations, partly because it was extremely difficult to muster the necessary performing forces. The size of the Palestine Broadcasting Service Orchestra had to be doubled, and an eighty-voice chorus had to be organized. With the onset of World War II in 1939 the efforts of the WCJMP suffered a tremendous blow. Despite the difficulties, the center pushed ahead with the performance, recognizing that it would be the last major event under the WCJMP aegis while Europe was embroiled in war.

The performance took place on 18 June 1940 in Jerusalem's Edison Theater. Karl Salomon conducted the Palestine Broadcasting Service Orchestra and Choral Society, and Vittorio Weinberg, who had sung the premiere in Prague, was soloist. Publicity and advertisements for the concert were extensive, and press reviews praised the concert as a moment of triumph for the WCJMP. Triumph or not, the *Avodat Hakodesh* performance was the final activity of the WCJMP; no archival evidence survives to indicate that the organization undertook additional projects after the 1940 concert.

The letters in the archives of the WCJMP, written on the eve of World War II, provide a profound documentation of Jewish cultural life in Central Europe during its final stage. For some individuals, for example Arno Nadel, the collector and compiler of Jewish folk and liturgical music, the letters may be the final documents of someone about to disappear forever in the Holocaust. Stretching over a period of several years, the letters address the changes endured by Jewish communities: first, the maintenance of separate organizations; then, the disruption of cultural activities; finally, the fear for survival. As an ardent Zionist, Salli Levi had hoped that the WCJMP would attract Jewish musicians to Palestine. Many correspondents held similar hopes and requested assistance in the location of positions that the WCJMP might somehow support. Indeed, some letters, such as the following from Hugo Adler, stressed that numerous musicians were prepared to immigrate, were only suitable positions available:

> Let's put it in the following terms. Let's assume that the new organization could take on the responsibility of helping its members emigrate. Above all, I believe this would be a positive signal and would also encourage a certain trust. With this mission you must approach those individuals who are in charge of appropriate positions and can

offer some sort of commitment. I know that whatever happens thereafter will be something quite different, but that matters not; the most
important thing is that this affair be set in motion and that our people —
who should indeed also be your people — can recognize that *you* understand their plight.[12]

By the late 1930s many had begun to realize that Jewish musicians
would not be able to survive much longer in Central Europe. Arthur
Bernstein, director of a concert agency affiliated with the *Reichsverband der
jüdischen Kulturbünde Deutschlands,* appealed in a 1937 letter that Levi
allow the agency to place its clients under the protectorship of the WCJMP;
Levi's inability to do so is clearly signified by his failure to respond. Subsequent letters also reflect increasing desperation, demonstrating unequivocally that, for many, postponed exit from Germany was not blindness to
what lay ahead, but the inability to secure the financial and political means
necessary for emigration.

For many reasons it is difficult to assess the lasting impact of the WCJMP.
First of all, the organization had a relatively short lifetime, after which its
activities came to an abrupt halt. Second, so much energy was spent organizing Jewish musicians outside the country that the center's influence
on musical life in Palestine was less than it might have been. Finally, the
almost total absence of references to the center by historical accounts of
musical life in Israel forces one to question the extent of its impact.

WCJMP records suggest four major reasons for the cessation of activity
in 1940: financial problems; organizational limitations in Palestine; World
War II; and the inability of the center to adapt sufficiently to the social
structures of the immigrant environment. There may well have been other
reasons for failure, but surviving records hold no clues to them. Financial
records of the WCJMP are scant and reveal little about its financial organization. On one hand, financial information was lacking because of the
center's dependence on massive expenditures of volunteer time, energy, and
money. Salli Levi diverted considerable funding from his dental practice to
care for daily needs at the WCJMP. On the other hand, the center's more
ambitious plans required substantial financial backing, more than the center
had at its disposal. To solve this dilemma, Levi enjoined colleagues and
committee members abroad to raise capital that could then be channeled
back to Jerusalem. As conditions abroad worsened and the war began, this
source of funding was completely arrested.

The WCJMP also faced some opposition within Palestine itself. That
Levi was only an amateur musician caused some to regard his plans with

suspicion. Emil Hauser, director of the Palestine Conservatory of Music, always reacted tentatively to Levi and only in later years offered support, never, however, enlisting full sanction from the conservatory. The Hebrew University, with no musicology department at the time, also offered no more than occasional verbal support to the WCJMP. Even though Levi conceived the WCJMP to provide a solid foundation for musical scholarship in Palestine, he received little cooperation from the country's still nascent musicological community; the recently arrived ethnomusicologist Robert Lachmann (1892-1939), for example, reacted negatively to the organization, never participated in its activities, and never contributed a completed article to *Musica Hebraica*.[13] It is not unlikely that, because *Musica Hebraica* attempted to do so much, its intended readership was somewhat ambiguous; it was neither fully a scholarly journal for the musicologist nor a periodical accessible to the broader public.

Most disappointing for Levi was his failure to bring about cooperation with the Palestine Orchestra. He had hoped that the orchestra would provide the institutional undergirding for a worldwide network of Jewish musicians. His extensive correspondence with the orchestra's management reveals that, to no avail, Levi tried to effect cooperation on numerous occasions. The difficulties with the Palestine Orchestra also undermined Levi's other plans for organization in Tel Aviv because of the orchestra's dominant role in the city's musical life. Levi compensated for the lack of cooperation within Palestine by strengthening his relations with musicians abroad, thus rendering the WCJMP dependent on outside contacts for survival. Clearly, his vision of a worldwide organization was very fragile in any case and dangerously so because of the impending war. The very structure Levi had created — a structure so necessary for those it served — was also a harbinger of its own demise.

The WCJMP never fully developed as an institution able to respond to and serve the changing ethnic culture of Palestine. The center remained essentially an institution of Central European Jewish culture and therefore succeeded in serving only that community in Palestine with a similar cultural background. Joachim Stutschewsky, whose youth in Eastern Europe should have enabled him to establish more extensive contacts with that ethnic community, never exploited that background while at the WCJMP. Although *Musica Hebraica* was a polyglot journal, it still bore the clear stamp of its editors' German roots. There can be no doubt that the WCJMP would have become more truly international — more representative of a "world center" — had World War II not intervened. Indeed, had the WCJMP survived the war years, the influx of new immigrant groups would have caused the organization to transcend the more restricted perspectives of the German *aliyah*.

Dissolution in 1940 notwithstanding, the WCJMP was immensely successful during its brief tenure. The center was a force of organization in the musical life of pre-statehood Israel and provides a means of reevaluating the musical activities of several of the nation's most important musicians during this period. The records of the center constitute one of the best surviving sources for the study of European Jewish musical life in the years immediately preceding World War II. Although the picture one discovers has many confusing elements, a perceptible struggle to find a viable solution to the problems at hand still remains; the World Centre for Jewish Music in Palestine and its endeavor to break new soil for the cultivation of Jewish music provided that solution, however tenuous, for many during the difficult transition from a European to an Israeli musical culture.

NOTES

1. Salli Levi, "Geschichte der Schaffung des World Centre for Jewish Music in Palestine," unpublished manuscript in the Archive of the WCJMP, n.d., prefatory page.

2. Salli Levi, *Das Judentum in der Musik* (Frankfurt: Salli Levi, 1929).

3. Ibid., p. 17.

4. Archive of the WCJMP, Mus. 33 V, A [5], a and b; during 1981-82 I prepared a complete catalogue of the contents of the Archive of the WCJMP and published it in "The Archives of the World Centre for Jewish Music in Palestine," pp. 241-52. Documents cited in this book utilize the reference system of that published catalogue.

5. Archive of the WCJMP, Mus. 33 III, 1 [c], p. 1.

6. See also *Musica Hebraica* 1-2 (1938): 51.

7. Hermann Swet, "By Way of Introduction," *Musica Hebraica* 1-2 (1938): 3.

8. See, for example, Ernest Bloch's comments in his untitled message, *Musica Hebraica* 1-2 (1938): 12.

9. Erich Werner, "Wanted: A Definition," *Musica Hebraica* 1-2 (1938): 6.

10. Anneliese Landau, "Jewish Music and Jewish Composers in the Diaspora: I, Germany," *Musica Hebraica* 1-2 (1938): 43.

11. Levi's wife, Else Levi-Mühsam, claims that the termination of the *jüdischer Kulturbund* by the Nazis — hence the elimination of the journal's primary readership and means of distribution — was the major reason *Musica Hebraica* 3 failed to go to press; personal communication to the author, 27 February 1985.

12. Archive of the WCJMP, Mus. 33 I — Adler, Hugo — 7.IV.38.

13. Apparently Lachmann was preparing an article for *Musica Hebraica* when he realized that Hermann Swet was not solely responsible for editorial decisions. Fearing that Levi's involvement might make the journal less scholarly, Lachmann withdrew his commitment of an article. See Lachmann's letter to Swet, Mus. 33 I — Lachmann, Robert — 17.II.38 (Archive of the WCJMP).

7

The Creation of an Urban Musical Culture in Israel

URBANIZATION profoundly transformed the Jewish community of Central Europe during the century prior to the Holocaust. Most Jews in the urban communities perceived urbanization as beneficial to their position in German society, and it is not surprising, therefore, that after immigration few should choose to abandon the growing influence of the city and the cultural advantages it had engendered. Palestine, however, was not an urbanized society at the beginning of the 1930s, in part because of the still-sparse population, but also because of the conscious decision of earlier immigrants to rebuild the Jewish nation on the land, not in the city. The *halutzim*, the pioneers, of previous *aliyot* had attempted to organize this agriculturally based society with a variety of rural communal settlements as its social core. Whereas the major cities of modern Israel—Tel Aviv, Jerusalem, and Haifa—had long histories, they were considerably smaller and rarely the focus of the sweeping changes envisaged by the early pioneers.

The immigrants from Central Europe implanted a new social order during the 1930s, one that brought about massive cultural changes. In direct contrast to the ideologies of the earlier immigrants, the Central Europeans turned to the city as the cultural and economic buttress of the new Jewish nation. Not only did the cities expand tremendously in size and importance, but they came quickly to support a cultural life previously unknown in Palestine. Near the neighborhoods inhabited by the Central European immigrants arose new cultural and educational institutions, concert halls and museums. Figure 22 illustrates the way in which the Central European neighborhood, Rehavia, came to form near the different cultural institutions of Jerusalem. Such institutions were supported financially by the industrialists and businessmen among the new immigrants, and they quickly came to support the tremendous influx of artists, musicians, and intellectuals fleeing Germany. The urbanization of the 1930s was as sweeping as it was sudden, but it propelled Israel along a course of cultural change from which it has yet to swerve.[1]

The musical culture of Central European Israelis bears the imprint of this urbanization to a remarkable degree. In all areas and genres of the musical culture—art, religious, popular, and even folk musics—one can readily observe the changes empowered by an urban environment. These changes occurred with the same swiftness and pervasiveness as the broader socioeconomic changes following the arrival of the immigrants from Central Europe. Within a decade Tel Aviv and Jerusalem both had orchestras; numerous music academies expanded the potential of the country to educate new musicians; a new broadcasting service and myriad ensembles of all sizes and complexions made for a thriving concert life and growing audiences. The concurrence of these changes in the musical culture depended entirely on the social structure of the city and in turn served to bolster that structure.[2]

The explosive proportions of urbanization during the German *aliyah* resulted from yet another historical factor: Because of the high degree of urbanization in European communities, the immigrant generation endeavored to reestablish urban institutions in Palestine. This motivation of the immigrant community has stimulated the process of change I call reurbanization, the transferral to another venue of central components from an urbanized social structure to maintain the cultural life of a particular ethnic group.[3] Reurbanization is distinctive also because it reverses the usual direction of change ensuing from the contact of a non-Western or folk music with Western and modern culture. It is therefore the immigrant group that largely determines the direction which cultural and musical change will follow, at least to the extent that such change depends on the city. In Israel the Central Europeans brought with them the tenets of Western culture, thus making it necessary to regard them as a Westernizing force, rather than simply a society undergoing Westernization.

One of the essential components of an urbanized musical culture is the prominent role played by art or classical music.[4] Above all, the Central Europeans wished to retain this prominent role for Western art music. They structured their musical culture to undergird this role, sometimes sacrificing other areas of musical activity. In the nineteenth century, Western art music had been a conduit for entrance into German society; in the twentieth century, specifically Jewish contributions to art music had even come to define aspects of a Jewish subsociety in Germany. Because of the highly symbolic function art music had acquired in the century prior to immigration, the Central European community in Palestine quickly established it as the cornerstone of their efforts to create a new musical life. For such efforts to be successful, urbanization was a precondition.

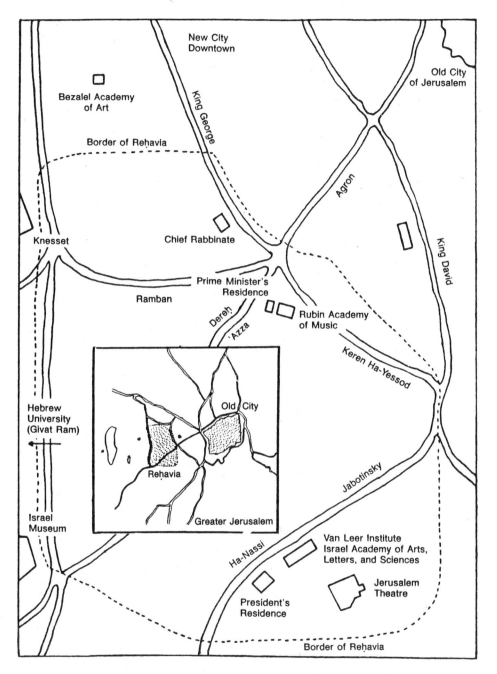

Fig. 22. The Reḥavia neighborhood, Jerusalem. Map: Florence Bohlman.

Urbanization exerted itself in the musical culture of the Central Europeans in different ways. For the symphonic orchestras urbanization rendered success immediate and abrogated the ethnic boundaries that might constrain the orchestras and stultify their development. Institutions of music education, too, depended on urbanization for a firm footing, but then were enabled by initial survival to serve a broad spectrum of ethnic groups. In different ways, Central European religious music and the musical activity of kibbutzim — neither of them constituents of an urban culture prior to the German *aliyah* — have responded to the expansion of Israel's cities. Urbanization has thus effected a multiplicity of acculturative responses from a wide range of musical institutions. To understand the extent of these responses one must also examine the organizations whose development they shaped. For some, Israeli symphonies for instance, urbanization has been a major factor in long-term success; for others, such as the kibbutz, urbanization has brought about considerable musical impoverishment. Each of the institutions, however, illustrates the different ways in which Israel's urban culture underlies musical change throughout the nation.

Prior to the 1930s numerous orchestral groups had been established in Palestine, only to suffer organizational and financial problems before foundering completely. Among the most notable of these were Fordhaus ben Tsissy's Palestine Orchestra and the orchestra of the Russian conductor Zvi Komanez.[5] These early attempts revealed that sufficient interest in orchestral ensembles did exist in Palestine, but that certain social and musical changes would have to come about before this interest could reify. In essence, the needed social change was the formation of an audience and a system of patronage that would assume permanent support of an orchestra; musically, a sufficiently large group of performers willing to serve as professionals was a prerequisite. These were precisely the changes that the German *aliyah* secured during the 1930s.

The first steps toward the establishment of the Palestine Orchestra (the Israel Philharmonic Orchestra after the founding of the state) were taken in 1934, when the conductor, Wolfgang Friedlaender, and about fifty instrumentalists formed a "Palestine Philharmonic Symphony Union." This loose confederation of musicians was soon joined by Michael Taube, a recent immigrant from Germany, where he had been a member of the Berlin State Opera since 1924.[6] Taube greatly expanded the activities of the symphony union by planning its concerts and developing educational programs inside and outside the group. With this foundation laid, the orchestra needed only to await the arrival of its chief architect, Bronislaw Huberman.

The well-known Polish violinist Bronislaw Huberman (1882-1947) dedicated himself to the task of building a new orchestra, quickly becoming the timely catalyst that transformed the Palestine Orchestra from idea to reality. Deeply affected by the Nazi ascension to power, Huberman redirected his creative energies, which had previously been devoted to concertizing in Central Europe, to mustering Jewish musicians from Europe and forming an orchestra whose existence and excellence would defy the cultural exclusion foisted on Jewish musicians in Germany. Huberman drew from three different groups of musicians to build the orchestra: those already in Palestine; those active in Germany, usually with one of the Jewish cultural organizations; and musicians in Europe, but not living in Germany. Of these groups, only the second consisted primarily of German-Jewish musicians, thus explaining the fact that Germans were not the dominant ethnic group of the orchestra in the 1930s.[7]

Documentary evidence suggests that Huberman maintained a somewhat ambivalent personal attitude toward German Jews while building the orchestra. This attitude may well have resulted from the physical distance caused by his steadfast refusal to reenter Germany after 1933,[8] but he realized that the fledgling orchestra stood to gain much from the participation of the highly skilled Central European musicians. The orchestra, moreover, could do much to extricate these musicians from the miserable artistic conditions they were suffering in Europe. Huberman knew that, if the Palestine Orchestra were to survive, it must turn to Central European musicians, both new immigrants and those still in Europe, to shore its ranks.[9] Huberman's initial ideological and artistic design, nevertheless, lay closer to Eastern than Central European Jewish cultural values. He envisaged building an orchestra in Palestine as an opportunity to bring classical music to a new type of audience, one lacking class distinctions and representative of no single ethnic or cultural group. Palestine, with its prevailing ideology of a pioneering society based on labor, was an ideal place to implement this philosophy. Huberman wrote in 1934, "If for no other reason than the unhappily differentiated European class structure that has prevailed for so long in the old country, the call to mold an orchestra that will bring the worker to the realm of music is even stronger. . . . The obligation of a Palestine orchestral organization must be deeply dedicated to bringing the worker to a level equal with the spirit of the music. Such an individual is, indeed, only a worker in the physical sense, but spiritually he belongs among the proudest pioneers of the land."[10]

Had such a philosophy rigidly applied to the orchestra's formation, a fundamental conflict with the cultural stance of many German musicians might well have ensued. Instead, Huberman turned over all responsibility for bringing musicians from Germany to Michael Taube, who succeeded remarkably in this project.[11] In its opening concert of 16 December 1936 under the direction of Arturo Toscanini the orchestra contained Jews (and apparently some non-Jews) of diverse ethnic backgrounds, thus realizing Huberman's ideological vision. Were he to have depended on the classless public for which he had earlier called, however, his orchestra would have passed the way of earlier attempts. Instead, the concert life that flourished during the next few decades shifted to the community of Central European immigrants.

The other major orchestra of Israel, the Israel Broadcasting Orchestra, also traces its origins to the 1930s, but the contributions of Central European immigrants were here more direct and obvious. These contributions were especially fortuitous because the Palestine Broadcasting Service Orchestra was founded in 1938 at a moment coeval with the largest influx of German musicians. Although the radio was under British control, its musical directorship was in the hands of Karl Salomon, an immigrant from Germany. Salomon depended almost exclusively on the presence of musicians already in Palestine who could perform in the sundry capacities necessary for a broadcasting service dependent completely on live performances. Unlike Huberman and Taube at the Palestine Orchestra, Salomon had no opportunity to organize a system that would bring musicians to Palestine. Salomon had at his disposal, nonetheless, one form of organization that had been imposed on the Jewish musicians in Germany. The *Kulturbund* organizations, like the Jewish orchestras in Frankfurt and Berlin, allowed for an extensive web of contacts among Jewish musicians throughout Germany. The activities of these musicians were well known even to the Jewish public, their primary means of support; for example, the Berlin *Kulturbund* orchestra had a subscription that reached 50,000 in the 1930s.[12] When members from these organizations immigrated to Palestine, they reestablished contacts among themselves. Such contacts especially favored the formation of the radio orchestra and accordingly produced an ensemble that was largely German in background and training.

The orchestra of the Palestine Broadcasting Service (PBS) functioned rather differently from its counterpart in Tel Aviv. It was a smaller, even *ad hoc* orchestra at the beginning and thus performed a more variegated repertory than the Palestine Orchestra. Chamber symphonic literature, chamber music, and light music received more attention. The orchestral player at the PBS was thus more diversified. His diversity tended to serve the immigrant community of the 1930s in a broader and more complete fashion. Many radio musicians, for example, also performed with ensembles playing popular music and jazz in the major cafes of Jerusalem — the Cafe Europa, the Cafe Vienna, and the Cafe Rehavia — all of which were vital intellectual and social magnets for Central European immigrants. Chamber music flourished within the conditions afforded by the broadcasting service, for its orchestra split up into myriad chamber groups as performance situations demanded them. As an orchestra that could immediately serve an urbanizing society, the PBS was well suited to the rapidly expanding musical culture of the Central European immigrants.

Soon after their establishment, the orchestras began to provide a means of exit from Germany for musicians. Accordingly, they were able to build and balance their ranks. The steps necessary to bring musicians from Germany were intricate and complex. The orchestras needed to procure both immigrant certificates from the British and exit visas from the Germans. This forced them, in a sense, to organize and institutionalize. At times they were forced to resort to elaborate schemes of falsification and forgery. Once the proper documents were in order, yet another matter had to be confronted: covering the considerable costs of the trip itself.[13]

Accounts of their memberships reveal that the Palestine orchestras were especially successful in bringing musicians from the standing Jewish orchestras in Germany. The Frankfurt *Kulturbund* contributed substantially to the wave of immigrant musicians, providing the basis for the wind section of the Palestine Orchestra. The contribution from Frankfurt intensified when its general music director, Wilhelm Steinberg (later William Steinberg), agreed to serve as principal conductor and rehearsal conductor for the Palestine Orchestra. The arrival of German musicians in the late 1930s seasoned the orchestras with a Central European flavor. In addition to important musicians like Steinberg, the management of the Palestine Orchestra was almost completely German. The first general secretary of the orchestra was Salo B. Lewertoff, prior to immigration the music director of the Rhein-Ruhr section of the Jewish *Kulturbund.* Succeeding Lewertoff in this position were Heinrich Simon and then Leo Kestenberg, formerly of the Prussian Ministry of Culture, who also assumed the post of general manager of the orchestra in 1938.[14] Faced by World War II, the orchestra's administrators confronted organizational tasks of enormous magnitude, but parried the problems they faced with amazing success. German musicians and management shaped both orchestras in many ways, and evidence of this influence persisted for many years. German, for example, remained the language of rehearsals well into the 1950s.

With their musical and administrative apparatuses in place, the orchestras had to confront the task of establishing and maintaining audiences that would support a rigorous concert life. Their attempts to accomplish exactly this goal were especially effective and largely indebted to the German *aliyah*. By extension, one may posit that the orchestras benefited directly from the urbanized musical culture that accompanied the Central Europeans. The initial concerts of the Palestine Orchestra were completely sold out, and even after the rehearsals were opened to the public, there were many unable to obtain tickets. Audiences exceeding 15,000 greeted Toscanini's eight days in Palestine for the initial concerts.[15]

Because the two orchestras functioned in quite different ways, they succeeded in generating several types of audiences, thereby broadening and strengthening the overall basis of concert life. The Palestine Broadcasting Service had originally hoped to use the Palestine Orchestra for its broadcasts. Huberman was completely opposed to such a role, realizing that the audiences he hoped to attract were not the same as those the radio could reach.[16] The radio orchestra, thus, had greater freedom to fill the gaps left by the Palestine Orchestra's specific appeal to subscribers.

The creation of a concert life in Palestine was a conscious undertaking by the immigrant musicians. Uri Toeplitz, a flautist and founding member of the Palestine Orchestra, described the task before the orchestras as one of forging completely new musical values within the audiences: "The public we had in the beginning were, of course, first of all the German immigrants who were used to go to concerts, and part of those Russians who had already adapted themselves to this kind of culture. But this fight to make music — as part of social life — was difficult because we had to change the support."[17] Because those engaged in the undertaking bore German musical tastes and had long been participants in the musical organization of European communities, the patterns established by the orchestras necessarily reflected the patterns of Central European musical culture.

The differences between the two orchestras meant that they served different audiences, thus producing the sort of specialization characteristic of urbanization. The Tel Aviv orchestra relied on more conservative musical tastes. It needed to attract audiences that would respond by renewing subscriptions year after year. Furthermore, its audience was primarily interested in large orchestral works that were not particularly experimental. The programs, performed on multiple occasions in Haifa and Jerusalem as well as Tel Aviv, generally avoided works that might induce widespread criticism. The orchestra in Jerusalem took shape in a completely different way. Whereas it too performed in public concert, this was only one of its activities; for its other activities, it had both to diversify and to specialize. It diversified by subdividing to provide performing ensembles for various needs; each of the resulting ensembles consequently specialized, some institutionalizing as musical groups of their own. The radio orchestra, therefore, depended on a different public. Subscription concerts and a season with popular appeal were not as necessary as in Tel Aviv. Experimentation was also easier for the radio orchestra, for one goal of the radio was to provide an outlet for new compositions by Israeli composers. Again, the radio orchestra could function in this way because of specialization. Both orchestras developed rapidly in the late 1930s because of the systems of patronage supporting them; both patronage systems, furthermore, reflected cultural values fundamental to the Central European community.

The orchestras were also linked to their audiences by new chamber music activities, those too reflecting specialization in the concert life. This link was extremely important because of the symbolic role accorded chamber music in the Central European musical culture. The chamber music activities of the radio orchestra were a direct outgrowth of its diversification; chamber music was performed daily on the radio, and a wide range of public chamber music series began during the German *aliyah.* In Tel Aviv chamber music became also an alternative to the conservative demands of subscription audiences. When, in 1936, the Tel Aviv Museum was founded, it initiated a chamber music series in which ensembles from the Palestine Orchestra performed. The public for these concerts was almost exclusively German, and enthusiastic audiences filled the two Saturday night performances.[18] These programs allowed for extensive performance of new music, as well as more authentic performance of pre-Classic music. These chamber repertories supplemented the general musical activity of the Palestine Orchestra, and the orchestra's patronage diversified accordingly.

Israel's major orchestras have developed a broad base of support from many ethnic groups since the 1930s. In this sense the orchestras have demonstrated urbanization to a greater extent than had the German imprint simply preserved community boundaries. Indeed, the speed with which institutionalization proceeded in the 1930s also suggests that the orchestras would not develop along parochial ethnic lines. There remains, however, considerable evidence of Central European roots in the orchestras. The most obvious case of this is the persistence of the Israel Philharmonic Orchestra as the most visible and important institution leading the fight against the proscription of Wagner. Even though many Central European Israelis are willing to perform his music only under relatively secretive conditions, the Israel Philharmonic periodically attempts to perform it publicly. The public and sometimes violent protest that has arisen from non-German ethnic groups serves as a clear reminder that certain emblems of German and German-Jewish musical culture remain unacceptable to some segments of Israeli society. Reurbanization has altered the Central European orientation of Israel's major orchestras, but some musical values inherent in that orientation remain intact, even in the face of protest.

Initial attempts to establish institutions of music education predated the German *aliyah*, but like the early orchestral endeavors these were largely unsuccessful because of organizational and financial problems. The first music schools appeared in Tel Aviv in 1910 and 1914, but little record of their activities survives; schools founded in Jerusalem and Haifa in 1918 and 1924, respectively, also leave little record. Not unlike the plight of early orchestras, the music schools found survival difficult because the social structure lacked sufficient urbanization to provide appropriate support and patronage. Again, it was not until the 1930s that the necessary urban musical culture would develop, making possible the establishment and survival of Israel's most important music schools.

The first music school to root itself firmly in the country was the Palestine Music Conservatory, which was founded by Emil Hauser. The Hungarian-born Hauser immigrated in 1932 after some years in Frankfurt as a member of the Adolph Busch Quartet and after founding the Budapest Quartet in 1917. Upon establishing the Palestine Conservatory, Hauser needed to confront two major problems: enrolling enough students and attracting qualified teachers. The solutions to both problems lay in the German *aliyah*. Music education, as a requisite component of *Bildung*, was an essential part of the cultural outlook of urbanized Central European Jews. They therefore welcomed the undertakings of Hauser and the new conservatory. Hauser found it impossible, however, to rely solely for his student body on the more limited immigration of the early 1930s. After the Nazi ascension to power, Hauser recognized the potential of the conservatory to provide escape from Germany for both students and instructors. The promise of employment and studies in Palestine were sufficient cause for the Germans and British to provide the necessary visas. For these reasons Hauser went to Germany to encourage students to immigrate to Palestine and pursue musical studies there. In the following account Shabtai Petrushka elaborates how

Hauser's efforts made immigration possible, even though each case was fraught with complicated and seemingly insurmountable technical en-cumbrances.

> In the summer of 1937 the director of the then Palestine Conservatoire, who was Professor Hauser, . . . secured some forged immigration cer-tificates from the British High Commissioner, Sir Arthur Walker. He gave these certificates to bonafide students. So he came to Berlin and put an ad in the paper that young musicians who are interested to continue their musical studies in Jerusalem are invited to meet him for an interview. At the time I wanted to leave. It was 1937, and it was very difficult to get an immigration certificate. They restricted immigration to 1,500 Jews a month, or some more, 2,000 per-haps. . . . My first wife . . . was a schoolteacher and was employed in a Jewish school. And I worked in the Jewish Orchestra. So, two people who were both working for Jewish employers had to wait. I knew the wait would be very long, so I'd try my luck with Professor Hauser. I went to an interview, and I brought him a few gramophone records that I had already from the Deutsche Grammophon [Gesellschaft],[19] and there was a Jewish gramophone company, where I was adminis-trative adviser. I showed him some scores. He said, "What do you want? I have no certificates for teachers, only for students." I said, "I want to get out, and I hope you can help me." So at that time there was actually a conservatoire especially for . . . music teachers in high schools. It was very important because there were not enough teachers. So he said, "If you are prepared to take this course, I can find for you a certificate." But I said, "If I do this, there should be certain subjects." He showed me the curriculum. And there were piano and harmony and solfège, which I didn't need. I said, "I'm prepared to pass an examination in all these subjects when I come there and get free from them." So he said, "That's all right." But I said, "If you have teachers in composition, I want to brush up my counterpoint," which I had not studied since the teens. He said to me, "We have a teacher, Hanoch Jacoby. He was a pupil of Hindemith, both in composition and theory." I said, "I could study with him.". . . In February of 1938, I went, and I took lessons with Hanoch Jacoby in counterpoint according to Hin-demith.[20]

There are no complete records to reveal exactly how successful Hauser was in bringing students from Germany, although German-speaking students were clearly the predominant group at the Palestine Music Conservatory in the 1930s and early 1940s. Teachers from this period note that about half of all classes were taught in German.[21] Its administrators structured the Palestine Music Conservatory to serve the urbanized musical culture of the Central European community. There were few, if any, alterations in the design of the conseratory's curriculum that reflected the pioneering ideology of earlier immigrant groups, for example, programs based on kibbutz folk songs. Because of the background and training of the predominantly Central European teachers, the early offerings thoroughly resembled the course of study in a German conservatory. This program of study also eased the acculturation of students to the new musical culture, for many had initiated their studies prior to immigration and found music education in Palestine a continuation of former pedagogical approaches. The new music academies provided yet another adaptive mechanism by preparing students for entrance into careers in other musical organizations, such as the new orchestras.[22]

At virtually all structural levels the conservatories bore the earmarks of a German system of music education. The conservatory was an institution separate from the university, just as it had been in Europe, and was charged primarily with the instruction of performers. The preparation of music teachers also took place in a separate institution, the best known being the Music Teachers' Training College of Tel Aviv, which had been established according to German models by the music-education reformer, Leo Kestenberg.[23] At times, the Central European structure stood almost in opposition to the reality of a Middle Eastern environment, but this resulted in neither elimination nor modification of opposing elements. For example, the Austrian organist Max Lampel served on the faculty of the Palestine Music Conservatory and later of the institution that superseded it, the Rubin Academy of Music, from its inception until Lampel's retirement in the 1970s. Jewish religious services in Israel, however, eschew the organ, and only one large performing instrument in Israel is not housed in a Christian institution, that of the YMCA in West Jerusalem.[24] Organ instruction was, nonetheless, a part of German music academies and continued as a vestige thereof in the Rubin Academy.

Early musicological and ethnomusicological endeavors were also largely the purview of immigrants from Germany. Already in the 1930s, musicological activity took place in several of the new musical institutions. Although none of its administrators were trained in musicology, the World Centre for Jewish Music in Palestine hoped to support research and study of Jewish music, and many of its most fruitful contacts were with musicologists in Europe and the United States. The Hebrew University, heavily influenced since its founding in 1925 by German academic traditions and by the influx of German-trained faculty members, invited Robert Lachmann (1892-1939) to inaugurate a Phonogram Archive for Oriental Music in Jerusalem. For Lachmann the setting could not have been more ideal, for his research had comprised studies of both Arabic and Jewish musics. Lachmann, until emigration the editor of the *Zeitschrift für vergleichende Musikwissenschaft,* the first journal devoted specifically to ethnomusicology, served as head of the Phonogram Archive only four years until his death in 1939, but musicology had achieved a place within the framework of an Israeli academic institution.

Following in the footsteps of Lachmann was another German-educated musicologist and ethnomusicologist, Edith Gerson-Kiwi. During her fruitful career Gerson-Kiwi has initiated music history programs in several Israeli institutions of music education, most significantly the Rubin Academy and the Tel Aviv University, and her efforts to record the traditional music of successive waves of immigrants have been nothing short of heroic.[25] Gerson-Kiwi's teaching appointments at different institutions from the 1930s until the 1970s symbolize an intellectual bridge between German musicology at the beginning of the century and the diverse traditions now practiced in Israeli universities. Musicology in Israel has necessarily grown to reflect the diversity of new scholars and fields of study; its foundations, nevertheless, remain securely shored by the traditions brought by musicological forerunners in the German *aliyah.*[26]

The urbanization of Jewish culture ineluctably altered the traditional roles of religion in Central European Jewish life. The urban center attracted increasing numbers of Jews from the *Landgemeinden* ("rural communities"), thus bringing about the demise of that form of community in traditional society. Against these forces, however, many aspects of Jewish traditional life did survive, if somewhat marginally. Even in those cities where Jewish life was relatively emancipated, there also stood an orthodox synagogue, despite the large number of community members attending the liberal synagogue. Such was the case in Mannheim, for example, where the Klaus Synagogue adhered to the more conservative tenets of orthodox Judaism, although most members of the Jewish community attended the *Hauptsynagoge,* the main synagogue.

An abandonment of some traditional music paralleled the abandonment of a traditional social structure. New forms of religious music and new genres of music unique to the community sprang up in place of the traditional forms, and these played a concomitantly important role in the determination of a community's cultural and religious identity. Just as the

religious life of an urban community often found expression in two synagogues, or several synagogues reflecting basically two religious philosophies,
two types of Jewish music emerged during the age of emancipation. The
first may be called liberal, the second, conservative. The liberal tradition,
largely a product of the urbanizing community, comprised a variety of
genres whose religious functions were often symbolic. The traditional music
of more conservative communities contrasted in its response to urbanization,
both before and after immigration. Traditional religious music, despite the
relatively small segment of the community practicing it, did survive during
the age of emancipation and continues to demonstrate tenacious survival
in Israel. Survival, however, has resulted primarily from preservation by the
older generation of immigrants.

Ironically, the traditional music of Jewish communities bore the impact
of the urbanization of another era. During the many centuries of repression
prior to the seventeenth century, Jews in Central Europe had always relied
on relatively closed communities for survival. This need for survival also
enclosed the repertories of Jewish traditional music, shielding it from many
outside influences. Certain aspects of internal change were allowed, but
change stemming from contact with other musics was often criticized.
Jewish communities in Central Europe during these centuries bore traditions
that were not dramatically dissimilar from the traditions of other Ashkenazic
Jewish communities in Europe.

In the sixteenth and seventeenth centuries the traditional culture of
Jews in Germany slowly began to undergo changes originating from contact
outside the community. Traditional music, for the first time, clearly evidenced traits distinguishing it from the music of other European Jewish
groups. One reason for this distinctiveness was the appearance of non-Jewish
tunes in the traditional repertory. The genre most influenced by non-Jewish
tunes was the *piyut,* a genre of religious poetry, usually with definite meter
and sometimes with rhyme, that was occasionally inserted into the fixed
liturgy. Because the *piyutim* texts were metric, melodies suitable to match
them were necessary, and cantors turned to one of the most obvious repertories of metric tunes, German folk songs.[27] By the end of the seventeenth
century, the religious music of German Jews formed a corpus that could
be distinguished from other Jewish groups because of the material absorbed
from the surrounding non-Jewish environment. At this point, however, the
process slowed and ossified; it did not again begin the process of absorption
once the era of emancipation was underway. Instead, while reflecting certain
aspects of the German cultural environment, the traditional religious repertory became increasingly isolated within it.

Just as consolidation broadly characterized many acculturative responses of the Central European immigrants, so too was it a dominant process in their religious life. For the smaller groups of more religious immigrants, however, fairly extreme preservation was often more likely than consolidation because preservation served explicitly to stem change. Members of an orthodox synagogue sometimes reestablished their community and chose to pray together in the same synagogue, not turning outside their religious community for members. This was true of the synagogue, *Binyon Zion*, in Rehavia. Those praying at *Binyon Zion* came primarily from the Klaus Synagogue in Mannheim, or they emigrated from the immediate environs of Mannheim. Hence, the traditions of *Binyon Zion* exhibit a stability of preservation. They are, nevertheless, largely preserved by an older community, for the average age of the community's members is probably well over fifty. Such communities are not common among the Central European immigrants of Israel. Not only did they constitute a minority in Germany, but they form an even more pronounced minority in Israel. In an urbanized society such communities remain unurbanized; during years of rapid change their traditions remain relatively unchanged. There remains little doubt that the traditions—as they persist today—represent the survival of a religious music unique to orthodox communities in pre-Holocaust Germany. As such, they are one of the few examples of marginal survival in the musical culture of the Central European community.

The identifying traits of German-Jewish religious music exist in virtually every genre of the tradition surviving in Israel. Many identifiably German elements have not disappeared. *Tzur mi-shelo* (fig. 23) comes from a repertory known as *zemirot*, songs generally used in the home on Sabbath before and after meals. This version was recorded in the small city of Shaveh Zion in northern Israel and clearly bears traits characteristic of German folk song. The melody itself is triadic and modally major, which is not true of the song in other European traditions.[28] Phrasing is very balanced with three four-bar phrases in both refrain and verse. Melodic sequence and textual repetition lend further symmetry to the phrases. March-like rhythm, present in the last two lines of both refrain and verse, is frequently evident in German-Jewish religious songs borrowed from non-Jewish sources. Harmonic implications also appear at strategic points throughout the song; for example, the final cadences of both refrain and verse are clearly built on dominant seventh to tonic cadences.

The same *zemirah* from a different ethnic repertory clarifies even more the influence of German folk music on the Shaveh Zion *Tzur mi-shelo*.[29]

Tzur mi-shelo

Fig. 23. "Tzur mi-shelo," as sung by Hillel Baum, recorded in Shaveh-Zion, Israel, 16 March 1980 (Phonothèque Y-3402). Source: Phonothèque, the Jewish National and University Library, Jerusalem. Transcribed by Philip V. Bohlman.

Text in Hebrew

Refrain

צור משלו אכלנו ברכו אמוני,
שבענו והותרנו כדבר יי:

First Verse

הזן את עולמו, רוענו אבינו,
אכלנו את לחמו, ויינו שתינו,
על כן נודה לשמו, ונהללו בפינו,
אמרנו וענינו, אין קדוש כיי.

English Translation

Refrain

    Bless the Lord, of whose countenance we eat,
    We have eaten and still left some food, as God has said.

First Verse

    The one who feeds his world is our shepherd and Father,
    His was the bread that we ate and the wine that we drank,
    Therefore, we shall give thanks to his name and praise him with our voices,
    Repeating: There is no one as holy as the Lord!

Drawn from probable Polish origin and bearing the clear imprint of Eastern European folk music, the version in figure 24 is in natural minor, with evidence of Phrygian modality at the second cadence of the refrain. The melody moves in a much more stepwise fashion than the Israeli version, and, whereas sequences of a sort are present, they bear melodic, rather than harmonic, implications. Both versions are relatively syllabic, but the rhythmic structure of the Eastern European version does not move with the march-like regularity of the German as a consequence of the former's more complicated rhythmic structure. These various characteristics cause Eric Werner to claim that the example is influenced by western Slavic folk song.[30] Whatever the exact influence on their melodic structures, the two versions are obviously taken from repertories that have long ago followed different paths of change.

Other religious repertories have witnessed change because of indirect response to the reurbanization that occurred in Israel. In such repertories, there has been consolidation of elements from ethnic music encountered only after immigration. Religious folk songs, perhaps more than other genres of religious music, usually bear evidence of multifarious non-Jewish influences. In a very different way, the reurbanization of musical life in Israel influenced the attitudes of Central European composers toward religious music. In the half century prior to immigration the composers active within the Jewish community set more and more Hebrew religious texts to music. In Israel this tradition acquired new impetus, and compositions with Hebrew texts and traditional religious melodies multiplied in number. Although this approach often relied on compositional craftsmanship secured in German music academies, its end result is clearly an example of the conflation of different musical styles in the immigrant culture. The immigrant composers began to lend new meaning to religious music within the Central European musical culture, in essence by classicizing it. The roots of this new expression lay only indirectly in the traditional music of the centuries preceding emancipation. Instead, the true path of inspiration derived from a redefinition of the German-Jewish community, before and after immigration.

In many ways the kibbutz stands in direct conflict with the reurbanization of Israel's musical culture. Musical activity on the kibbutz is today very different from that of urbanized segments of society, but it has felt the impact of urbanization nevertheless. In certain ways the kibbutz has felt this impact to an even greater extent than the institutions of the city, for on the kibbutz musical organizations have changed dramatically as a

Tzur mi-shelo

Fig. 24. "Tzur mi-shelo." Source: Eric Werner, *A Voice Still Heard . . . The Sacred Songs of the Ashkenazic Jews* (University Park: Pennsylvania State University Press, 1976), pp. 277-78. Reprinted with permission.

direct result of reurbanization, which has effected an overall impoverishment of musical activity since the early decades of the kibbutz's history.

Although Central European immigrants of the 1930s chose to settle in the cities more intensively than any previous immigrant group, there were those who settled in rural areas and on the kibbutzim. For many musicians without immigration certificates the kibbutz served as a means of entry into Palestine. Lacking large-scale musical organizations that could guarantee employment for musicians, many turned to the kibbutz as a recognized source of employment that did not demand special training or skills. Anyone willing to work on a kibbutz also increased significantly his or her chances of receiving an immigration certificate. Josef Tal, for example, entered Palestine in 1933 as a photographer — according to his papers — on Kibbutz Gesher, although soon thereafter he left to resume his musical career in the city.[31]

Of those Central European immigrants who first worked on kibbutzim, there were many who decided to remain there and settle. Some settled in ethnically mixed kibbutzim, others in kibbutzim largely inhabited by German-speaking immigrants. Many German immigrants discovered the kibbutz quite by chance. Unlike many potential emigrants in Eastern Europe, relatively few Central European Jews undertook training programs for kibbutzim prior to their exit.[32] Many of those who did turn to the kibbutz as an alternative means of support after encountering frustration elsewhere later found that the lifestyle there was quite to their liking.

One musical organization whose members discovered kibbutz life in this serendipitous fashion was the "Ha-Nigun" Chorus. "Ha-Nigun" formed in 1933 and comprised a membership largely of Jewish singers who had been forced from their positions in Germany by the Nazis. Based in Paris, the chorus performed throughout Europe during the 1933-34 season and enjoyed considerable success. In 1934, the manager arranged a tour for the chorus in Palestine. Upon reaching Palestine, the chorus discovered that no word of its tour had reached the country, and a schedule of concerts had yet to be arranged. With no immediate means of support at their disposal, the choristers of "Ha-Nigun" decided it would be wise to work for a while on various kibbutzim. They would stay there until the manager could arrange concerts, at which time they would again gather together as a chorus. While waiting for the promised tour to reify, many of the singers became attached to their kibbutzim and decided to remain as full members. This decision was fortuitous for all because a series of concerts for "Ha-Nigun" never materialized.[33]

When an immigrant musician began to labor on a kibbutz, his involvement in musical activities did not necessarily cease, but the nature of his professional status as a musician generally underwent considerable alteration. Musical undertakings on the kibbutz itself — lessons, concerts, composition — were considered as part of service to the kibbutz. Musical activity in an urban setting away from the kibbutz, however, was regarded in quite a different way. The musician usually channeled any money received for performances in the city, for example a guest appearance with an orchestra or on the radio, directly to the kibbutz. The kibbutz, moreover, did not evaluate such performances as part of normal labors, but as activity outside the kibbutz.

The value of a kibbutz musician was measured foremost by her contributions to the cultural life of her own kibbutz, that is to say, to her own relatively closed society. Only secondarily were her contributions to the cultural life of Israel in general regarded as valuable. A kibbutz composer, therefore, was not necessarily judged successful by his own community if he achieved national or even international fame from his creative achievements. His work also had to serve the many musical needs of the kibbutz, such as its festivals or programs of music education. Then as now, in this sense the kibbutz enforced a sharp dichotomy between itself and the cultural life of urbanized society.

Although Central Europeans constituted a minority in the kibbutzim, many of their musical activities stand as significant contributions, especially when evaluated in relation to musical life. The Central European composers from the kibbutz all fall within a certain age group (ca. 55-75). Most made their major contributions during the three decades from 1940 to 1970.[34] Among the best-known composers from this background are Yehudah Oren, Yehudah Engel, Haim Arvel, Yitzhak Dror, Theodor Holdheim, Shlomo Yaffe, and Yehudah Sharret.[35] Such composers left a cultural setting in Europe not significantly different from that of other composer-immigrants. Their musical background, however, contrasts quite dramatically with their urban counterparts. By and large the kibbutz composer of German background received his compositional training in Israel and within the educational context encouraged by the kibbutz. Many studied privately with other Israeli composers; others received a more formal education, albeit one supported financially by the kibbutz.[36] Inevitably, this has produced a different attitude toward music in general and composing in specific. Not only does the kibbutz require that the kibbutz composer serve a somewhat different, nonurban audience, but her musical studies have prepared her specifically to serve that audience.

Most kibbutzim, especially during their early years, had only limited and primitive concert facilities. A few, however, constructed large auditoriums and sponsored quite complete concert series that drew from the urban areas of the country. Most active of this type of kibbutz has been Kibbutz Ein Gev, not insignificantly so because of its Central European heritage. Soon after the establishment of the Palestine Orchestra kibbutz members from Ein Gev invited their former acquaintances from Germany to vacation at the kibbutz. Many accepted, and during their sojourn at Ein Gev orchestra members performed chamber music in the evenings together with kibbutz members. Within a few years the vacation period began to occur annually during the Passover season, and evening concerts became a regular feature, sometimes with invitations sent to other kibbutzim in the Galilee area. From this beginning emerged the Ein Gev Festival, an annual series of concerts by the Israel Philharmonic Orchestra during Passover. Now highly organized and drawing visitors from the entire country, the Ein Gev Festival takes place in the 2,500-seat auditorium at the kibbutz.[37]

For the vast majority of kibbutzim that did not adapt to the urban institutions of musical life in Israel, widespread musical activity has generally declined during the past few decades. In his studies of kibbutz musical life Natan Shahar has documented this decline, placing it in four distinct periods: (1) 1921-36; (2) 1936-48; (3) 1948-67; and (4) 1967-80. During the first two periods, musical life on the kibbutz exhibited great vitality. Most music was created by the members themselves, who formed their own musical groups and constituted the bulk of the audiences. The second period further reflected an increased performance of compositions by kibbutz composers.[38] During these initial historical periods, the composer's status shifted from one of amateur who composed in his spare time to one of semi-professional, whose musical activities, especially teaching, were part of her labors in the kibbutz.[39]

The musical activities of the kibbutz consistently diminished throughout the third and fourth periods. Performing groups on the kibbutzim disappeared and were only occasionally organized for special events. Kibbutz-wide attendance of concerts by visiting artists ceased, and such events became the domain of only a few individuals with formal musical training. Kibbutzim turned increasingly to the outside for musicians to perform at special events, and these commissioned or sponsored fewer and fewer new works by kibbutz composers.[40] Whereas the kibbutz acknowledged the composer as a professional with some esteem at the beginning of the third period, he began increasingly to perceive that his real audience lay outside the kibbutz, hence producing some ambivalence and conflict between kibbutz and composer regarding the latter's exact role.[41] Even the inter-kibbutz ensembles, such as the Kibbutz Chamber Orchestra, rallied less support within the kibbutzim and turned gradually to non-kibbutz audiences. The accumulated effect of this decrease in activity on kibbutz composers is not surprising: as a type of musical specialist, the kibbutz composer is disappearing. Writing in 1978, Natan Shaḥar found that already 61 percent of all kibbutz composers were over the age of 51.[42]

The impact of urbanization has been profound in the kibbutzim. In general, musical activity has passed from relative activity to obvious passivity. Effecting this dwindling musical activity was the kibbutz's inability—or even refusal on philosophical grounds—to adapt to the emerging urbanization of Israeli musical life. The increased specialization of urban institutions was never fully accepted by the kibbutz. A concert life with the consistent participation of a musically educated audience also did not endure. Hence, even outside performers have found it difficult to generate enthusiasm and support when visiting kibbutzim.[43] Virtually all kibbutz musical activity has become dependent on Israel's urban society, which reflects the degree to which urbanization—often propitiously, sometimes adversely—has affected the music of the entire nation.

The musical culture of Central European communities had achieved a remarkable degree of urbanization prior to immigration. Even more remarkable was the power of that urbanization to reassert itself and dominate the musical culture of Israel within only a few years after immigration. And it did so even while itself undergoing considerable change. Almost no area of Israeli musical life remained untouched by the force of urbanization riding the coattails of the German *aliyah*. Musical professionalism became immediately specialized as performing ensembles with very specific functions appeared. Many of these functions served or were served by the burgeoning mass media. Musical literacy became relatively widespread as an abundance of carefully conceived and well-staffed music academies appeared in the larger cities. Although many Central European immigrants had been trained according to rather specific German academic models, they perceived the wealth of other traditions confronting them in Israel and allowed for diversity, rather than uniformity, of style. Most important, the high degree of urbanization of the German-Jewish musical culture had institutionalized its own system of patronage and a dependable, financially sound concert life. The audiences that had supported the *Kulturbund* orchestras in Berlin and Frankfurt and Hebrew oratorios in Mannheim now became, in part, the audiences that supported the Palestine Orchestra and evenings of chamber music at the Tel Aviv Museum. Already by the late 1930s, the musical life accompanying the German *aliyah* was on firm footing. Unquestionably, this musical life remains one of the clearest symbols of an ethnic community's power to reurbanize its musical culture with extraordinary speed.

NOTES

1. An urban population of 75.9 percent made Israel the third most urban nation in the world by the 1960s, only a generation after statehood and two generations after the initial arrival of the German *aliyah;* see Isis Ragheb, "Patterns of Urban Growth in the Middle East," in *The City in Newly Developing Countries,* ed. Gerald Breese (Englewood Cliffs, N.J.: Prentice-Hall, 1969), p. 108.

2. The most concise description of the components of an urbanized musical culture is Bruno Nettl, "Introduction," in *Eight Urban Musical Cultures: Tradition and Change,* ed. Nettl (Urbana: University of Illinois Press, 1978), p. 6. Adelaida Reyes Schramm has contributed significantly to the theory and understanding of musical change in the city; see especially her "Ethnic Music, the Urban Area, and Ethnomusicology," *Sociologus* 29 (1979): 1-21, and "Explorations in Urban Ethnomusicology: Hard Lessons from the Spectacularly Ordinary," *Yearbook for Traditional Music* 14 (1982): 1-14.

3. Philip V. Bohlman, "Central European Jews in Israel: The Reurbanization of Musical Life in an Immigrant Culture," *Yearbook for Traditional Music* 16 (1984): 67-83.

4. Nettl, "Introduction," p. 9.

5. Elsa Thalheimer, *Five Years of the Palestine Orchestra* (Tel Aviv: Palestine Orchestra, 1942), pp. 10-11.

6. Ibid.

7. Most Israelis, when questioned about the ethnic makeup of the Palestine Orchestra, will report that it was almost completely German during its formative years.

8. Huberman's public rebuttal of Furtwängler's attempts to persuade him to resume concertizing in Germany was published in the *Manchester Guardian,* 13 September 1933, and is excerpted in Thalheimer, *Five Years of the Palestine Orchestra,* pp. 14-16.

9. See ibid., p. 18.

10. This ideological vision is most clearly outlined throughout this letter to Mayor Dizengoff of Tel Aviv, dated 27 January 1934 and postmarked the "Dead Sea"; the letter is reprinted in "Secretary of Bronislaw Huberman," ed., *Bronislaw Huberman Builds the Palestine Orchestra* (Letters of Bronislaw Huberman in the Central Music Library of Israel) (Tel Aviv: [Americans for a Music Library in Israel], 1966), p. 8.

11. Letter of 10 September 1935 from Bronislaw Huberman, postmark Abano presso Padova, to Michael Taube, Berlin, p. 1; in ibid., p. 16.

12. Interview with Shabtai Petrushka, 30 April 1981, Jerusalem. *Kulturbund* publications had a total circulation of 350,000; see Düwell, "Jewish Cultural Centers," p. 297.

13. See the letter from Bronislaw Huberman to Michael Taube, 10 September 1935, in "Secretary of Bronislaw Huberman," p. 1.

14. Thalheimer, *Five Years of the Palestine Orchestra,* p. 31.

15. Ibid., p. 26.

16. Letter of 30 September 1935 from Bronislaw Huberman, postmark Vienna, to Emil Hauser, Jerusalem; in "Secretary of Bronislaw Huberman," p. 17.

17. Interview with Uri Toeplitz, 29 April 1981, Tel Aviv.

18. Ibid.

19. Petrushka had retained his position as a producer and engineer at DGG into the Nazi period.

20. Interview with Shabtai Petrushka.

21. Interview with Edith Gerson-Kiwi, 10 December 1980, Jerusalem.

22. Both orchestra leaders and conservatory directors regarded the symbiotic relation between the organizations to be among their most important goals; see, for example, the letter of 8 September 1935 from Bronislaw Huberman, postmark Abano presso Padova, to Emil Hauser, Jerusalem, in "Secretary of Bronislaw Huberman," p. 16.

23. Kestenberg's achievements as a German music educator were considerable. In the 1920s he instituted important reforms in German music-education programs, still known as the "Kestenberg-Reform." While living in Prague during the early 1930s, Kestenberg founded the International Society for Music Education. See also his autobiography, *Bewegte Zeiten* (Wolfenbüttel: Moseler, 1961).

24. The YMCA is arguably also a Christian institution, but it serves largely Jewish residents of Jerusalem in almost all respects.

25. Her field recordings number almost 10,000.

26. Gerson-Kiwi has twice assessed the development of musicology in Israel; see her "Musicology in Israel," *Acta Musicologica* 30 (1958): 17-26, and her more recent article, co-authored with Amnon Shiloah, "Musicology in Israel, 1960-1980," *Acta Musicologica* 52/2 (1981): 200-216.

27. Eric Werner, *A Voice Still Heard . . . The Sacred Songs of the Ashkenazic Jews* (University Park: Pennsylvania State University Press, 1976), p. 89.

28. Ibid., pp. 277-78.

29. Ibid.

30. Ibid., p. 139.

31. Interview with Josef Tal, 20 November 1980, Jerusalem.

32. An exception, however, was the *Blau-Weiß,* whose members were often imbued with this spirit.

33. Interview with Johanan Ron, 11 May 1981, Ramat Ha-Sharon.

34. Natan Shahar, "Ha-malhin ba-kibbutz, makomo be-seder ha-hevrateh ba-kibbutz ve-yetzirato ha-musikalit" ("Musical Life and the Composer in the Kibbutz: Historical and Socio-Musical Aspects"), M.A. thesis, Bar-Ilan University, Ramat Gan, Israel, 1978, Chapters 3 and 4, pp. 49-87.

35. Ibid., pp. 246-51.

36. Ibid.

37. For a discussion of kibbutz festivals in general see Matityahu Shelem, "Kibbutz Festivals," *Encyclopaedia Judaica,* 2nd ed., vol. 10, columns 959-63.

38. Shahar, "Musical Life and the Composer, p. B.

39. Ibid., p. D.

40. Ibid., pp. B-C.

41. Ibid., pp. D-E.

42. Ibid., p. E.

43. When queried whether he had performed in recent years on kibbutzim as much as he had formerly, Uri Toeplitz responded: "No, I can't make them [kibbutz audiences] programs that attract me." Interview with Uri Toeplitz, 29 April 1981.

8

The Immigrant Musician

CHANGE ASSUMES many forms in the musical culture of an ethnic community. The broad processes that stimulated the reurbanization of Central European musical life in Israel might well seem sweeping in their impact. Furthermore, the speed with which they transformed some of the most basic musical activities might seem to reduce individual contributions to meaninglessness or irrelevance. Lest these urbanizing processes of change become too monolithic, lest they blind us to the particularity that is also a part of musical change, I shall turn in the next two chapters to the role played by the individual musician against the background of a changing musical life. Even the most pervasive processes of change are bereft of motivation and direction without the decisions and actions of these individuals. It is important for us to remember also that the individual musician is not as concerned with overall patterns of change as with situating given performances within the framework of his or her community, that is establishing a cultural link based on communal responses to personal creative expression. The musician serves as the essential link in the musical life of an ethnic community on many levels. If we are to understand the diverse forms of musical activity in an ethnic community, we must also recognize and examine the roots of variation and the decisions that spawn change. It is precisely these that constitute the realm of the individual musician.

The character of a cultural institution in the ethnic community often derives from the actions and personalities of its most active members. To a large degree any musical tradition is a conglomerate of individuals and survives in the immigrant culture only because they strive to maintain it. Many individuals also participate in numerous institutions and in a wide range of musical activities, creating by their involvement the interface at which different forms of musical expression interact and together form the structural undergirding for music in the ethnic community. Thus, the musical institution, whether small or large, private or public, serves as a vehicle for each individual's musical contributions to the larger community.

166 · "The Land Where Two Streams Flow"

An examination of individual musicians in the Central European community will therefore also shed light on the musical institutions with which he or she is associated. Similarly, it will illumine the degree to which the musical culture of an immigrant is as much a product of individualized, even idiosyncratic, activities as the result of external social, political, and economic forces.

Within any given tradition there are usually several musicians who stand out as unusual members of their ethnic community. Whether this exceptional quality has positive or negative ramifications depends on the various judgments that influence individual responses to the tradition itself. In the Central European community in Israel, Western art music, especially that of the German-speaking countries of Europe, has acquired greater prestige than many other repertories of music. In many other Israeli ethnic communities, one can witness a repudiation of this same music, with the works of German composers regarded as the antithesis of Jewish tradition. Individual musicians, nevertheless, are sometimes able to bridge the contrasting attitudes toward the Central European traditions of Western art music in Israel. They are able to introduce new types of music into the traditions that previously concentrated on Central European repertories, thus creating a context within which German music might be presented to those who previously considered it culturally unacceptable. Creativity of this sort often characterizes the roles of a few exceptional musicians. Such musicians come to play an especially significant role in a society dominated by cultural pluralism and constantly in flux because of the confrontation of different ethnic traditions. Such individuals are constantly engaged in a process of mediating differences.

The several musicians whose contributions to the Central European ethnic community form the basis of this chapter have left lasting impressions on the institutions with which they were associated. These immigrant musicians injected their traditional values into the institutions of their ethnic community in very different ways that reflect not only the different types of institutions but quite distinctive personalities. All of these musicians actively participated in a wide variety of other musical institutions as well, those within the ethnic community and those elsewhere in Israeli society. Though such individual musical activities seem at first glance remarkably stable, more thorough examination makes it apparent that each immigrant musician effected a remarkable degree of change throughout his or her career. As exceptional representatives of their ethnic community, these musicians and their musical activities stand as testaments to the lasting influences of the Central European community on the music of Israel.

Although chamber music occupies a special position in the musical life of virtually the entire Central European community in Israel, its sustenance depends on a few specialists, namely the performers and those who maintain the intricate fabric of performers and audiences, and open their homes to the frequent performance of chamber music in the setting often referred to as *Hausmusik.* Without these individuals the vitality of chamber music in the community could not have survived until the present. These individuals are responsible for determining the structure of each evening of *Hausmusik,* and they have become the primary conduit between the institution and Israeli society outside the Central European community. Accordingly, they are responsible not only for preserving the tradition, but for encouraging the participation in it of those from other ethnic groups, a participation that has proved necessary for its maintenance.

In the various urban areas with Central European communities or neighborhoods, several individuals are notable as the predominant forces behind the *Hausmusik* tradition. In Jerusalem's Rehavia neighborhood the tradition has asserted itself to become vital to the community in the home of Alice Sommer Herz. Born in Prague in 1903, Alice Sommer Herz was active as a chamber musician from her earliest years of piano study, especially within her own family, for her siblings were also musicians. Like most Jews in Prague, she was a member of the German-speaking minority, a situation naturally conducive to a complex pluralism and community strucure in which Central European chamber music traditions could flourish.

During World War II, Sommer Herz was incarcerated in the concentration camp at Theresienstadt (Terezín). Here, too, she played a material role in the musical life of the camp, which permitted cultural and artistic activities, if under very primitive conditions, in order to give the impression that the concentration camp was no more than a temporary ghetto occupied by Jews for the duration of the war. Of all the musical activities in Theresienstadt, chamber music and small solo recitals held special meaning for the internees because they took place in private chambers or could utilize the limited facilities afforded the musicians, for example a piano lacking legs. Even under such conditions Alice Sommer Herz performed approximately one hundred concerts. For the survivors of Theresienstadt musical activity had provided a sense of community in spite of the tragedy and deprivation that they encountered daily. Many would seek that same sense of community again when they settled elsewhere after the war.[1]

Surviving Theresienstadt with her son, Raphael, Sommer Herz immigrated in 1949 to Israel, where she settled quickly in Jerusalem and assumed a teaching position at the Rubin Academy. In Israel she was active in many different musical activities that demanded her talents as a pianist; not only did she have extensive teaching duties at the Rubin Academy, but she performed frequently as a soloist and chamber musician throughout the country. The artistic conditions in Israel during the early decades of statehood encouraged the intensification and spread of chamber music traditions. Audiences were still insufficient for the large-scale solo performance of music. It was necessary during these early years to take performances to the public wherever one might muster an audience. If this meant a kibbutz far from Jerusalem, then musicians needed to travel to the kibbutz and perform with whatever facilities were available. The most suitable genre for this sort of concert was chamber music, usually involving a pianist and a string player, sometimes even a full piano trio. During the early decades after her immigration to Israel, Sommer Herz traversed the length and breadth of Israel presenting concerts of chamber music. She performed with many other musicians, some of whom, like the Tel Aviv composer and violinist, Hanoch Jacoby, remain in close contact and perform chamber music at her home whenever they are in Jerusalem. Thus, Sommer Herz's predilection for chamber music received reinforcement from the many musical institutions in which she was active after immigration. Because these provided a musical environment similar to that she had known in Prague, her cultivation of a chamber music tradition in Israel grew continuously from its Central European roots, again finding nourishment in the ethnic community in Israel.

Teaching has always been the avenue through which Alice Sommer Herz most directly affected the musical attitudes of young Israeli musicians. Among the traditions she attempts to impress upon her students are those that *Hausmusik* and the Central European chamber music tradition most clearly symbolize. For example, she encourages students to perform within a chamber music setting at a very early age. Not only do such experiences serve to demonstrate to students the value of a communal environment in which musical ideas are shared mutually among many participants, but the students learn to understand that the music and ideas it represents transcend the unilateral focus that often attends solo performance on a large concert stage. Sommer Herz's teaching endeavors have also become one of the best conduits for the introduction of new blood into the *Hausmusik* tradition in the Reḥavia neighborhood. Perhaps 50 percent of the participants in neighborhood chamber activities are former students, which further accounts for the high percentage of young and middle-aged participants.

The tradition therefore avoids disintegration as the first-generation immigrants have aged and passed away.

The traditions of chamber music in Sommer Herz's home possess aspects of both preservation and change. The traditional aspects that she is most careful to maintain are those lending themselves to formation of the infrastructure. The repertory performed at concerts in her home, for example, is generally conservative and rarely includes twentieth-century music. When a performance of contemporary music does take place, the musician is usually a student or a guest, and the work is that of a contemporary Israeli composer. Thus Sommer Herz is careful to make apparent to all that her own musical taste clearly articulates a distinct value system and does not waver. Music from other traditions, albeit not eschewed, is always introduced by someone else. The strength of the underlying value system allows change by serving as a bulwark against disintegration.

Sommer Herz permits change to enter the chamber music traditions of the Central European community without serving as the agent for that change herself. This dialectic relation exists because, despite her own personal interest in a standard core repertory, she is not overly protective of the need for preservation. On the contrary, she encourages others to bring about change. Sommer Herz recognizes that her most valuable contribution to the tradition is to provide for its stability by preserving specific aspects of it. She is quick to recognize that others are better able to introduce elements of change, and she leaves this role open to them, indeed encouraging them to innovate. Preservation and change are processes that are constantly and concurrently ongoing, and rarely does one stultify the other in Reḥavia's concerts of chamber music.

Most important, Sommer Herz symbolizes the expressive role of music in the value system of the Central European community for young musicians and for others who attend the concerts she organizes in her home. Not only does she represent the tradition to its fullest, but her active participation is emblematic of the musician in modern European Jewish history and by extension the triumph against tremendous odds of an individual Jew. These various qualities transform the experience of chamber music in her home in very special ways. First, the community regards it as a positive cultural force and hence a living tradition. This prevents the growth of antiquarian trappings, or the view that the tradition is a curious vestige of another time and culture. Second, chamber music in the community becomes truly a group experience because all participants contribute their own special qualities; moreover, all contributions receive the same support and respect. Third, participants become aware of a phase of Jewish history with which they have only scant familiarity and negative associations. Many younger musicians are not aware of the complex role played by Jews in the musical culture of Central Europe prior to the Holocaust. Arousing their consciousness of this role increases their understanding of their own musical culture. That an individual such as Alice Sommer Herz can bring about such awareness bears witness to the creative force that she symbolizes in the Central European community, even while purveying her own traditional values.[2]

For some immigrant musicians, the community has served more as a means of sheltering musical activity than as a basis for allowing it to expand into other sectors of Israeli society. A retreat within more closed community musical activities occurred in the case of Felix Sulman and his amateur choral society, who first attempted to establish themselves outside the boundaries of the community, but were eventually forced to retrench within. The roots of the Sulman choral society stem from Germany, where Sulman and his wife were active members of the *Blau-Weiß* movement in Berlin. That movement had generated a folk-song tradition related to other German youth movements, but the *Blau-Weiß* had also assumed specifically Jewish and Zionist directions since the early decades of the twentieth century. An ardent Zionist, Sulman's musical education and orientation were completely tied to these German-Jewish traditions: "Wandering was our main connection with nature, was our main sport, with our Romantic background to be acquainted with the Jewish music as a means of communication and expression of our feelings and sensations."[3]

Trained as a researcher in veterinary medicine and pursuing a career in that field as professor at the Hebrew University, Sulman has organized various types of amateur choruses throughout much of his life. After immigration to Palestine in 1933 he organized a choir to perform religious works and served as its conductor. Both Sulman and his choir soon found that the choral music of the synagogue did not suit their musical interests, and they began to meet in order to sing German choral works. Sulman's efforts received additional impetus from the influx of new immigrant musicians from Germany, for he and his wife lived during the 1930s above the Palestine Conservatory of Music, which served as a constant source for new choristers. He recalled, "I was acquainted then with all the pupils arriving on student certificates from Germany. And we gathered them on the roof of the conservatoire which was then in the ha-Nevi'im Street [Prophets Street], a roof of fantastic dimensions, and we sat there. We turned

to our German songs, our German books, and later on musical instruments. . . . It was a Romantic time because, [where]as other people suffered
from the lack of anything interesting to do in the evening, we enjoyed the
curfew!"[4]

During the 1930s and 1940s Sulman's choral activities conformed generally to the traditions of *Hausmusik.* Friends gathered frequently in various
homes, usually his, and there they performed from the Central European
Jewish folk-song tradition and other German choral traditions. After the
foundation of the state, Sulman increased the activities of his choral group
by attempting to expand them beyond the boundaries of the Central European community even to include Christian institutions. In 1949, he founded
the Abu Ghosh Festival at the monastery of that name on the road between
Tel Aviv and Jerusalem. There he and his choir, joined by other musicians
from throughout the country, annually performed major works from the
Central European choral tradition. After several years, rabbinical authorities
voiced opposition to the singing of such works by a Jewish choir in a
monastery and succeeded in forcing the public performances of the choir
to take place elsewhere and eventually to cease after 1961. Sulman's own
account of the birth and eventual decline of his festival is a bittersweet
combination of hopefulness and resignation to reality:

> We got so much inspiration from going out to Jerusalem, to the Via
> Dolorosa. That was really our world then. The development went
> further when members of the group went together with us, touring
> in the country. Once we arrived . . . at Abu Ghosh. . . . When I sat at
> the organ they had and played some music, our friends immediately
> joined in, and we sang Mozart's *Ave verum corpus.* So immediately
> the monks and nuns of the place came in and joined in. They said,
> "You must come. That was a new sensation because we never had
> such a thing here and we would like to hear you often." Which we
> did then. So, we developed a certain program for the Abu Ghosh Festival,
> which we had in our hands for about . . . ten years. Then the rabbis
> interfered. People participating in it were ostracized. They had enough
> possibilities for ostracizing them. We did *The Creation* in the church,
> and the Bible was read out by the director of the radio [Karl Salomon].
> They could blackmail him, which they did, at the radio. They tried
> to blackmail me at the University, which they could not. The whole
> situation became very fragile. . . . There was a large echo of all this in
> the country because it was at the time when nobody ventured to sing
> secular music, which was a Christian art.[5]

Subsequent to the rabbinical attacks on the Abu Ghosh Festival the choir has functioned only within the boundaries of the ethnic community, re-hearsing every week or two in the home of a choir member and usually concentrating on reading works rather than polishing them for performance. Though forced to capitulate under the pressure from the larger society, Sulman still calls attention to the positive role his chorus has assumed in the Rehavia neighborhood in Jerusalem. He is, however, saddened that the ideal from which the Abu Ghosh Festival arose has yet to find widespread support in Israel: "The idea was that a Jewish choir would sing in an Arabic village Protestant music in a Catholic church. [This] would be the most concentrated point of ecumenical meeting."[6] Beyond the boundaries of the ethnic community such an ideal would find scant support in Israel even today.

Although it is a cultural institution of national proportions, *Kol Israel* ("Voice of Israel") is one of the most important musical institutions for the Central European community. The Israel Broadcasting Authority has been vital to the musical activities of the ethnic community, both historically at the time of the German *aliyah*, when the radio provided positions to immigrant musicians, and in contemporary Israeli society. Many within the community rely heavily on the radio for daily concerts and broadcasts of recordings, which Central Europeans generally do not collect in large numbers. The radio is also a source of employment for many musicians who have been involved in a variety of capacities at the network. The radio has both influenced and been influenced by change elsewhere in the musical culture. Change, moreover, often came to bear on the radio because of the activities of a few individuals who sought to achieve a central role for the medium in the cultural life of the country. The influence of few at *Kol Israel* was as far-reaching as that of Arieh Sachs (1908-80), a German immigrant who began his service with the radio on the day of its founding in 1936 and terminated that service only upon retirement almost forty years later.

It is significant that the radio network, first called the Palestine Broadcasting Service (PBS), was founded during that period when German immigration to Palestine was at its peak. Though the British government founded PBS and modeled it closely after the BBC, German immigrants soon managed it, playing an especially prominent role in the determination of programming policies. The first music director was Karl Salomon, who founded the orchestra of the PBS and sponsored many performances of new works by Israeli composers, as well as by Jewish composers in the Diaspora.[7] Of perhaps greater consequence, Salomon assembled a talented staff of young musicians for the broadcasting service from the scores of musicians then pouring into Palestine from Central Europe.

Arieh Sachs was in many ways typical of this assemblage of young immigrant musicians. He was somewhat atypical, however, because of his decision to direct his musical energies toward a single profession, albeit a profession that demanded a tremendous breadth of musical ability.[8] Like many Central European Israeli musicians, Sachs did not actually become a professional musician until after he immigrated. While still in Berlin, Sachs had obtained a law degree, yet his musical training and traditions had grown from German roots, and throughout his career he continued to draw upon those roots. He felt that these traditions were fundamentally in conflict with Israeli society, yet he hoped and strove during his tenure at the radio network to eliminate conflicts between the musical traditions of his former and new homes.

Sachs was among the first group of musicians to be hired when the PBS was established. He attracted the attention of the system's administrators largely because of his wide-ranging musical activities, especially his involvement with a small jazz ensemble that performed frequently in Tel Aviv and Haifa. Accordingly, the duties for which he was responsible during the early years at the PBS were diverse, requiring the skill of a pianist who could read quickly and perform in a variety of styles. Because radio performances were always live, Sachs had to accompany virtually anyone who performed there, whether cantor or popular singer, chamber ensemble or singer of *Lieder*. To the extent that he could concentrate on a particular style, however, Sachs became an advocate of baroque chamber music, for he had access to the only harpsichord in the country at the time. Even this instrument owed its existence in Palestine to Sachs, who had arranged for one of his German classmates, Wilhelm von Bläse, to bring the harpsichord with him when he moved to the country for a short time. The conditions at the radio were rather primitive, but the largely Central European staff was full of enthusiasm for the cultural tasks they were undertaking, the musical mission they had before them. The first studio of the PBS was in the Palace Building, which now houses offices of the Ministry of Industry and Tourism. A number of other buildings in the city also functioned for radio activities, such as the YMCA, in which chamber and orchestral concerts sometimes took place. One of the earliest challenges to the radio's survival was the War of Independence, when the studio was in the zone reserved for the Arab population. Largely through the foresight and ingenuity of Arieh Sachs, however, the PBS scores and recordings were spirited to the

Jewish zone and there housed by Sachs, thus rescuing them from certain destruction during the war.[9]

Sachs gradually ascended to positions of greater importance and influence at the PBS. In 1942 he assumed the positions of Programme Assistant and Producer. When the broadcasting service fell under the administrative purview of the new Israeli government in 1948, Sachs took the position of Senior Producer; this appointment was followed by another in 1953, to head of the instrumental-music department, the post he would hold until his retirement in 1973. Upon retirement he continued to accompany instrumentalists and singers, solo and ensemble. He turned, furthermore, to music criticism, a new career that would frequently bring him again to the concert hall. Even his music criticism demonstrated the breadth of the vision Sachs held for Israel's concert life, for he wrote reviews for the left-wing newspaper, *Al ha-Mishmar.*

There were many aspects of Sachs's life that benefited from sheer serendipity. Indeed, the very fact that he pursued a career in music after preparing more diligently for one in law bespeaks the intervention of chance. But the serendipitous events marking Sachs's musical career were not that unusual among the musicians of the Central European community, thus identifying yet another distinguishing characteristic of the community: many who had not been professional musicians in Germany embarked on musical careers after they settled in Israel. General education in Germany always included music as one of its components. One needed not plan a career in music to study it with considerable intensity throughout one's education. Music was, in fact, almost an indispensable part of humanistic *Bildung* for the Jewish community. Such musical training accounts substantially for the level of musicianship demonstrated by the trained amateurs who participated so intensively in the chamber music traditions of Central Europe and later of Israel. It was at this level that Arieh Sachs had prepared himself. The need for his diverse talents in Israel, however, would force him to transcend this level and to use his German musical *Bildung* to fulfill the demands of the professional music world.

Arieh Sachs was the driving force that championed several genres of music at *Kol Israel.* Most important of these was chamber music. Not only did he organize many of the ensembles that performed at *Kol Israel,* but he performed in many, indeed in most during the earliest days of the network. Sachs thereby played a significant role encouraging the broadcasts of chamber music reaching Israeli homes. Again, his Central European background influenced his choice of repertories. *Kol Israel* has always organized chamber music series in Jerusalem; historically—and yet today—these have taken place in the Jerusalem YMCA, from which the radio network simultaneously broadcasts them. This institution of public chamber music, which has done much to increase general interest in chamber music, owes a considerable debt to the special stewardship inspired by Sachs's Central European musical aesthetic.

Baroque music was another of the special areas in which Sachs was very active. Quite early in the development of music at the broadcasting service, Sachs argued for the stance that the music of earlier eras demanded a studied approach that incorporated authentic instruments, at least to the degree that this was possible in Israel. Radio programs should therefore serve as a means of musicologically educating the public. Sachs's interest in early music extended primarily to the early eighteenth century, especially to Johann Sebastian Bach and the Bach sons, and Israelis most often remember him for the performance standards he set for music from that century.

Sachs also furthered the cause of contemporary Israeli music. He was in charge of the radio department that organized and sponsored new music, and in that capacity premiered many works on the radio because of his accompanying and chamber music responsibilities. Sachs approached the contemporary music of Israel with the conviction that it had the power of symbolizing and advocating the musical development of the country. He stressed the greatest possible breadth in the programming of new music, encouraging a diversity of styles that he felt more accurately reflected the pluralistic nature of Israeli culture.

Both preservation and change are implicit in Arieh Sachs's conceptualization of possible roles for Western art music in Israel. Throughout his life he remained firmly committed to Central European traditions, and these were the traditions that his personal musical activities most often stressed. Still, he was aware of the need for the Israeli musical culture to develop an identity of its own, based perhaps on Central European traditions, but not solely dependent on them. He opposed governmental actions that aimed to limit and stultify a broad approach to the incipient musical culture. This opposition extended directly to musical censorship, and he worked to eliminate the proscriptions against Wagner and Strauss, as well as the avoidance of music that suggested strong connections with Germany. Throughout his career he remained a patient crusader for the performance of German music in Israel. His crusade took many forms, some successful, but many not. Not only did he ally himself with the pro-Wagner and Strauss forces, but he fought so that the German language would not be expunged from *Lieder.*

The proscription against Wagner and Strauss still remains in force today, but the general exclusion of German culture and music has slackened. In part, some of this change is due to the efforts of Arieh Sachs. His efforts may have been largely unseen, but their patient pursuit has yielded some successes. Perhaps the most notable were those that strengthened contact between Israeli and German musicians. His efforts to stimulate the exchange of musicians and ideas paved the way for many of the cultural exchanges that have now become commonplace. The struggle was, however, a slow and arduous one that was more often than not beset by detractors and critics.

Symbolic of the role that change played in Sachs's concept of musical life in Israel was his encouragement of young musicians. He viewed the radio as an important testing ground for young Israelis who wished to make careers as performing musicians both in Israel and abroad. Frequent broadcasts highlighted young musicians, and as the musicians grew older and gained maturity, they often recorded for the radio. Sachs also realized that young musicians needed to study and perform abroad if they were to gain the experience that a small country like Israel could not offer. This, too, served to keep cultural communication between Europe and Israel open and served to stimulate a broader awareness of musical ideas. Within Israel several of the younger musicians encouraged by Sachs have widened the musical awareness of the Israeli public. One of the most notable examples of such musicians has been Cilla Grossmeyer, a German-born singer who has brought about a resurgence of interest in German *Lieder* in Israel. Grossmeyer performs frequently on diverse Israeli stages, both for the general public and for more closed gatherings of Israelis in the Central European community. Thus, through Sachs's championing of a singer well-suited to sing in this previously suspect genre of music in Israel, German art song achieved an inroad, however tentative, into Israeli musical life.

Although some of the musicians during the first waves of immigration had managed to establish a few musical institutions in the early twentieth century, it was not until the 1930s that immigrants from Central Europe would bring sufficient organizational skills to ensure the more permanent implementation of a musical life supportive of the traditions of Western art music. Central European musicians were especially eager that the limited musical life in Palestine—limited, that is, in its fulfillment of the musical values and needs of the immigrants—be transformed to possess the same opportunities they had known in Europe.

As a single cultural institution *Kol Israel* effected the most widespread transformation of these limitations in the late 1930s. Not only did it extend the possibility of performance to established chamber ensembles, but it formed its own orchestra in 1938. For the performance of choral works the Palestine Broadcasting Service also maintained a chorus. All of these ensembles premiered new works, as well as a more classic repertory. The orchestra and chorus also served other organizations. The major concerts sponsored by the World Centre for Jewish Music in Palestine, for example, utilized the performing forces of the PBS. Although the membership of many ensembles at the PBS was constantly in flux, they were a source of employment for immigrant musicians, allowing many to survive the financial problems contingent with adjustment to the new country.

The initial British design for the radio system in the mid-1930s was that it should be a public enterprise whose financial health relied on license fees and the customs duties charged for every imported radio receiver; the Mandate authorities allowed no commercials. From its first days the authorities intended that the radio serve the entire spectrum of ethnic groups in the region, and it offered broadcasts in each of the three major languages, English, Hebrew, and Arabic. This policy of multilingual broadcast continues until the present, when broadcasts in French, Russian, Romanian, Ladino, and Yiddish regularly occur. Ironically, the only major exception to the policy was a failure at any time to broadcast in German, a policy stemming from the negative views many had of the language. The founders of the Palestine Broadcasting Service felt that it should somehow serve the diverse groups settling in the country. Exactly how this might be effected, however, presented the founders with a complex problem. Should all ethnic differences be addressed? Or should the PBS, contrariwise, strive for a single, unified cultural front as a symbol for the culture of an emerging nation? Which religious traditions should be addressed, and how? In part, the British answered these questions during the Mandate by stressing the need for the equality of all traditions.

For many of the Central Europeans active in the music departments of the radio this solution was not completely satisfactory. Arieh Sachs, particularly, was unwilling to sacrifice the special place that the early group of Central Europeans had won for Western art music. Although Sachs was sensitive to the different problems that immigrants from diverse backgrounds faced when coming to Israel, he believed that the radio must strive for a common cultural product, and that new immigrants should come to respect that cultural goal just as they came to adapt to the new nation.[10] Sachs and his colleagues in the music departments prevailed in their assertion that the musical content of one broadcasting band of *Kol Israel* not give itself over completely to unrestricted diversity. This band, now the first, might serve better by not compromising in its presentation of a single genre, Western art music. Its prototypes clearly lay in the musical culture of the Central European community, but its influence gradually became multi-ethnic in nature, achieving thus a different type of diversity, one more reflective of the nation's cultural pluralism.

Sachs was frequently a promulgator of radio's educational agenda. Uplifting and building the cultural activities of the listeners took precedence over entertainment. Sachs, moreover, was responsible for planning many of the network's educational programs, especially when these pertained to music. His planning of such programs often reflected his own interests, as well as those of the Central European community. These interests emerge, for example, in Sachs's description of several of the radio's concert series during the early 1950s, which he had designed to acquaint listeners and audiences with both chamber music and early music:

> "Kol Yisrael" also acquainted listeners all over the country with two new ventures in the field of chamber music initiated in the Capital by musicians and staff members of the broadcasting service's music section. The one, called "From Duo to Octet," presents Chamber Music of the classic, romantic and modern period[s] according to the numerical composition of the instruments employed, thereby stressing also the variety in combination between string-and-wind-instruments. The other series, called "Collegium Musicum," is primarily concerned with the cultivation of pre-classical music. The participation of organ and harpsichord, and the variety of combinations, solo or ensemble, vocal or instrumental, serve to remove every danger of monotony which many listeners fear when they hear about pre-classical music.[11]

Sachs believed that the educational programs of the radio would institutionalize the musical traditions that they espoused, for he recognized that the appropriate audiences already existed in Israel. He reported further about the programs described above: "The educational value of these broadcasts may well be seen in the fact that a number of rural settlements have commissioned for their holiday concerts special instrumental combinations and programmes of preclassical music."[12] In short, Sachs and others at *Kol Israel* were striving to reconstruct a musical life fashioned from the musical institutions of the Jewish community in Central Europe.

At the core of this conceptualization of musical life stood the need for a well-established concert schedule. *Kol Israel* was well aware that an active concert life was always vital to the Central European immigrants. The founders of the broadcasting service took it upon themselves to make the radio the foundation of concert life. Because of the dominance of Central European immigration at the time of the radio's establishment in the 1930s, the orchestra and other ensembles quickly attracted performers with a German musical background who strove to recreate a concert life like that in Central Europe. Karl Salomon had founded the first orchestra in Jerusalem at the Hebrew University, but this ensemble enjoyed only short-lived success because of the lack of proper indoor performing facilities.[13] Salomon, however, was a masterful organizer, and, with the failure of the Hebrew University orchestra behind him, he assembled the performing ensembles of the radio on firmer footing. After the foundation of *Kol Israel,* concert life in Israel, especially in Jerusalem, burgeoned and spread quickly.

One long-standing impediment to a growing concert life was the dearth of adequate performing facilities. At the time of the radio network's inception facilities were very limited, especially for larger ensembles. One of the earliest halls used by the radio orchestra was the Edison Cinema, a fairly large structure, nonetheless beset with other problems, such as a tin roof that produced percussive counterpoint to the orchestra during inclement weather. The broadcasting service experimented with several other halls, but settled on the concert hall of the YMCA, an edifice built with American financial support in 1932. This hall continues to serve the radio as the site of its weekly chamber concerts. Various other theaters also housed the ensembles of *Kol Israel,* in some cases helping to establish those halls for other purposes as well. After the Khan Theatre's conversion into a performing facility, the radio used it to stage chamber music concerts and a series of new-music concerts. Thus, in a very physical sense, the activities of the musical ensembles of *Kol Israel* were a major force in the institutionalization of Israeli musical life.[14]

Though essentially conservative in its concept and creation of a new Israeli concert life, the broadcasting service has always sought to encourage young Israeli composers. Each year, the orchestra sponsors several concerts of music by Israeli composers, and the radio itself frequently includes Israeli compositions in its programming. Again, such patronage at *Kol Israel* reveals persistent institutionalization. The radio provides a constant and permanent forum for the performance of new works and thus functions as a conduit between Israeli composers and Israeli society. *Kol Israel* is itself not strictly an institution of Central European culture; rather, it represents the transformation of many such institutions, however implicit within its complex structure, into a concerted Israeli musical institution. Any examination of the radio as a thread of cultural history in Israel must therefore also recognize the ways in which its components—its many constituent institutions—function. It is these components that bear the clearest imprints of the individuals who, in the 1930s, established the radio system and utilized their own experience—an experience growing primarily from Central European roots—to effect a new musical culture that would represent a pluralism of cultural experiences.

Throughout his career at *Kol Israel* Arieh Sachs sought rapprochement of the conflicts between the voices calling for a single Israeli cultural base and the pluralistic representation of ethnic differences. Although he worked always to bolster the emerging Israeli musical culture, he often turned in private to the Central European traditions that he knew could only partially integrate into the new national image. Because of his labors the many genres of music that were such a vital part of his own cultural background in Germany found their places among the most important offerings of the radio. Sachs's labors, like those of so many other immigrant musicians, formed a link between Central European and Israeli traditions. His lifelong goal was to establish the latter more firmly, yet he himself wandered not far from the former.

The course of musical change very often depends on the interaction of a few musicians whose participation is central to the survival of a community's musical traditions. Individual musicians may stabilize traditions, or they may introduce change. When particular values have accrued to traditions, individual participation usually avoids the conscious instigation of change. Some immigrant musicians, Felix Sulman for example, attempt to recreate the musical institutions of the pre-immigrant society, thereby protecting their own particular values and stemming change. Other immigrant musicians, Alice Sommer Herz for example, may believe that the tradition cannot survive for long without consciously introducing change. Conscious change may also be the creative goal of certain individuals who recognize the need for coupling stability and change, especially within the immigrant culture where unforeseen collisions between traditions are usually commonplace. The vital contribution of such musicians lies in their ability to maintain and control that facet of a musical tradition which they know best, whether it be a particular folk-song repertory or a type of chamber music. When immigrant musicians allow change to occur within this context, tradition usually stabilizes, if indeed with a new vigor stimulated now by change.

NOTES

1. The musical life of Theresienstadt is documented in Joža Karas, *Music in Terezín 1941-1945* (New York: Beaufort, 1985); for a discussion of the camp's chamber music activity and Sommer Herz's role therein, see Chapter 5, "Chamber Music and Recitals," pp. 37-62. One of the major proponents of *Hausmusik* in the Tel Aviv area, Edith Kraus-Bloedy, was also interned in Theresienstadt.

2. In the winter of 1985-86 Alice Sommer Herz moved to London, now the home of her son, Raphael.

3. Interview with Felix Sulman, 30 April 1981, Jerusalem.

4. Ibid.

5. Ibid.

6. Ibid.

7. Brod, *Die Musik Israels*, p. 46.

8. An extensive series of interviews with Arieh Sachs's wife, Esther, conducted during 1982 and 1983 form the basis for this discussion of the musician's life and work. The information contained in several unpublished and fragmentary memoirs written by Sachs shortly before his death and now in the possession of Esther Sachs is also fundamental to this discussion.

9. Arieh Mirken, "Der öffentliche Ehrungen Scheuende," unpublished manuscript in the possession of Esther Sachs, pp. 3-4.

10. Sachs addressed these concerns in an article he wrote shortly before his death, "Broadcasting in Israel — and before," typescript, 28 April 1978, publication details unknown, in the possession of Esther Sachs.

11. Arieh Sachs, "Israel's Musical Life in 5713," *The Jerusalem Post*, 9 September 1953, p. 8.

12. Ibid.

13. Arieh E. Sachs, "Konzertsäle in Israel," typescript, 26 December 1968, publication details unknown, p. 1.

14. Ibid.

9

The Immigrant Composer

THOUGH A written tradition heavily dependent on an urbanized culture, Western art music is no less susceptible than other musics to the changes resulting from culture contact in the immigrant environment. Audiences and their tastes are suddenly quite different; performance possibilities are both quantitatively and qualitatively different; patronage systems may not support musical life in an accustomed fashion; conflicts between disparate ethnic groups exacerbate ethnic differences marking style and public reception; tradition must confront these demands for change.

By extension, the composer is also subject to these pressures, and he or she must choose to respond to them according to the patterns of change present in the immigrant environment. The composer's response may range from deliberate preservation to rapid adaptation or assimilation. These responses may occur either rapidly or slowly, depending on the composer's ability or willingness to accept change. Art music, like folk and other types of traditional music, is not an isolated means of cultural expression; rather, it is a part of other institutions maintained by the immigrant group and becomes a factor in the change or preservation that these institutions permit.

Composers of art music may choose to cross the ethnic boundaries engendered by these institutions, but they must then seek out new institutions in the larger society if they wish to maintain their careers as composers. More common, however, is a gradual transformation of immigrant institutions — even those upon which written art-music traditions depend — thereby expanding the audience for the composer beyond his or her own ethnic community. In this sense, written traditions function no differently from oral traditions, although the degree to which individuals, namely the composers, can bring about change is significantly greater, as is the speed with which they truly stimulate the transformation of institutions, both in the ethnic community and in the larger society.

Many of the musicians coming to Palestine during the German *aliyah* were also composers, whether accomplished professionals, promising students, or enthusiastic amateurs. Many of these had contributed to the renascent musical activity that had begun in Central European Jewish communities in the early decades of the century. The reinstitution of an urban musical culture led to conditions under which this new tradition could endure. But the immigrant composer also had to adapt Western art music to a new cultural environment. In the course of adaptation, Western art music demonstrated a wide range of responses, not unlike those one would expect from other genres. In many ways, these responses are similar to folk and ethnic religious genres; in some ways, they differ from genre to genre. Taken together, these many responses illustrate that art music is no less bound to the impact of culture contact on musical change than are other areas of musical activity.

One of the most immediate acculturative responses of any immigrant composer is consolidation, which results because the composer absorbs new influences and expands his or her technical vocabulary and aesthetic palette. Certain social conditions may also encourage consolidation. In the rapidly developing cities of Palestine, for example, the influences that were potentially susceptible to consolidation were also more concentrated, more immediately available to the composer. The urban setting also intensified the range of ethnic influences bearing upon the immigrant composer, increasing the degree to which ethnic boundaries might be crossed simply by pulling those boundaries closer together. Thus, the changes accompanying consolidation formed in accordance with the very institutions that in turn gave such vitality to art music in Palestine.

The immigrant composer must confront many cultural constraints whose sources do not lie within the ethnic community. These constraints are often more direct and explicit than they are for traditional music, for example when the composer must mold new works in order to serve the host nation or a conglomerate of several ethnic groups. Stated otherwise, the immigrant composer must often grapple with expectations of nationalism to which he or she is expected to conform; indeed, many in positions of political and institutional power may well perceive failure to conform to aesthetic demands as failure to adapt to the new culture. The composer, as a professional, must carefully consider individual responses to these expectations, for overt unwillingness to respect them may also limit audience acceptance and financial support. Consolidation thus viewed may become a type of nationalization, the throwing off of one cultural cloak and the donning of another.

The institutions necessary for the support of Western art music undergo transformation in the immigrant environment in a variety of ways. Some rapidly conform to the new social structure, whereas others may reappear in essentially transplanted versions. Institutions specific to one ethnic community may, in due course, bring about other types of change, generated within the community, but influencing the whole of society. It is this pattern that characterized the contributions of Central European immigrant composers. A rather large group of composers arrived with the German *aliyah*, many more than in previous waves of immigration. But it was not a thirst for Western art music that greeted the composers. Rather, they faced a series of very pointed nationalistic demands to which immediate response was expected. Their responses varied according to individual aesthetic values, as well as the ways in which they perceived that the nationalistic demands could truly represent the new nation beyond the immediacy of the moment.

Just as Israel remained a composite of different ethnic groups, so too did individual compositional responses to the national culture emerge as parts in a larger composite response. The diverse components of that response point to the oversimplified model of an immigrant society that would have one try to identify "German-Israeli elements" in the music of the Central European ethnic community or "German-Israeli influences" in any other community. Though quite significant, the contributions of Central European composers were hardly as clear-cut as specific musical elements. Rather, their chief contribution was to intensify the receptivity of the larger society to the diversity that enriches any immigrant nation. The immigrant composers therefore encouraged a musical culture in which composers from many ethnic groups and subsequent generations could create new compositions and find diverse audiences. It was, perhaps, the most important quality of this contribution that it could tolerate and then foster diversity, instead of clinging to shaky notions of which music was or was not Israeli.

The necessity for attention to diverse styles and changing public tastes was nothing novel for Central European immigrant composers, because many had already confronted the need to consolidate musical activities in Germany. The processes of acculturative change appropriate in Israel were not so completely different from those long underway in Europe. The specific demands were distinct in the two settings, but the ability to consolidate within a pluralistic social and musical setting had long been a distinctive quality of the composer's mediation between Jewish and non-Jewish society. Most composers had long navigated both cultural streams of German-Jewish society. The ability to respond to a variety of aesthetic demands within the bounds of their own musical tradition would serve the immigrant composers well and ultimately empower their major contribution to the burgeoning Israeli musical culture. This capacity was a corollary of the firm grounding these immigrant composers had in the fundamental theory and practice of Western art music. In this sense, they differed somewhat from many of the immigrant composers from other European areas. Though compelled by pioneer zeal and inspired by the visions of Zionism, Eastern European immigrant musicians had often not endured the rigorous academic training that was common in the Central European community. This did not mean that the contribution of many Eastern Europeans to the immigrant culture was less, but it was more circumscribed by the boundaries of specific styles and approaches to the musical materials available in Palestine. Nor did many Eastern Europeans possess the breadth of experience with musical life outside the community that would allow for a broadening of particular approaches. The more specific boundaries of Eastern European compositional approaches further limited the transmission of new styles to others, particularly to younger generations through programs of academic music education. Many Central European composers, in contrast, situated the music academy within their concept of tradition, thus causing them to provide ways whereby the tradition would be conveyed to others.

From the 1930s until the early years of the state, the ability of the immigrant composers to consolidate became one of the most important means to gain acceptance. Many composers accepted consolidation as intrinsic to the Jewish musical experience, recognizing that historically Jews had succeeded in different cultural settings because of their ability to synthesize from diverse sources. Many Central European Jewish musicians had successfully incorporated this ability in their musical tradition. Writing in 1951, Max Brod describes the transformation of diverse and individual Jewish characteristics into a concerted whole as, perhaps, the only possible way of defining Jewish music: "One can first designate as Jewish music that which is created by the Jews. We would, nevertheless, like a tighter and more precise definition, so we would only call music Jewish when it exhibits a Jewish character. Or indeed many Jewish characteristics, a multitude. Thus, from this point on one will not maintain that there is a single type of Jewish music or that one ought to be able to recognize a single archetype behind a variety of appearances."[1]

Although Brod is speaking subjectively here, his "definition" does describe accurately the musical culture of many Central European communities in the renascent period prior to the Holocaust. In Mannheim, for example, the different musical organizations were constantly reorganizing and regrouping throughout the 1920s and 1930s. Instead of many different and mutually exclusive musical genres within the community, a more cohesive amalgam of new forms emerged, which can only be described as Jewish, albeit derived particularly from Jewish culture in Central Europe. It was exactly this pattern that many immigrant composers were able to institute in Palestine.

An aesthetic of art music in Palestine based on Central European traditions hardly enjoyed a positive reception in the beginning. Whereas those who represented the tradition realized the impossibility of a single "Jewish" or "Palestinian" voice, their pioneering predecessors were wont to call for exactly such a unified voice. Responding in a rebuttal to such calls in 1938, Erich-Walter Sternberg pointed out the inseparability of diversity from Jewish tradition and the composer's need to find a way of transcending that diversity in the search for a more unified approach: "Native of every quarter of the globe, product of the most diverse schools, he [the Jewish composer] has a public to deal with whose musical tastes and standards are of the most heterogeneous kind. Under these circumstances, so it seems to me, a composer has only one course to follow: to care nought for what is expected of him, be it Palestinian folklore, or synagogical music, or pieces in the Russian manner, but to go his own way, to speak his own tongue according to the dictates of his Music."[2]

To greater or lesser degrees, the Central Europeans observed the principles of their tradition. Some, like Paul Ben-Haim, preferred to compose in several different styles that they hoped would reflect the new culture. Such styles, however, must never abandon well-honed compositional techniques as their foundation. Other composers, for example Josef Tal, looked for diversified styles that more fully represented their own personalities and experiences, and in so doing they succeeded in extending the definitions of which musics constituted an Israeli approach. Accordingly, a wealth of styles had already emerged during the first generation. These had early on transcended the narrow expectations of the 1930s and had laid the groundwork for even greater diversity. The immigrant composers had produced a heterogeneous unity rather than the homogeneity that was earlier expected of them. Such a diversity might have proved a destructive force. Because of the strength of Central European musical traditions, however, and the concomitant continuity it permitted during the years of rapid cultural change, diversity became the foundation for Israeli composers of the first several generations.

When immigrants enter a new cultural environment, they encounter pressures, explicit or implicit, to conform to the culture of the new country. In all cases, these pressures touch most of the individuals and groups within the immigrant subsociety; in some cases, additional pressures are very specific and focus on particular groups or professions. Pressures of the second type often came to bear on the immigrant composers during the 1930s and 1940s. These pressures were due, in part, to considerable distrust of the cultural values that other ethnic groups felt intrinsic to the Central European community and, obversely, extrinsic to their own. These values, so some Eastern Europeans argued, too often originated outside Jewish society and thus needed to undergo complete transformation in order to embody an emerging Jewish nationalism.[3]

Critics enjoined immigrant composers to infuse new compositions with an immediate and explicit spirit of nationalism, although most enjoinders stopped short of clearly defining such a spirit. The composers responded to these ideological pressures in many ways.[4] In some cases, they effected the compromises necessary for the appeasement of critics. In other cases, there was no appeasement to be had. Definitions of an Israeli music usually identified what it was not, rather than what it was. For some composers, attempting to appease the cries for nationalism would have meant restructuring the very essence of their pre-immigration compositional style. Erich-Walter Sternberg, for example, composed a work entitled *The Twelve Tribes of Israel* for premiere by the Palestine Orchestra during its second season. Though Sternberg had unquestionably based the work on a theme from Jewish history, some critics deemed *The Twelve Tribes of Israel* musically unacceptable. These detractors claimed the work was not grounded in a Jewish national idiom, failing, however, to spell out that idiom. In the pages of *Musica Hebraica* Sternberg responded to his detractors: "The efforts made by Jews in their quest of a new internal and external basis have awakened general interest in the desire for some new form of Jewish culture. In the domain of music there is much divergence of opinion as regards the aesthetics of Jewish music in its new garb-to-be, and no lack of 'authorities' ready to define its precise future aspects, apparently oblivious to the fact that all our efforts are foredoomed to failure so long as there exists no possibility of a mutual musical approach on the part of composers and public — no common ground where both sides can meet."[5]

The confusion over the proper representation of a Jewish national idiom was complicated not only by the choice of what to represent, but also by how one achieves such a representation aesthetically and musically. Some concepts depended more on ethnic and historical background; others arose completely from social ideologies. Unquestionably, the confusion resulted in large part from the numerous historical and ethnic differences that had come to characterize Israel's pluralistic society.

The first composers to settle in Palestine were, like the members of the other waves of immigration in the early twentieth century, from Eastern Europe and imbued with the same pioneer spirit. The musical roots of the early composers were evident in their participation in Jewish nationalist activities in Russia, among which the St. Petersburg Society for Jewish Folk Music was the most influential musical organization. Understandably, the musical aesthetic of the pioneer composers derived from Eastern European musical genres, especially Yiddish folk song. When they settled in Palestine, they continued to pursue these interests as both collectors and composers. For them, the musical culture of Eastern European Jewry, isolated in so many ways from non-Jewish society, was the obvious surrogate for a Jewish national music in newly settled Palestine.

The composers from this generation turned most frequently to folk song for inspiration and source material. Their compositions often consisted of arrangements of folk songs for small ensemble or chorus, often those of the kibbutz. In this sense, they were limited not only by their musical sources, but also by the performing forces at their disposal. Among the composers of this generation were Joel Engel, David Schorr, Arieh Abileah, and Solomon Rosowsky. Their contributions were noteworthy because they stressed the preservation of Eastern European traditions from the early decades of the century and the kindling of a keener interest in and support of art-music traditions. The ideologically motivated music of this generation could not, however, survive the urbanization of the 1930s or the influx of new ideologies accompanying other ethnic communities.

In the late 1930s a new concept of Levantine Jewish music supplanted the predominance of the Eastern European pioneer aesthetic. The new concept attracted partisans with surprising speed, many of them Central European composers. Somewhat later, the loose group espousing the new concept took the name "Eastern Mediterranean School," primarily because its adherents aimed for a sound ideal they thought typical of that geographic region. There was consensus on only a few components of that ideal, but sharp disagreement concerning others. At its broadest, the new aesthetic encompassed elements of musical style from Greece, Turkey, and Arab areas of the Middle East, as well as the music of Oriental Jewish communities. More specific, however, was the focus on Sephardic and Yemenite musics, especially the latter, which symbolized for many the most ancient Jewish traditions.

The interest in Yemenite and Sephardic music seems to have arisen for two reasons. First, Yemenite religious music was believed to bear a stylistic resemblance to music in the Jewish synagogue before the destruction of the temples; the accentuation of Hebrew in this music served as further evidence of this cultural and historical proximity to ancient Israel. Second, the Yemenite singer Bracha Zephira commissioned new song literature based on Yemenite and Sephardic melodies from almost every major composer in the land. These composers, by extension, became spokesmen for the role of Yemenite and Sephardic music in a new Oriental-Jewish aesthetic of Israeli music.[6]

Composers from different ethnic groups began to utilize this approach, albeit in quite different and distinctive ways. Those from Central Europe, such as Paul Ben-Haim, relied on a Hindemithian concept of harmony, while employing coloristic devices borrowed from Impressionism. Composers with a closer affinity to Hungarian music, such as Oedoen Partos, interpreted Middle Eastern folk song in an approach derived from Bartók and Kodály. In the end, it was these diverse techniques of composition, rather than Eastern Mediterraneanism itself, that achieved a firmer footing during this period (ca. the late 1930s until the early 1950s). Indeed, the entire period comprised an evolution of function for these techniques, providing them with a new vocabulary and new modes of expression. By the early 1950s the compositional techniques of Western art music had acquired a firm position in the Middle Eastern cultural environment.[7]

Despite its rich possibilities, the Eastern Mediterranean movement never became more than the aesthetic gesture of immigrant composers, hence still wanting the total potency of an Israeli national school. Eastern Mediterraneanism had formed a bridge to a younger generation of composers who had been born in Israel and had more intuitively internalized the sounds presumably unique to that region. Many critics believed that this generation could somehow acquire the techniques of the immigrant generation, but mold from them an aesthetic uniquely Middle Eastern. As this generation began to mature artistically soon after Israeli independence, it symbolized an optimism for an almost utopian cross-fertilization between Western and Middle Eastern musics.[8] If Hindemith and Bartók had provided the underlying techniques for the previous generation, the Middle East and its musical traditions might theoretically yield new principles to the young Israelis; in the wildest throes of optimism some even believed that *maqām* could replace Western modes, and improvisational forms akin to *taqsīm* might supplant Western formal structures.

Despite the optimism of the 1950s and early 1960s, a synthesis of East and West has not occurred in the work of Israeli composers. Rather than turning to its immediate physical and cultural environment, the younger generation again turned outward to international styles of composition. Though not completely neglected, music from the Eastern Mediterranean region is not a dominant influence upon Israeli composers; some aspects of the Middle Eastern musical environment, most notably Arabic music, which is heard almost daily in some form by Israelis, play almost no role whatsoever in the most recent compositions by Israeli composers. The genres in which Middle Eastern music was most influential were actually popular or light musics, where it is still used at times to create a special, Israeli sound. Thorough examination of Israeli composers since the 1930s reveals that the national style so polemically argued by many has failed to develop. Instead, Israeli composers continue to write in a number of styles, and their works continue to reflect the international character of the immigrant society that still prevails.

Even though diversity has dominated the trends of Israeli composition, there are certain attitudes toward musical sound that most composers share. These attitudes entered Israeli music at a critical point during the 1930s and have since become the basis for numerous stylistic developments. Most important, by their very nature these attitudes lend the compositions that reflect them a particularly Israeli stamp. The first of these attitudes derives from biblical cantillation; the second from the modern Hebrew language. Cantillation, though found in different musical and linguistic dialects, had been a common element for Jews throughout the Diaspora for two thousand years. In the search for an identifiably Jewish musical sound among the immigrant groups in Israel, cantillation became an obvious early source of inspiration. It further provided a means of linking classical Hebrew with particular melodies, many of which then became familiar to different audiences. Cantillation fostered the consolidation of compositional techniques by providing a focus around which they could converge. Even those composers unwilling to capitulate to the demands for folkloric compositions, such as Josef Tal, used biblical themes and thus succeeded in finding new directions for their music while staving off criticism. The increased exploration of cantillation as a source for Israeli composers even led Max Brod to suggest that the modern music of Israel had become a vehicle for a wider interest in cantillation itself and its many styles.[9]

The other source unifying the work of most Israeli composers is the use of modern Hebrew. This source is, of course, not unrelated to the increased interest in cantillation and its interrelation of text and melody. Modern Hebrew's association with the modern state of Israel, however, is significantly more intense. The musical setting of modern Hebrew demanded from the composer a new realization of the language's accents and inherent melodic characteristics. Many immigrant composers found that their musical style began to change most dramatically at the point of discovering they had mastered modern Hebrew. Thus, the daily encounter with Hebrew in their sound environment in turn altered their perception of and response to that environment. The emergence of modern Hebrew as the language of modern Israeli composition symbolizes the transition of its many styles from the amalgamation of the immigrant generation to the consolidation of a new ethnic community.[10]

Although they faced conditions of great physical difficulty, the Central European immigrant composers arrived at a moment when the institutions most supportive of their art were first forming. In effect, this meant that most could depend on not one, but several of these institutions for support. This situation was especially favorable to the immigrant composers, many of whom were also accomplished performers and teachers. They could teach harmony and composition classes at a music academy in the morning, rehearse with performance ensembles at the radio network in the afternoon, and perform jazz or popular music at one of the numerous cafes or hotels featuring such music in the evening. A combination of salaries from all of these endeavors was rarely enough to support more than a meager existence, especially in the 1930s, but it did prevent the composers from having to turn away from music to find employment. Moreover, such extensive involvement in diverse areas of the musical culture of Palestine increased the composers' adaptability to that culture, while concurrently increasing their sensitivity to its diversity.

Several musical institutions were well suited to the activities of the immigrant composer. The Palestine Broadcasting Service, for example, afforded immediate opportunities for the performance of new compositions. New music was encouraged by the director of music at the broadcasting service, Karl Salomon, himself a German immigrant composer. Even though the bulk of the radio audience may have had fairly conservative musical tastes, the radio nurtured and broadcasted a considerable amount of new music from its inception. The willingness of most immigrant composers to teach also served the cause of new music in Palestine, for younger musicians had the opportunity to learn and experiment with new compositional techniques, thereby expanding the audience for new music in the process. For some young students, their lessons with immigrant composers were their first real contact with new music.[11] The generation of immigrant composers from Central Europe had, in this way, considerable power to cultivate and influence an audience interested in new music.

The composers immigrating during the German *aliyah* largely ranged in age from twenty to thirty. Most had left Germany soon after or during their studies and before they had developed mature styles. They did not have immutable expectations of the difficulties they would have to surmount. Many showed a particular willingness to experiment with different compositional styles, responding as they could to availability of performers. Those composers who were somewhat older had either to alter their styles quite dramatically, as Paul Ben-Haim was successfully able to do, or to retain their compositional approaches in the face of criticism, as Erich-Walter Sternberg preferred to do. Still, viewed as a group, the immigrant composers were fortunate to be at a stage in their careers at which their personal compositional styles were still forming.

Just as the wealthier immigrants of the German *aliyah* formed new residential districts along the peripheries of the larger cities, the young musicians could establish themselves in social settings not unlike those in which the musicians in Germany's urban centers had lived. In Jerusalem one such area surrounded Zion Square, whose restaurants not only provided employment because of their need for musicians, but also were attractive because of the artistic and intellectual milieu they engendered.[12] Many young composers came to depend on these social settings for their main source of income, and unusual was the immigrant musician who did not support himself or herself by playing in jazz or dance bands in these urban districts at least during the 1930s and 1940s. Indeed, the boundaries of such districts symbolized in yet another way the cultural boundaries of the ethnic community itself.

Like the rest of the German *aliyah*, the young composers gravitated to urban areas and did not settle in large numbers in rural settlements. Prior to immigration, the system of patronage on which they depended was urban in nature; it was only natural, therefore, that they should seek the support of similar patterns of patronage after immigration. In the urban environment of Palestine there was little sense of the pioneer spirit of Jewish nationalism prevalent on the kibbutzim prior to the influx of Central Europeans. The immigrant composers thus viewed the musical activities spawned by Eastern European nationalism from afar—arranging folk songs, for example—but rarely participating in them. Instead, they chose an alternative route, responding relatively quickly to the demands for a national music within the patronage system more immediately at their disposal.

Adaptation to the new musical institutions in Palestine was also a factor of individual motivation and acceptance of the exigencies of change. Although he immigrated at the age of fifty-five, Max Brod came to symbolize the ability to adapt to the new culture for the younger generation of musicians. He learned Hebrew quickly and became a director and writer for the theater company, Habimah. He immediately redirected his Central European cultural aesthetic to make important contributions to the country's musical life. For example, Brod wrote the libretto for the first opera composed in Israel, Marc Lavry's *Dan ha-Shomer* ("Dan, the Watchman") (1945). His *Die Musik Israels,* written in 1951, was the first comprehensive survey of Israeli music and remains the classic work on the subject. Alexander Ringer has described Brod's importance to the younger generation as a source of "ideological tutelage."[13]

There were other immigrant musicians and composers who chose not to respond to the pressures and demands for change. Stefan Wolpe, who had emigrated from Berlin in 1933, exemplified this pattern of acculturative response. Wolpe's compositions were the most avant-garde of the young composers, and he quickly gathered about him a group of students. To these students he taught the most advanced styles of the day, encouraging them, for example, to explore the many possibilities of the twelve-tone technique and to find personal directions of their own. Wolpe also taught at the Jerusalem Conservatoire, and he participated actively in the World Centre for Jewish Music in Palestine; but his unwillingness to compromise his compositional approaches succeeded in winning him only small audiences. Ironically, many of the fine students he had attracted either left Israel with him in 1939 or at a later date. Several of those students established themselves as important composers elsewhere: Wolf Rosenberg and Peter Jona Korn in West Germany, and Herbert Brün in the United States. Only Ḥaim Alexander, whose music bears little resemblance to that of Wolpe, remained to establish a compositional career in Israel. It is with Stefan Wolpe that one sees, perhaps, the stylistic limit that the musical environment of Palestine in the 1930s would or would not tolerate. A former student of Anton Webern, Wolpe was the only major composer who arrived in Palestine already heavily influenced by serialism. In Palestine he found only resistance to that tradition of Central European art music, and he left the country frustrated. The styles and techniques of the immigrant composers did encounter some limitations that were insurmountable.

If the immigrant composers from Central Europe differed on the basis of their diverse concepts of an appropriate aesthetic direction for new music, they shared a common grounding in and respect for the tradition of music theory and practice that spawned the craftsmanship inseparable from Central European approaches to composition. This compositional craftsmanship acted as a framework for the Central European aesthetic, distinguishing it from the sundry techniques utilized by the earlier generation of Eastern European composers. In the immigrant environment such a framework permitted not only the considerable reestablishment of the Central European tradition, but also a means of experimentation and searching out new directions. As an acculturative response this framework was essential to both preservation and change.[14]

The Central European framework contained two primary components. First, the immigrant composers were well versed in all aspects of tonal harmony. This meant not only classical harmony but the extended tonality and chromaticism of the late nineteenth and early twentieth century. Second, they composed in larger and more variegated forms. The inability to effect an expansion of form had been a severe limitation to the earlier composers, who concentrated instead on smaller forms, such as setting folk melodies in a variety of ways. In contrast, the Central Europeans were able to use a single folk melody as thematic material for an entire movement, or even an entire multi-movement composition. This manipulation of thematic material and larger forms also influenced contrapuntal styles, which by extension was another essential component of the Central European framework.

Within this framework and as a result of its undergirding craftsmanship, the Jewish folk melody or theme derived from biblical cantillation lent themselves to techniques not previously essayed in Palestine. The same theme might undergo development in the sonata movement of a symphonic work or in the subject of a contrapuntal work for keyboard. Some composers chose to use a more extended chromatic harmony, while others adapted a post-Impressionist style to the new materials. Composers who felt the Central European framework too limiting could extend it, or even de-emphasize the role it played.

The variation that thematic development permitted was essential to the Central European composer. Many chose, therefore, to turn rather quickly after immigration to the technique of theme and variations, thinking that through this approach those less accustomed to the complicated treatment of thematic material would understand how it might lead to the evolution of larger forms. Erich-Walter Sternberg used this formal concept in his early work for the Palestine Orchestra, *The Twelve Tribes of Israel*, only to be greeted by sharp criticism of its putatively non-nationalistic sound. In response, Sternberg chose to defend the use of theme and variations for its ability to capture a deeper sense of musical sources traditionally a part of Jewish culture and history. In his rebuttal to the critics, Sternberg explains his choice of theme and variations, and provides an eloquent apologia for the present and future role of the Central European compositional framework in the music of Israel:

> My music is . . . more concerned with an idea than a series of images; it appeals to the emotions rather than to the imagination. My aim was to underline some expression characteristic of its particular subject. Details did not interest me; nor was I out to show the idea of any particular stage or stages of its development. . . . The theme is the source from which all the tribes derive, the variations depend for their role on the extent in which they enhance the theme itself. By adopting this method of treatment I was able to infuse my work with a common pathos, to knit it together in a general atmosphere of tension; in fact no other form could provide so close a musical link between the various parts of a composition.[15]

The Twelve Tribes of Israel has since survived the criticism directed against it to become one of the monumental works of the 1930s. The formal treatment espoused by Sternberg and other composers of his generation was later employed by other composers and became one of the primary conduits through which the Central European framework came briefly to form a common practice. That this treatment of thematic material possessed the ability to extend unity to internal diversity would empower the Central European framework to function in many different compositional approaches well beyond the immigrant generation.

The Israeli composers of the immigrant generation fall into three broad groups, based in part on their employment of different techniques afforded by the Central European compositional framework and in part on their attitudes concerning music's role in Israeli society. Unquestionably, the three groups overlap. The Central European composers have responded to rapid cultural change in Israel in very distinctive ways. Some composers stand midway between two groups; others might even occupy more than one group at a given time. Still, the tripartite classification lends itself to the discussion of general trends among these composers. It further makes it possible to correlate these general trends with other patterns of change in the ethnic community.

The first group contains composers who adapted their compositional approaches to the broad stylistic shifts through which Israeli music passed. In some cases, the Central European composers simply followed these stylistic shifts; in others, they were among the main advocates of the movements that a particular shift stimulated. It is the second of these responses that was characteristic of Paul Ben-Ḥaim and which will serve as a backdrop for the following discussion of Ben-Ḥaim. The second group comprises composers whose reactions to the stylistic shifts were more conservative. Though not opposed to an increased attention to folk songs or themes derived from biblical cantillation, these composers were more reticent to abandon a compositional approach acquired during their pre-immigrant studies. These composers often found it necessary to compose on two different levels, one intended for public consumption and another truer to the Central European framework and reserved entirely for the community. Hanoch Jacoby clearly represents the ability to respond to quite different audiences in this fashion. The composers of the third group have written in diverse and cosmopolitan styles. Although these composers did not completely eschew the treatment of Israeli national themes, such treatment was never more than secondary to a concern for compositional developments abroad. In the broadest sense, the composers of this group, represented in the following pages by Josef Tal, recognized that unity could only exist if diversity were also subsumed as a part of the broad cultural streams flowing through the ethnic community.

Although his work has become known throughout the world, Paul Ben-Ḥaim was hardly a cosmopolitan; rather, Israeli musicians knew him as a quiet man, a composer controversial neither in his philosophy nor his approach to music. Ben-Ḥaim settled in Palestine at a time when the pressure to conceive and compose in a Jewish national style was just beginning to gain impetus. Already prior to immigration Ben-Ḥaim had attracted some attention in Germany, and he could lay claim to a decade-long public career stretching from the early 1920s.[16] A career already firmly established would suggest an unwillingness to conform to the expectations of those calling for a Jewish national style, but Ben-Ḥaim's life and work reveal little evidence that such an unwillingness ever materialized. He never participated in polemical battles over acceptable aesthetic and ideological limitations. On the contrary, even his first works in Palestine during the early 1930s manifested characteristics that would later draw him toward the Eastern Mediterranean movement.

Born in 1897, Paul Ben-Ḥaim received his musical education in Munich, there undertaking studies in violin, piano, and composition.[17] Ben-Ḥaim's earliest compositions generally evoke a post-Romantic style of extended chromaticism, at times quite reminiscent of Gustav Mahler. Soon after his student days, however, Ben-Ḥaim embarked along new aesthetic and philosophical paths. Encouraged by the composer Heinrich Schalit, Ben-Ḥaim began to explore Jewish themes and to employ these as the basis for new compositions. Primarily during these years, he explored different choral media, such as psalms and motets, and drew his texts from biblical sources, most notably from the books of Job and Isaiah, in addition to the Psalms.[18]

Many works from Ben-Ḥaim's Munich period, such as his oratorio, *Joram* (1933), bear a strong resemblance to new compositions performed in the Jewish community of Mannheim during the same period, especially those composed by Hugo Adler. Both composers turned to the choral and orchestral forces of the Jewish community and conceived large oratorios based on biblical texts. Although Adler's *Balak und Bilam* was the first major work performed under the aegis of the World Centre for Jewish Music in Palestine, the composer did not himself immigrate. Ben-Ḥaim did immigrate, providing one of the most visible links between the renascent musical culture of the Central European community and the musical life of Palestine. The inspiration that the Central European community provided for his early works simply found new avenues of expression in the immigrant environment, a further manifestation of the cultural continuity between the two communities. Ben-Ḥaim's earliest works in Palestine already show a programmatic penchant responsive to the character of the new land. Although he immigrated in 1933, he produced his best-known works from the first decade after immigration. In both the *String Quartet* (1937) and the *Piano Trio* (1939), for example, there is already clear evidence of his interest in a new sound aesthetic. This same interest is perceptible in the *First Symphony* (1939-40), composed for the Palestine Orchestra.[19]

By the mid-1940s, the interest in a sound characteristic of the region had fully manifested itself in a new style, Eastern Mediterraneanism. Although this style at first appears as a dramatic departure, a more gradual and consistent development is evident upon examination of its various aspects. On the surface there is attention to programmatic aspects; certain passages clearly evoke images of the Israeli landscape and the way of life, however overly idealized and idyllic, that is associated with that landscape. The frequent use of open harmonies and parallel treatment of fourths and fifths suggest a further bow to Impressionistic techniques. Still, the larger formal structure derives from the Central European framework, relying to a large degree on the harmonic approach of Paul Hindemith. Ben-Ḥaim clearly borrows from many sources — some of them seemingly contradictory — but from them he molds a unified whole that does not betray the underlying diversity, producing a technique Alexander Ringer has dubbed "eclectic conservatism."[20] The gradual and conservative response of Ben-Ḥaim to stylistic change is further demonstrated by his unwillingness to engage certain gestures to exaggerate the Oriental sound of a composition. His orchestrations, for example, do not employ Oriental instruments nor do they utilize microtones. Instead, Ben-Ḥaim substitutes Western instruments, such as the harpsichord for the *qānūn*.

His Eastern Mediterranean style was already fully stated in 1944 when he wrote the well-known keyboard work, *Five Pieces for Piano*, op. 34.[21] The "Orientalisms" that Ben-Ḥaim attempts to achieve are quite evident even to the listener without extensive knowledge of Middle Eastern music, which may explain why the pieces are popular with young pianists outside of Israel. The first movement, "Pastorale," suggests musical qualities of the Middle East both programmatically and technically. The melodic line, with its attention to rhythmic details and ornamentation, exemplifies many of the characteristics of the *nai*, an end-blown flute common throughout the Middle East and associated by Western listeners with a pastoral setting (see fig. 25). The work is tonal, but the melodic structure always bears evidence of its derivation from a modal concept, suggesting the improvisational unfolding of *taqsīm*. The openness of perfect fifths frequently underlies the harmony. The overall aim of the "Pastorale," then, is to employ aural means to create a visual image in programmatic fashion.

In other movements of the *Five Pieces for Piano* Ben-Ḥaim exploits different aspects of the Eastern Mediterranean technique. The abstract third movement, "Capriccio Agitato," contrasts with the "Pastorale" regarding the degree to which one can perceive programmatic intent. The "Capriccio Agitato" suggests a more general instrumental virtuosity, one that might remind the listener of certain qualities of the *qānūn*, yet never a slavish reproduction of *qānūn* techniques. Even the variety within the different movements of *Five Pieces for Piano* shows that Ben-Ḥaim's concept of Eastern Mediterraneanism was not one of a singular style, but of breadth, even musical pluralism. This concept depended not only on a masterful control of the compositional craftsmanship of the Central European framework, but also on a rich and fertile imagination.

Paul Ben-Ḥaim's influence upon younger Israeli musicians and composers has been significant. He symbolizes for many the first European

Fig. 25. Opening movement, "Pastorale," from *Five Pieces for Piano,* op. 34, p. 1, by Paul Ben-Ḥaim. Source: Paul Ben-Ḥaim, *Five Pieces for Piano,* op. 34 (Tel Aviv: Edition "Negen," 1948), p. 1. Reprinted with permission of Israeli Music Publications, Ltd.

immigrant composer who set forth in new directions to constitute a style uniquely Israeli. Even though he has his detractors, Ben-Haim's music is known outside of Israel better than that of any other Israeli composer. Ben-Haim's contribution may also be measured by his influence on other Israeli composers. Many composers, both of the immigrant generation and subsequent generations, have studied with Ben-Haim, most of them pursuing their own individual directions thereafter. Whereas Ben-Haim taught his students the value of craftsmanship, he encouraged them to employ that craftsmanship as a means of seeking new and diverse aesthetic directions. As one former student expressed this influence: "A teacher like Ben-Haim . . . didn't impose on you only technique, but [he was the type of person] who had a huge influence on your attitudes towards music and towards the way of life."[22]

Though a musician of diverse talents, Hanoch Jacoby considers composition his most important musical activity. Composition, however, demands in Jacoby's philosophy a concentrated approach that depends on consistency and uncompromising mastery of the technical skills inherent in the Central European framework. Because he found these requisites wanting in Israel, his work bears evidence of the push and pull of conflicting forces over which he, as a composer, never gained complete control. Jacoby's approach to composition has been essentially conservative and thus often at odds with the rapid change of Israeli society. Some of the works he regards as his best never receive performances, whereas those he considers relatively weak have achieved a large measure of popularity. His career has been that of an immigrant composer who never fully adapted the Central European framework to the Israeli musical culture.

Hanoch Jacoby was born in 1909 in Königsberg (now Kaliningrad in the Soviet Union), long a center of German and Jewish culture in East Prussia. He undertook musical studies in Berlin, there distinguishing himself as the only private composition student ever accepted by Paul Hindemith. This experience was so profound that Jacoby's conservative craftsmanship has consciously borne many earmarks of the Hindemithian tradition ever since. Jacoby's early career was frustrated when the Nazis made it impossible to perform in German musical ensembles, and in 1934, when he was invited by Emil Hauser to serve as the violist in the newly formed Hauser Quartet, Jacoby immigrated to Palestine.

The contact with Hauser was fortuitous for the young immigrant, for it included immediate association with the Palestine Conservatory of Music. Jacoby's teaching duties at the conservatory covered the entire gamut of the curriculum: violin, viola, chamber music, orchestra, harmony, and composition. In this position he was the first theory and composition teacher for many of the young musicians immigrating to the country. Jacoby served in various capacities as a teacher in Jerusalem music academies, even as the director of the Jerusalem Music Academy from 1954 until 1958. In 1958, he abandoned teaching completely to begin a new career as violist in the Israel Philharmonic Orchestra. Jacoby's was a career of quixotic pursuit, of searching for an orderliness in Israeli musical life that continually eluded him.

Jacoby's compositional aesthetic is exemplary of the role played by thematic development within the Central European framework. In his compositions thematic unity is seldom restricted to a single movement, but frequently extends to all movements of a multi-movement work. Although he rarely strays from harmonic principles derived from Hindemith, he is wont to employ Middle Eastern music and Jewish folk music in primary thematic statements. Jacoby asserts that his treatment of such materials is unlike that of any other Israeli composer because of his preference for contrapuntal, rather than homophonic, manipulation of his themes. Such treatment is justified, according to Jacoby, by the essentially polyphonic potential of the Middle Eastern melos, making it possible to treat this music "like the *Inventions* of Bach."[23]

In his early works utilizing Middle Eastern thematic material, Jacoby worked closely with Bracha Zephira, as Ben-Ḥaim and adherents of the Eastern Mediterranean movement had done. This cooperation was relatively short-lived, although he did write a considerable number of songs for Zephira. Late in the 1940s and in the early 1950s, Jacoby began to create his own melodic material, conceiving it however in a style similar to Middle Eastern music. He expanded this practice in subsequent years, and even his most recent compositions reflect the practice. More than most composers from the immigrant generation, Jacoby admits freely to strict fidelity to the Central European framework, stating that "some of my friends suggest that people should send my compositions to Germany to show the Germans how an Israeli preserved the German spirit of music."[24]

Jacoby's compositional approach is also marked by the degree to which a single theme can be used as the basis for an entire work. Even when the theme is not actually stated at early stages in a composition, a work should be ineluctably unfolding along a particular path as if to discover and elucidate its elemental theme. It is not surprising, therefore, that one of his favorite compositional devices has been theme and variations. The composition for which he is best known, *King David's Lyre* (1948), illustrates clearly how Jacoby has sought to portray aspects of Israeli nationalism without departing from the Central European framework. Composed on 15 May 1948, the day on which Israeli independence was granted, the work has but a single theme. That theme appears in each variation to symbolize a different episode in Jewish history. Through successive variations the same theme appears as biblical and Babylonian tunes, a lullaby, a pioneer song, and in the stentorial tones of a national anthem.

In many of the compositions Jacoby regards as his most personal statements, the complex, even abstruse, treatment of thematic material reveals itself only upon analysis. During the late 1940s and early 1950s his inability to stimulate critical interest in the intricacy of such works caused Jacoby to begin composing for two audiences: the first, a more general audience not particularly interested in unraveling complex works; the second, a smaller audience willing to plumb beneath surface responses to undertake more critical analysis of the works. The recognition of the audiences further brought about the production of two repertories with specific ethnic associations. For the general audience an eclectic, almost chameleon-like amalgam of approaches was mustered according to the requirements of a particular commission or performance setting. For the second, smaller audience works were composed that utilized techniques from the Central European framework. It is not surprising, thus, that the second audience attracted few from outside the German-speaking ethnic group. The works intended for this audience, moreover, represent those genres with symbolic meaning for the Central European community, especially chamber music and compositions without programmatic intent. Jacoby describes these works as especially Germanic in spirit, so designated by their tightly controlled thematic unity. To illustrate this spirit Jacoby points to the *Wind Quintet* (1951; originally published as a quartet in 1946). The first movement states the thematic material immediately at its beginning (fig. 26). The theme is developed throughout the first two movements using quite traditional methods, though in complex and intricate ways. The third movement begins as theme and variations, in which the relation to the initial theme is not exactly clear. Again, the thematic variation is quite complex, if purposely obscured, until the sixth variation, in which the theme is finally stated, but in cancrizans fashion, with the initial note actually the final one of the composition. Hence, it is not until the final section of the entire quintet that the theme fully emerges again, even though there its statement is in reverse order (see fig. 27).

For Hanoch Jacoby Western art music contained explicit ethnic boundaries that were defined by both compositional approach and audience. His own awareness of these ethnic boundaries allowed him to fabricate them within his own corpus of compositions, hence rendering that corpus a measure of Jacoby's acculturative responses. These responses were many, and yet they were inextricably bound to the multiple undertakings during his career: teacher, performer, critic, and composer. In each of these capacities Jacoby remained adamantly loyal to the techniques and traditions he had acquired as a student in Germany, revealing thereby the equivocal and multifaceted conservatism of one composer's response to cultural change.

It is unjust to imply that Josef Tal (born 1910 in Posen) represents any single group of composers, or a single way of approaching composition. He is the most individualistic composer of the immigrant generation from Central Europe. But it is because of his individualism that he represents the broad range of concepts constituting the third group of Central European composers. Tal is, moreover, the most successful of the composers who stood firmly against the pressures to write in an Israeli national style. In contrast to the different patterns of conservatism characterizing the work of Ben-Haim and Jacoby, Tal's compositional style was always embarking along new directions, expanding upon the framework gained through his studies in Germany, rather than simply exploring it. He relied upon the unity of the German framework as a foundation for diversification and thus endures as the composer from the immigrant generation whose work opened the most doors to musical styles developing abroad.

Like Hanoch Jacoby, Josef Tal led a diverse career; unlike his fellow composer, however, Tal's career always focused on the pedagogical aspects of music. He first served on the faculty of the Palestine Conservatory in various capacities, and he was later the initial faculty member in music at the Hebrew University in 1951, after the twelve-year hiatus since the death of Robert Lachmann. Tal expanded his service to the Hebrew University in 1961 by establishing the Israel Centre for Electronic Music and serving as its director. In 1965, when the Musicology Department at the Hebrew University was founded as the first program of musicology in Israel, Tal became its first chairman.

Just as Tal was a pioneer in Israel's programs of higher education in music, so also did he stand at Israel's compositional vanguard. From his earliest compositions following immigration in 1933, he demonstrated a tendency toward a cosmopolitan and international approach. He exhibited a firm independence, preferring not to ally himself with either avant-gardist

Fig. 26. First page, opening movement of Hanoch Jacoby's Quintet for woodwinds, first published 1951. Source: Hanoch Jacoby, Quintet (Tel Aviv: Israel Music Institute, 1987). Reprinted with permission of current copyright holder, Israel Music Institute (IMI), Tel Aviv.

Fig. 27. Final page, final movement of Hanoch Jacoby's *Quintet* for woodwinds, first published 1951. Source: Hanoch Jacoby, *Quintet* (Tel Aviv: Israel Music Institute, 1987). Reprinted with permission of current copyright holder, Israel Music Institute (IMI), Tel Aviv.

groups, such as that associated with Stefan Wolpe, or the movements striving to develop a Jewish nationalist idiom. He was especially ill at ease with the Eastern Mediterranean approach. He recalled in 1980, "I wasn't very fond of these kinds of using Eastern music. That means, if you write a symphony, the first subject will be a quotation of, let's say, a Yemenite folk song, and then you put it into the frame of a classical symphony, and you invent a second theme. You develop out of the Yemenite folk song a symphony of forty minutes with all that we know about a European symphony. And I regarded this always as a kind of a rape on the folk song."[25] Although he disliked the techniques of the Eastern Mediterraneanists, he did recognize that traditional Jewish music could serve as a valuable font for the Israeli composer. Not only was traditional music a receptacle of history for all Israelis, but it symbolized the ingathering of Jews on a soil both ancient and modern. Rather than completely ignoring Jewish folk music, Tal determined that it could lend itself to techniques inherent in the Central European framework, but not yet developed. One such incorporation of traditional Jewish music as thematic material formed the basis of his *First Symphony* (1952):

> When I had been asked to write my first symphony here, it was the Israel Philharmonic Orchestra. I took an old Jewish-Persian tune, which I found in the big *Thesaurus* by Idelsohn, which I thought was quite a sophisticated tune. In the tune were quite a lot of cells, each one which was interesting from the point of view of the intervals [it] used, from the point of view of rhythm. In fact, before I quoted the tune in full, which comes quite late in the symphony, I started to use the single cells of this piece and to work it out. I was free of harmonizing it in any style, be it modal harmony or tonal harmony or chromatic tonality. I could even do that dodecaphonically, if I wanted to, but I didn't do that because I thought that it's also not folk in twelve-tone music. I was absolutely free, so I chose whatever I chose to do.[26]

Even more efficacious than such treatment of traditional melodies, Tal found that setting the Hebrew language could unite different cultural symbols from contemporary Israel with his own personal aims. He therefore composed numerous works with Hebrew texts, especially those extracted from the Bible. This, in turn, led Tal to opera, a genre in which he has composed to a far greater extent than any other Israeli composer. Ironically, his work with opera forced him to rely on performance organizations outside of Israel, for Israel had no adequate company of its own. Two of his last three operas, *Ashmeda'i* (1970) and *The Experiment* (1975), received their premieres in West Germany, which has consistently responded favorably to Tal's compositions.

His intense involvement with the operatic medium while a citizen of a nation in which opera receives scant attention is indicative of Tal's belief that the composer must respond primarily to his own aesthetic concepts, not to pressure from audiences and critics. A self-described *enfant terrible*, he has never bowed to public pressure urging him to make his work more broadly consumable in Israel. Instead, he has preferred always to search for new approaches, constantly refining and expanding his personal aesthetic. Undoubtedly, the most dramatic expansion of his personal aesthetic was his incorporation of electronic media into compositions beginning in the 1950s. Having studied and composed at several European and American studios, Tal created the first Israeli studio in 1961. He has employed electronic techniques for almost every genre, including two operas and three piano concerti.

Because of his experimentation and the underlying philosophy that impels it, Josef Tal wrote not in one compositional style, but in many. Some works are quite tonal; some completely lack tonality. Just as he utilized Jewish traditional music, so also did he compose dodecaphonic music. Always, however, there exists the unifying motive of turning outward to discover new ideas and aesthetic concepts. Tal's music can even capture a deep sense of nostalgia, reflecting on an earlier era and the cultural climate then prevailing. Such is the spirit of *Else-Homage* (1976), a retrospective glance at Else Lasker-Schüler's years in Jerusalem.[27] A reflective work such as *Else-Homage* reasserts Tal's own recognition that the early immigrant decades fostered his experimentation. Josef Tal's influence on Israeli musical life is evident in many different areas. He is respected both as an experimenter and as a teacher, both as a cosmopolitan and a musical intellect with deep concern for the future of Israeli musical activities. Throughout his career he has maintained that the unique character of Israeli culture was not its unity but its diversity, its openness to numerous cultural streams. At times he has defended such a position against the onslaught of considerable criticism. Tal's position, nevertheless, has endured and persists as an acculturative response that embraces change in Israeli culture, rather than eschewing it. Within this full engagement with change lies the true steadfastness of Tal's intellectual and musical contribution.

When the immigrant composers from Central Europe arrived in Palestine in the 1930s, they were proponents of a compositional framework acquired after rigorous musical studies in Germany's music academies. In Palestine they encountered pressures demanding that these techniques be diverted to ends quite unlike those for which the framework was suited. The varied responses of the immigrant composers produced a diversity of considerable richness. That diversity reflected the many components of the nascent Israeli culture, as well as the struggle of many components to survive. Although some streams of development, such as the Eastern Mediterranean movement, once seemed to point to a potentially unified expression, diversity has instead prevailed until the present.

The prevalence of diversity illustrates that consolidation, the predominant acculturative response at work elsewhere in the immigrant culture, and cultural pluralism, the primary result of that response, are also inherent in the art-music traditions of the Central European Israelis. The diverse approaches of different composers symbolize the myriad influences that the immigrant environment brings to bear on musical attitudes and values. The institutionalization of these approaches within the social structure of Israeli culture illustrates the success with which processes of consolidation came to foster musical life in the Central European community.

If the diverse approaches of the immigrant composers contribute to the formation of a pluralistic musical culture, then it is the composer who serves as the conduit across the boundaries separating the ethnic community from other groups in the culture. Although most of these composers received their early training in the institutions of the pre-immigrant culture, the burden was placed on them after immigration to respond to a cultural environment that was completely foreign. The resulting pluralistic response negated the possibility of creating an aesthetic that was only German or simplistically Israeli. The aesthetic was, instead, a multifarious combination of both European and Israeli musical and cultural streams, with many new cultural influences tendered by the continued diversity of new immigrant groups.

The consolidation of German-Jewish and other ethnic traditions parallels other patterns of consolidation characterizing the culture of Central European Israelis. One can even go so far as to state that consolidation has come to depend on many of these patterns. The changing responses to religion and language necessitated by the immigrant environment also spawned new approaches to music. Likewise, the music academies established by the Central European immigrants had to be responsive to music students with quite different ethnic and musical backgrounds. The composer's ability to consolidate was also essential to his or her ability to introduce and stimulate change in the art-music traditions that subsequently emerged. Today, it remains clear that the diversity of Israeli music is but another measure of the acculturative responses of the constituent groups in Israeli society. That the generation of immigrant composers from Central Europe was able to quicken this diversity, while concomitantly channeling it along several new directions, is the true measure of its contribution to Israeli musical life.

NOTES

1. Max Brod, *Die Musik Israels,* pp. 14-15.

2. Erich-Walter Sternberg, "The Twelve Tribes of Israel," *Musica Hebraica* 1-2 (1938): 24.

3. Occasionally, this attitude was voiced as a dichotomy, wherein Eastern European culture and music bore the seeds of a "more Jewish" tradition in contrast to Central European traditions, which were "less Jewish." Such attitudes even find their way into recent works; see, for example, Zvi Keren, *Contemporary Israeli Music: Its Sources and Stylistic Development* (Ramat Gan: Bar Ilan University Press, 1980), p. 69.

4. The controversy stemming from some ideological struggles might linger for many years; see Jehoash Hirshberg, with David Sagiv, "The 'Israeli' in Israeli Music: The Audience Responds," *Israel Studies in Musicology* 1 (1978): 159.

5. Sternberg, "The Twelve Tribes," p. 24.

6. See Gila Flam, "Beracha Zephira — A Case Study of Acculturation in Israeli Song," *Asian Music* 17/2 (Spring/Summer 1986): 108-25; and idem, "Shiluvoh shel ha-shir ha-temeni ba-mimsad ha-tarbuti be-eretz yisrael shel shanot ha-shloshim al-yadeh Bracha Zephira" ("The Interweaving of Yemenite Song in the Cultural Establishment of Eretz-Yisrael during the 1930s by Bracha Zephira"), *Araḥot Temen* (1984): 339-52.

7. One of the most thoughtful and concise discussions of the Eastern Mediterranean movement is Alexander L. Ringer, "Musical Composition in Modern Israel," in *Contemporary Music in Europe: A Comprehensive Survey,* ed. Paul Henry Lang and Nathan Broder (1965; New York: W. W. Norton, 1968), p. 283.

8. Keren, *Contemporary Israeli Music,* p. 81.

9. Brod, *Die Musik Israels,* p. 20.

10. The new interest in cantillation and the setting of Hebrew to music was facilitated by the research of two scholars from a Central European musical and academic background: Robert Lachmann and Abraham Zvi Idelsohn. Immigrant composers frequently cite Lachmann's study *Gesänge der Juden auf der Insel Djerba* (1940; Jerusalem: Magnes Press of the Hebrew University, 1976), published posthumously, for stimulating initial examination of the interrelations of Middle Eastern music and biblical cantillation. Idelsohn's monumental thesaurus of melodic material gleaned from diverse Jewish ethnic groups provided a wealth of thematic material for many Israeli compositions, especially during the immigrant

generation; see A. Z. Idelsohn, *Hebräisch-orientalischer Melodienschatz*, 10 volumes (Berlin: Benjamin Harz [et al.], 1914-32).

11. Haim Alexander, for example, recounted of his first lessons with Stefan Wolpe: "When I came here, I showed my compositions to my teacher, Stefan Wolpe, and he said that everything is very nice, now throw it away and start again" (Interview, 14 December 1980, Jerusalem).

12. The importance of this urban bohemia is the subject of Jehoash Hirshberg, "Joseph Tal's Homage to Else," *Ariel* 41 (1976): 83.

13. Ringer, "Musical Composition in Modern Israel," p. 282.

14. See Bathja Bayer, "Israel, State of (Cultural Life): Music and Dance," *Encyclopaedia Judaica*, 2nd ed., 9, column 1009.

15. Sternberg, "The Twelve Tribes," p. 25.

16. Jehoash Hirshberg, "Heinrich Schalit and Paul Ben-Haim in Munich," *Yuval* 4 (1982): 131-49.

17. Brod, *Die Musik Israels*, p. 63.

18. Ibid., p. 58.

19. Ben-Haim himself describes his early years of settlement in Paul Ben-Haim, "Ali'iti le-eretz yisrael" ("I Immigrated to *Eretz Israel*"), *Tatzlil* 13 (1973): 172-73.

20. Ringer, "Musical Composition in Modern Israel," p. 284.

21. Published by Edition Negen in 1948. The *Five Pieces for Piano* are sometimes known as the *Suite for Piano*.

22. Interview with No'am Sheriff, 20 May 1981, Tel Aviv. For a more complete assessment of Ben-Haim, see Jehoash Hirshberg, *Ben-Haim, haiav ve-yetzirtoh* ("Ben-Haim, His Life and Works") (Tel Aviv, 1983). See also Ben-Haim's autobiographical comments in his "Netivut la-'olam ha-gadol" ("Movement into the Large World"), *Tatzlil* 15 (1975): 142-45.

23. Interview with Hanoch Jacoby, 8 May 1982, Jerusalem. Others of the Central European immigrant generation have espoused similar views; see, for example, Peter Gradenwitz, *Musik zwischen Orient und Okzident: Eine Kulturgeschichte der Wechselbeziehungen* (Wilhelmshaven: Heinrichshofen's Verlag, 1977), p. 355.

24. Interview with Hanoch Jacoby, 8 May 1982, Jerusalem.

25. Interview with Josef Tal, 20 November 1980, Jerusalem.

26. Ibid.

27. Jehoash Hirshberg describes the influence of the cultural environment of the German *aliyah* on *Else-Homage* in "Joseph Tal's Homage," pp. 83-93.

10
Hausmusik

HAUSMUSIK HAS HISTORICALLY served as an essential means for maintaining social cohesion in the musical culture of the Central European ethnic community. As a cultural institution it is important for several reasons. First, *Hausmusik* lends continuity to a genre of music that not only has intense emotional meaning for most Central European immigrants, but also one that distinguishes the ethnic group from others: chamber music. Second, it creates a web of social relations based specifically on music. If one or several parts of the social events surrounding a home concert must be deleted, it is never the concert itself. Third, *Hausmusik* plays a vital role in estab-lishing and maintaining communication among the members of the com-munity. Some members meet only occasionally during the evening of a concert, content to converse with whoever happens to be in attendance; others consciously use the opportunity to meet with friends whom they see in no other context. Finally, because the performance of chamber music occurs most frequently in several homes according to a rather fixed calendar, it has also become a metaphorical articulation of ethnic geography and the ritualization of Western art music in the Central European community.

The social relations established through concerts of *Hausmusik* are very complex and grow from those existing prior to immigration and shared during the initial transferral of the ethnic community to Israel. Such re-lations, moreover, tend to cross generational boundaries, thus providing a means of entrance into the musical activities of the community for its younger members born in Israel. If chamber music had not reemerged as a pervasive setting for ritualized musical behavior soon after immigration, it is questionable whether the musical culture of Central Europeans could have persisted as emphatically as it has.

Although Central Europeans are not the only ones present at chamber concerts in the home, they are most often the organizers. Indeed, the importance of chamber music to the Jewish communities of Central Europe has an extensive history. The rise of chamber music in the Western tradition was coeval with the rise of liberalism during the second half of the eighteenth century.[1] Chamber music achieved even more importance as a musical genre and social setting during the period of nineteenth-century emancipation. During an age of burgeoning public and professional musical life, chamber music occupied a private and amateur sphere. Just as Jews had benefited from the rise of liberalism, so too did chamber music provide them a special venue for interaction outside the Jewish community. The Jewish salon was a place where Jews and non-Jews met in an atmosphere of equality. The genre, with its democracy of musical parts and its elimination of barriers separating performers from audience, further reflected this spirit of equality.[2] Jews also excelled in amateur chamber ensembles in the nineteenth century (and later in professional ensembles), so much so that the history of chamber music in some German cities unfolded largely within their Jewish communities from the mid-nineteenth century until the 1930s.[3] So pervasive was this role of chamber music in the Jewish community that the *jüdischer Kulturbund* created a special administrative category to sanction and support chamber music after the exclusion of Jewish musicians from public performance outside the community in 1933.[4]

Multiple layers of ethnic meaning had already surrounded chamber music in Central Europe. Both Friedrich Nietzsche and, even more explicitly, Theodor Adorno identified a quintessentially Central European historical process in chamber music.[5] Few Israelis would deny that this historical process is also inseparable from the genre's resurgence in Israel. *Hausmusik,* with its central element of chamber music, is thus a ritual of the home in the Central European community. The most explicit instance of ethnic boundaries within the art-music culture of Israel forms from the dichotomy between Eastern European emphasis on virtuosity and solo performance and Central European stress of the shared experience of chamber music. Immigrants of Russian descent rarely attend concerts of *Hausmusik,* either as members of the audience or performers.[6]

The non-musical aspects of chamber music are also frequently distinctive of the Central European community. Many regard the chamber concert as the preferred setting in which to discuss literature and art, and to participate in cultural activities retained from Europe. During the early decades of statehood these activities were often symbolic of the two cultural streams of the recent immigrants: whereas they passed most of their days laboring outside the home, the immigrants reserved special moments for the evening, when they might re-create the milieu of artistic exchange in their homes. As a means of preserving European customs, the conscious cultural bifurcation was primarily restricted to the immigrant generation and as such encompassed a closed world, one reflective of bygone days.[7] The contemporary Israeli *Hauskonzert* contrasts with the closed world of the early immigrant in an important way: it is not closed to the outside, but open, and as such frequently draws outsiders into its musical experience. Its survival relies not on the abilities of community members to preserve, but on the willingness of outsiders to participate. Thus, the characteristic form that it has acquired during several generations now defines it as Israeli and no longer as European.

The concert of chamber music has developed highly ritualized forms in Israel. The ritual of the concert itself spawns various levels of organization, all of which are vital to the role chamber music plays in the Central European community. On one level, ritual extends to the evening and events contingent with the concert. On a second level, organization extends to the ethnic community and the necessity of establishing a regular position for chamber concerts in the course of weekly events. Finally, it is because of the ritualization of chamber music that concerts serve as a means of organizing interaction with those outside the community, making it possible for them to attend and participate in an event that is otherwise highly structured and potentially exclusive.[8]

Three types of participants are necessary for a successful evening of chamber music: the host or hostess; the performers; and the audience. Of these three types, the first comes almost certainly from the ethnic community, and the third only rarely does not include participants from outside the community. Each evening of chamber music unfolds as a series of specific events or phases, which together may last as long as five or six hours. Successful organization of chamber music events depends on several groups, some specific to the event, others more general in function. Of the first type, a core group attached to one home or host is the best example; I refer to the core group as such because its members rarely miss a concert of chamber music in a particular home, thus ensuring an element of audience and ritual stability. The Rubin Academy of Music or the Hebrew University in different ways characterizes the second type of organization.

The repertory of chamber music in Israel is very specific, thereby undergirding its symbolic role in the ethnic community. Standard works come from an historical period stretching from the mid-eighteenth to the mid-nineteenth century, roughly parallel to the period framed by Bach and Beethoven, the dyad fundamental to Carl Dahlhaus's notion of absolute music,[9] though also including early Romantics like Schubert, Mendelssohn, and Schumann. Again, this period has special significance for the Central European community, for it was historically a period of liberalism and initial emancipation. It was a period when the community first discovered new promise and philosophical resonance in *Bildung*. Just as *Bildung* became a sort of secular religion for many Central European Jews, so too did the music of the Classic and early Romantic periods acquire a deeper cultural significance: in essence, this repertory was one of the means whereby Jews could declare full and willing participation in the traditions of Western culture.

The association of a standard chamber music repertory with classicism is also a salient determinant of that repertory's symbolic role, for this has further meant a dissociation from nationalism and sacred functions of music. The chamber works of Mozart or Beethoven are therefore not perceived in the Central European community as German or Austrian, but as higher art forms that signal a higher value system. Within the community a few other genres have functions similar to those of chamber music, the best example being art song, *Lieder*. [10] Thus, the boundaries of the chamber music repertory are the products of a specific past and present, of an ethnic community that has always been Jewish and yet has always witnessed the confluence of other cultures in its intellectual and musical endeavors.

The custom usually called *Jause* initiates the evening of *Hausmusik*. Taken from Austrian dialect, but used by Central Europeans with other national origins, *Jause* designates late-afternoon tea or coffee, which in Jerusalem almost always begins at about 4:30 P.M. *Jause* itself usually takes place in a room separate from that of the concert. Serving coffee and cake initiates the introductory phase of the evening and provides several practical functions. First of all, punctuality is seldom observed — no matter what the occasion — and the initial, more informal nature of *Jause* therefore prevents the embarrassment of late arrival during a performance. Second, *Jause* acts as a period of transition from the frantic activities of the work day to the more intimate and subdued mood prevailing during the concert. Third, attendance is relatively flexible, and new participants are present fairly often; hence, the initial phase allows time for introductions and informal discussion. Therefore, even though *Jause* has a social function of its own, it is inseparable from the *Hauskonzert* in the Israeli context.

Jause generally lasts approximately one hour and never any longer. Its conclusion is signaled by the movement of its participants to a completely different location, the setting for the concert itself. This room is almost always a living room as well, although the small size of Israeli apartments means that the dominant occupant of the room is a piano (see figs. 28 and 29 for the two most common patterns arranged for the *Hauskonzert*). The concert does not begin immediately, even when the musicians seemingly prepare to play and take their places with instruments in front of the audience. Again, a necessary transition occurs. During the second phase conversation takes an important turn: previously it had focused on general topics; now it must focus on music. Musical discussion lasts from twenty minutes to a half hour. Its complexity and direction, moreover, vary according to who is present in the audience. Sometimes, specific questions about the forthcoming concert are asked; at other times, participants pose less pertinent questions, such as an inquiry about recent concert experiences.

The performers usually do not participate during this second phase, unless it is to act as inquisitors. They do, however, control the second phase, for it is they who terminate the discussion. The decision to terminate the second phase arises when the performers are confident that the attention of the audience is sufficiently concentrated on music. Termination is quite sudden—even abrupt—and is rarely accompanied by more than a single statement, such as "Wir werden jetzt mit der Musik anfangen" ("We will now begin with the music").

The program prepared for a concert of chamber music is never a random assortment. Although the *Hausmusik* setting is very different from that of a public concert, many of the same concepts and ideals of program order are observed. The first piece is shorter, more modern, or less demanding of the audience's concentration. The second is a longer work, often with multiple movements and obviously chosen to occupy a dominant position in the program. If a solo pianist performs, for example, the second work is almost always a sonata by a late-eighteenth- or nineteenth-century composer. Upon the conclusion of the second work a period for discussion often follows, much as an intermission would during a public concert. Its function, however, differs slightly from that of an intermission, for during the *Hauskonzert* it is not necessarily a moment of rest for the performers, who now discuss the music, usually the work just performed. This discussion specifically relates to the performance setting and unquestionably intensifies the chamber music atmosphere. The discussion never focuses on the performance itself, rather on the insights the musicians have developed concerning the music. Always, such discussions heighten the intensity and involvement of both audience and performers.

The second part of the concert begins as abruptly as the first and is again initiated by the performers. The third work frequently relates to the

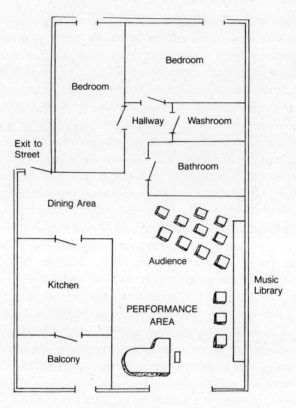

Figs. 28 and 29. Common floor plans and furniture arrangements for apartments in which *Hauskonzerte* frequently take palce. Drawings: Florence Bohlman.

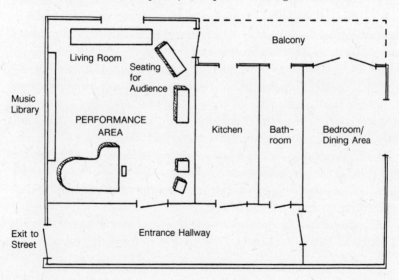

second, either because of similarity or contrast of specific points. The audience is never aware of the exact program and rarely seeks to discover it in entirety beforehand. Only the performers know which work will follow the discussion, and they are careful to shift the discussion toward that work so that the transition to it is logical and natural. Like the second work, the third holds a place of esteem, being regarded by all present as a major composition from the chamber music repertory. Fortified by the previous discussion, the audience maintains its intensity through this work, which ends approximately one hour after the concert's beginning. The intensity of both performers and audience is so great at this point that it would be quite impossible to end the concert without a lighter work. With a framing function not unlike the first work of the program, the finale is relatively short and contrasting in mood vis-à-vis the central works.

At this moment it would seem that the concert is concluded. But, again, there occurs a counterpart of the public concert. Although never calling them encores, audiences almost always request additional pieces from the performers. These particular works usually reflect the personality or specific national background of the performers. An immigrant from Czechoslovakia might, for example, play a group of Czech dances for these concluding pieces. Those who know the performers well usually request the concluding works by name or style. Performers favor such requests, thus symbolizing to all in attendance that the concert has achieved the high degree of intimacy customary to the ritual.

A period of conversation like that preceding the concert also follows it. This conversation period serves just the opposite function as that at the beginning, namely acting as a transition from the music to discussion of more general topics. The shift in discussion is necessary because most members of the audience have now been present for about three hours. With only about half of them either amateur or professional musicians, the introduction of new topics into the discussion becomes a means of more actively involving the non-musicians. The shift away from music also makes it possible for those who must leave to do so; it would be considered quite impolite to leave immediately after the performance, but the half hour of conversation separating the conclusion from early exit generally suffices as suitable homage toward the performers.

Although group involvement is stressed during the discussion following the concert, this phase contains several other important functions. Many evenings with *Hausmusik* are attended by special guests, very often a visiting professor at an Israeli university or a foreign visitor in the home of an audience member. This phase affords an opportunity for special guests to talk about their backgrounds, about the countries from which they come, or about the activities they are undertaking while in Israel. The momentary focus on the evening's guests serves functions of both courtesy and communication. Frequently, the function of communication is heightened when guests acquaint themselves with other audience members whose professions or backgrounds are similar. The emergence of individual dialogues between special guests and their new acquaintances also signifies the shift from general discussion to numerous smaller conversations throughout the room, which again reaffirm the involvement of the entire group in the evening's activities. The individualization of conversation also recognizes the social and cultural differences among audience members. Small conversation groups often form according to shared mother tongues; similar professions also stimulate the formation of small groups. These groups, in which all members fully participate, symbolize the complete abandonment of social and cultural tensions, and ensuing conversations may last from a half hour to several hours.

The individualized discussion shared by all attending the concert effectively signals the end of the evening. Because people are speaking in small groups, one needs to take leave with apology only to one's partner in discussion; hence, there is never a feeling that a person leaving during this phase is doing so because he or she is bored with the evening or feels uninvolved. Conversation also shifts away from the concert itself to music in general. In this sense, the final phase serves as a transition away from the *Hauskonzert*, just as *Jause* at the beginning served as a transition into it.

At many concerts of *Hausmusik*, though by no means at all, the final phase of group activity is followed by yet another, more intimate phase. The central activity of this phase is dinner, most of which has been prepared in advance by the host or hostess. For many reasons the dinner is the most intimate event of the evening and yet a phase essential to maintaining the *Hausmusik* tradition. First of all, conversation usually takes place in the mother tongue of the host, which is more often than not German. Because only three or four people are present, each must share that mother tongue or be freely conversant in it. Second, conversation refocuses on the concert itself, and the performer leads the discussion of the program. Other musicians often recount teaching and performance experiences relative to the program. Past performances by others, especially in Europe, are remembered and even critiqued. Music almost always dominates as the topic of conversation during the final phase; although there is no exclusion of other topics, they generally relate directly or indirectly to experiences associated with music. In short, the core group must be more than passively interested in music. The final phase serves primarily to reinforce the core that provides a necessary stability for the *Hauskonzerte* in a particular home or those attended by a particular group of people. For some core groups, especially those undergirding *Hauskonzerte* that occur regularly and frequently, the demands on time may be considerable. If the cultural evenings occur once a week on a specific evening, the core group may find it necessary to devote that evening to the concerts two or three times each month. When concerts occur more frequently than once a week, several core groups may form; this happens, for example, when one group attends regularly on Friday night and another on Saturday night.

The stability of the *Hausmusik* tradition symbolizes its importance to the Central European community. Concerts persist only because community members devote considerable time and energy to strengthening the stability that underlies them. In Israeli society it is often difficult to arrive at such stability. At numerous times during the year the regularity of the concerts is challenged by intervening holidays and the frequency with which members are abroad. Often, when a hostess has been abroad, she must work for several weeks to reestablish her core group and the former regularity of performances. The persistence of challenges to stability has recast the institution of *Hausmusik* in such ways that it can meet the demands of Israeli society; accordingly, the institution has transformed its role in the musical culture of Central Europe to one reflecting the new demands of the Israeli ethnic community.

The traditions of *Hausmusik* depend on several other social institutions of Israeli society for their continuation. These institutions fall into two broad categories: those specifically related to the Central European community and those generally associated with the larger Israeli society, but well supported by the ethnic community. Such institutions therefore reflect the generally pluralistic structure of Israeli society. They retain their own character while not conflicting with musical activities elsewhere. Indeed, the social organization of chamber music within the ethnic community is virtually a model for the cultural pluralism characteristic of Israeli society.

A clear example of an institutional superstructure specifically related to the ethnic subsociety is the Central European urban neighborhood, such as Rehavia in Jerusalem. The urban neighborhood provides support for a number of reasons, not least of which are practicality and convenience.

Many older participants are unable to travel long distances; many younger participants must be able to travel to and from the *Hauskonzert* quickly in order to meet other obligations. In those areas where Israelis of Central European background live close to the homes of musicians who frequently organize concerts, general support is stronger and the existence of such factors as a core group of participants is more likely.

Chamber music in the home has enjoyed relatively little success in other ethnic communities. Within a neighborhood like Rehavia most residents view chamber music as a traditional component of musical life. Most expect that cultural evenings will occur with some frequency, and participants from the community seek out the events in addition to relying on invitations. Those living in the urban neighborhood are also accustomed to planning their homes so that *Hauskonzerte* neither necessitate the rearrangement of furniture nor present special inconveniences for the musicians. If chamber music is performed, the host must always be able to provide music stands. Hosts who are themselves frequently performers usually possess a wealth of musical scores in their libraries, thus allowing for spontaneous readings of music. All of these traditions are more characteristic of the Central Europeans than of other groups.

Central Europeans frequently brought their pianos with them at the time of immigration. They often arrange the living room so that the piano is the focal piece of furniture; the "stage" exists without the need of special arrangement. The excellent music libraries of many Central Europeans also accompanied them to Israel. The presence of an extensive music library in the home especially marks the Central European community, for a well-stocked music library exists only after several generations of collecting and is very difficult to come by in Israel, where musical scores are extremely expensive.

The urban neighborhood is supportive for several other pragmatic reasons as well. Within such neighborhoods one finds more participants who speak German fluently or as a mother tongue. The foodways of such a community are similar. *Jause* with its coffee and cake at 4:00 P.M., though not customary among other ethnic groups in Israel, takes place in many Central European homes regardless of a subsequent chamber concert. The size and proximity of most Israeli apartment houses are also factors that influence the tradition. Not all Israelis are tolerant of the music making of their neighbors, even during those hours when playing the piano is socially permissible. Were frequent objections from neighbors to confront *Hauskonzerte*, the ritual would soon cease to exist.

To some extent *Hausmusik* takes the place of some other social activities. One institution supplanted in this manner is religion—or, more properly, the assembly for services on *Erev Shabbat* and *Shabbat* (Friday evening and Saturday). Very often, the most important concerts of chamber music occur at these times. The reasons for this substitution of function are several, none of which can alone totally explain the phenomenon in Central European neighborhoods in Israel. First, not only is Friday more convenient for audience members, but it is sometimes the only evening on which the musicians who might take part in chamber music are free from other obligations. Second, Central European Israelis are, as a group, less observant than certain other groups; for many of the participants in *Hauskonzerte*, praying in the synagogue has never been customary. Finally, Israeli families and friends may gather together in a multitude of contexts on Friday evening. Some gather after services in the synagogue; others delegate observance to the home. The performance of chamber music on Friday night acts as an extension of these traditions, albeit secular in nature. The core group of participants is not unlike the circle of friends that always celebrates the arrival of the Sabbath together. The meal following the concert is similar in its timing and function to that in religious homes; indeed, because obligations following the concert are fewer on Friday night, participation in the meal is usually somewhat greater. Even the music may be interpreted as a substitution for the prayers and songs of the Friday evening religious celebration. Through this transferral of function the *Hausmusik* on *Erev Shabbat* has assumed a symbolic significance in Israel that it did not possess in Central Europe.

Hausmusik in the Central European community interacts with and depends on other musical institutions in the urban neighborhood. In Jerusalem the Rubin Academy of Music is a source of both performers and audiences. It is significant, thus, that the academy is situated in Reḥavia, therefore within walking distance of the homes in which *Hauskonzerte* most frequently occur. In some instances the concerts serve as extensions of the academy's activities. Very often the performers are instructors at the academy; many of the older, retired performers were instructors in music academies throughout most of their careers. The relation to formalized music training also serves as one of the most important means of refurbishing the chamber music tradition with young participants. Some attend the concerts because of invitations from their teachers; others perform at the cultural evenings, perhaps to rehearse for a public concert. There is no attention given to the ethnic background of younger musicians participating in the tradition in this way. All participants welcome performances by younger musicians and consciously avoid making them feel uncomfortable by speaking languages other than Hebrew. Whereas the tradition remains Central European, those who maintain it willingly include participants from other ethnic backgrounds and just as willingly alter the character to make younger participants feel welcome.

The *Hausmusik* tradition interacts with the symphony orchestras of Israel to a lesser degree, primarily for reasons of practicality. Israeli orchestral musicians are very busy almost all the time and have extremely erratic schedules. Not only do concerts take place during the times at which chamber music concerts occur, but Israeli orchestras spend much of the year abroad. Thus, orchestral players would find it much more difficult to participate in *Hausmusik* on a regular basis. Because performance for orchestral musicians is always professional, they seem less willing to perform freely within the amateur context afforded by *Hausmusik*. Occasionally, chamber ensembles assemble on the spot and actually read through the music for the first time as an ensemble. Whereas such performances may lack polish, the audience is far more interested in the music itself than the degree of professionalism. Moreover, the performers in such ensembles may demonstrate quite different levels of competence; complete amateurs may perform with veterans. Orchestral musicians also fail to provide the same link with younger musicians that instructors from the music academies frequently admit to the tradition. This, in itself, would be no reason to exclude orchestral players, but it is another example of their failure to bolster the *Hausmusik* in the same way as other participants.

In Jerusalem the Hebrew University has become an institution that indirectly supports *Hausmusik*, in fact for reasons similar to those for which the symphony orchestras do not. Probably one third of all participants at most Jerusalem chamber music concerts are directly associated with the Hebrew University, either as faculty or students. Many are amateur musicians, and none could properly be classified as a concertizing musician; the Hebrew University maintains no program in applied music, nor does it regularly support performance organizations. For many *Hausmusik* participants from the Hebrew University, such evenings are their primary musical activity, especially during seasons when there are few public concerts. Support comes from the university for other reasons as well. In Jerusalem many university faculty members live in Rehavia, where they have easy access to the cultural evenings of the neighborhood. Knowledge of German, especially among older faculty members and scholars in the humanities, is far more widespread than in other professions in Israel; this is even more the case for younger faculty members. *Hauskonzerte* are thus able to attract new participants from the university community, often regardless of ethnic background.

The German language, too, functions to solidify the *Hausmusik* tradition. Its presence during the evening may be as subtle or dominant as the participants wish it to be. Insistence on using the language, however, never excludes participants or closes the tradition to the rest of Israeli society. Several factors control the specific choice of language. Certain topics lend themselves better to discussion in German, whereas language is not a determinant with other topics. With still other topics the use of German is generally preferable, but all participants defer willingly to the language most acceptable to the group in attendance.

The topics usually discussed only in German are those directly associated with pre-immigrant cultural experience or ones for which German plays an extremely important role. German literature, preferred by most older members of the community, brings about discussion in which the participant must have some knowledge of the literature itself, must exhibit some sensitivity to the literary forms and themes of Central European literature, and must be able to understand readings or quotations around which certain points of discussion may turn. Although these topics rely on the German language to some degree, they are also bound to the experiences of those with a Central European humanistic education or with considerable recent experience in Germany. Situating discussions of literature and the other arts in the context of *Hausmusik* further inculcates chamber music as an aspect of *Bildung.*

Because many and sometimes most of the musicians performing *Hausmusik* are non-professionals, most participants need to develop a sensitivity to the cultural role of musical amateurism. In this context musical amateurism acquires meaning specific to the Central European community in Israel. Amateurism does not mean that the musicians were trained as children and young adults but have long since abandoned performance and only occasionally practice. On the contrary, most of the amateur musicians practice regularly and will even teach their instruments. Only about half of the musicians performing *Hausmusik* regularly pursue music in ways that can be construed as professional, and most are not full-time professionals. Neither amateur nor professional feels ill at ease playing with the other; moreover, the audience members accept both as equals and show no particular preference for concerts in which professionals alone perform. In short, amateurism in the context of the *Hausmusik* tradition is an attitude characteristic of those whose training may be extensive, but whose livelihood does not come from music. Amateurism has achieved a level of respect in Israel that it did not possess in the pre-immigrant cultural setting, where there was a pronounced distinction between musical *Kenner* and *Liebhaber* (in this usage, experts and amateurs). In fact, some musicians who were amateurs prior to immigration later became professionals in Israel.

Chamber music in Israel has become primarily centered in the *Hausmusik* tradition. The Israeli concert-going public is not particularly supportive of chamber music. Subscription series that feature chamber music attract relatively small crowds, whereas tickets for the major symphony orchestras are often difficult to obtain. Simply stated, the Israeli public is more interested in symphonic music than chamber music. The same generalization is not true of the Central European community that supports *Hausmusik.* Many participants in the tradition claim to prefer chamber music to orchestral music, a claim verified by their rare attendance of symphonic concerts. Not unrelated to this preference is the willingness of the Central Europeans to claim the chamber music repertory of the past two centuries as their own; other Israelis seem never to feel the need to challenge this claim.

Chamber music becomes synonymous with *Hausmusik* on a number of different levels. First, both emphasize the intimacy of the musical experience. The size of the room and the closeness of the audience stress that performance is shared by musicians and audience. Second, chamber music is regarded by those present as a more intellectual and sublime genre of music, one in need of a more cultivated atmosphere than orchestral music. The various discussions of music further accentuate the intellectual conceptualization of chamber music. Third, because amateurism encourages participation by many, the evening's social democracy parallels the emphasis on equal roles in the music itself.

Whereas *Hausmusik* seems ostensibly to serve as an agent of preservation in the Central European community, it depends on an ability to change for survival. Symbolizing this change is the degree to which younger Israelis become involved in it. The tradition does serve as a means preserving certain aspects of culture, but preservation and change always coexist. Encouraging change is the ease with which new members may cross the boundaries of the tradition and fully participate in the ritual of chamber music within a short period of time. Although the *Hauskonzert* is not a public concert, recognition of its existence circulates freely about the Israeli musical community. If someone wants to attend such events, it is usually not difficult to secure an invitation. Upon initial attendance, the new participant may come to future concerts as often or as infrequently as desired.

The general character of *Hausmusik* is one of preserving the ethnic particularity of the community. Chamber music maintains an association with Central Europe, and the repertory includes very few compositions that bear witness to post-immigration experience, either works of Israeli composers or new music in general. Preservation is especially evident during the concluding works of a program, when individual performers sometimes choose works they feel represent themselves in a special way. Non-musical activities during the evening also bear the mark of preservation. The foodways, for example, are unquestionably Central European and never include Middle Eastern dishes. The discussions that frame a concert are also imbued with a sense of preservation, relative both to what is and what is not discussed. When literature is discussed, it is almost always German classical literature and never Israeli works; contemporary literature under discussion is generally European and more often than not works by more conservative, non-experimental writers such as Siegfried Lenz. The lack of attention devoted to politics and contemporary affairs in Israeli society also serves as a symbol of preserved values and the conscious avoidance of a more volatile reality outside the community.

The balance between preservation and change is determined by the individuals who host and perform at the evening of chamber music. The host controls attendance, through invitations and by carefully structuring the evening. The performers determine the balance between preservation and change by choosing the repertory. The host also makes the overt gestures that render *Hausmusik* attractive to new participants. The tradition of *Hausmusik* constantly depends for its vitality on the individuals who maintain it within their homes. The tradition's ability to survive, altered or unaltered, depends on the ways in which these individuals establish a balance between preservation and change, between the maintenance of the musical values of the Central European community and their promulgation elsewhere in the musical life of Israel.

NOTES

1. Theodor W. Adorno, *Introduction to the Sociology of Music*, trans. E. B. Ashton (New York: Seabury, 1966), p. 86.
2. These factors increasingly undergirded the processes of reflexivity that accompany many forms of ritualized artistic performance; cf. John J. MacAloon, "Introduction: Cultural Performances, Culture Theory," in *Rite, Drama, Festival,*

226 · "The Land Where Two Streams Flow"

Spectacle: Rehearsals toward a Theory of Cultural Performances, ed. MacAloon (Philadelphia: Institute for the Study of Human Issues, 1984), pp. 10-13; and Bruce Kapferer, "The Ritual Process and the Problem of Reflexivity in Sinhalese Demon Exorcisms," in MacAloon, ed., *Rite, Drama, Festival, Spectacle,* pp. 179-207.

3. See, for example, Herrmann, *Musizieren,* passim.

4. S. Adler-Rudel, *Jüdische Selbsthilfe unter dem Naziregime 1933-1939: Im Spiegel der Reichsvertretung der Juden in Deutschland* (Tübingen: J. C. B. Mohr [Paul Siebeck], 1974), pp. 146-48.

5. Adorno, *Introduction,* pp. 88-89.

6. At the approximately one hundred *Hauskonzerte* I attended during two years in Israel, Russian-Israeli musicians performed on only one occasion. Whereas such an observation should not be interpreted as statistical evidence — I was rarely afforded the opportunity to attend concerts at the homes of Russian Israelis — it does support the distinction most commonly held by Israelis.

7. Saul Friedländer reflects eloquently on the world recreated by the Central European immigrants during the early decades of their settlement in *When Memory Comes,* trans. Helen R. Lane (New York: Farrar, Straus and Giroux, 1979), pp. 8-9.

8. The ritual associated with chamber music therefore comprises elements of both structure and anti-structure, which in Victor Turner's concept of ritual represent the dialectic of stability and change; see Victor Turner, *The Ritual Process: Structure and Anti-Structure* (Chicago: Aldine, 1969).

9. Carl Dahlhaus, *Die Idee der absoluten Musik* (Kassel: Bärenreiter, 1978), pp. 118-19.

10. There is considerable precedence for including art song among the genres of chamber music; see, for example, Adorno, *Introduction,* p. 85.

11

A Sense of Community, a Sense
of Nation

THE MANY facets of the Central European ethnic community are always evident at a concert in Israel. During the intermission, one need not wander too far before hearing a conversation in German. Sometimes, that conversation is among older individuals, several of them undoubtedly immigrants in the German *aliyah*. At other times, older Israelis and much younger individuals share the conversation. The accent and vocabulary of the younger conversants reveal that they come from Germany and are probably in Israel to study or teach. Yet another conversation in German is between an older musician and a younger one, this time an individual born in Israel but from a home with German-born parents. In general, all of the conversations center about the concert or other musical events during the present season in Israel. These events clearly occupy a central place in the lives of the conversants, taking precedence over politics, inflation, or conflicts with other Middle Eastern nations. Instead, the nation's musical life has come to serve as a rallying point for these Central European Israelis. They take pride in the abundance and excellence of that musical life, never forgetting the vital nurturing role played by their own ethnic community.

Attending a concert in Israel leaves one with no doubt that a sense of Central European community still remains. One might say even that the concert actually forms a real locus of crystallization for the community's ethnicity. Do the elderly conversants speak equally as freely in Hebrew to younger Israelis? Why do young Germans find such easy access to and acceptance by the Central European community? Does the second-generation musician spend most of the musical season in Israel or Europe? Such are the suspicious queries and negative reactions that many outsiders might harbor. They wonder why, after fifty years, German is still heard at all in Israel. They wonder why these Central European concert-goers continue to dress as if they were attending the symphony concerts in Berlin rather than in Jerusalem. Why is it that the Central Europeans continue to be different, and why are those differences so visible during the intermission of a concert?

The complex organization of musical activity through the implementation of new musical institutions has provided the Central European community a complex social structure within which its ethnicity could persist. Historically, most musical institutions clearly bore the earmark of ethnicity and reflected the pluralistic social organization of Central European Jewish culture, both before and after immigration. But there have been cases in which the community's musical activities have differed sharply from those permissible in the larger Israeli society, thus producing conflict. In such cases, music itself has bolstered an impermeable ethnic boundary separating part of the community from the larger society. The reactionary nature of certain musical activities, moreover, has caused the ethnic boundaries to become even more entrenched. Accordingly, the musical culture of Central European immigrants still stands apart in some areas, even though these belie the larger pattern of ethnic interaction characteristic of the entire community. The musical life thus persists in both the community and the nation, the two predominant cultural streams for German-Israelis a half century after the German *aliyah.*

Just as its musical culture continues to influence certain patterns of ethnicity, so too does the Central European community rely on a wide range of musical values to determine the acceptable patterns and limits of cultural pluralism. If other Israelis prefer to limit the performances of certain Central European repertories because of the historical experiences with which they are associated, the community carefully excludes such limitations. When the only support for music with German texts deemed unacceptable in Israeli society comes from non-Jewish segments of that society, some Central European musicians turn to those segments for support rather than alter their musical activities. In many areas of the musical culture, the persistence of the Central European community's musical values has produced change elsewhere in Israeli society; in other areas, conflicting attitudes will occupy different sides of the ethnic boundaries, at least for several more generations.

The musical culture of the Central European community has effected a pluralistic relation with Israeli society in ways that have elicited both positive and negative responses from that society. Nonetheless, the community has never undermined or weakened the national culture and has always transformed negative societal responses into positive contributions to the larger culture. Though still defined in many ways by distinct patterns of ethnicity, the Central European community has generated through its musical culture an intense support of the national culture and the place of music in it. Music has historically provided one of the cultural interfaces where interaction between the ethnic community and the nation was at its greatest and thus has functioned as a primary conduit for the pluralistic interrelation of community and nation. Without such an interface the structure of the Central European community would have long ago collapsed and the cultural life of contemporary Israel would be very different from the thriving one so evident today in the diverse domains of musical activity.

For various reasons certain musical events in which outsiders generally do not participate occur within the Central European community. Sequestering musical activity in this way has two fundamental ramifications. First, outsiders viewing the community from a distance might well not understand the musical event they were observing and its impact on the community. The most obvious case of such an event is one in which the German language is used throughout or plays a particularly significant role. Second, certain types of concerts in the community have been greeted by considerable criticism when they included more than the German-speaking ethnic group. At times this criticism has reached such proportions that those involved with the concerts have needed to retract public accessibility so that the community's boundaries shelter particular musical activities. The community institutionalizes such events as a form of cultural self-defense.

The persistent use of German in the ethnic community has long provided a subject for criticism. This criticism intensifies and can become even more vitriolic when public performances include German. Several times each year, residents from the Central European community gather to honor a particular German poet, for example Heine or Schiller. A community organization sponsors a concert in which the poet's works are read and settings of the poetry as *Lieder* are performed. Such cultural evenings would unquestionably raise vocal objections were they completely public. If they simply took place in the context of *Hausmusik*, there would be no need to worry about protest from outside the community. But such a physical restriction would not be completely feasible because of the potential for large attendance resulting from the broader value for the entire community. Instead, organizers seek a sponsoring institution that can also provide a large concert hall and organize the distribution of invitations to those who will attend. Because of the sensitive nature of such arrangements, several organizations, for example a university department and the Goethe-Institut, usually combine forces to deflect the pressure from any single institution.

The various celebrations honoring the 150th anniversary of Goethe's death generally took this form of organization. During the winter and early spring of 1982, several concerts of Goethe *Lieder* and recitations of his poetry

and prose works took place in Jerusalem, virtually all of these events un-
beknown to the public. Some of these events used the auditoriums of Israeli
cultural institutions, such as the Van Leer Institute; the institutions of the
German government, such as its embassy, also sponsored several Goethe
evenings. Attendance was effectively open only to those whom one of these
institutions had invited. Beyond personal invitations there was no publicity
whatsoever. The distribution of invitations depended entirely on the infrastructure of the Central European community and its involvement with
the institutions of musical and artistic activity, both Israeli and German.
Such restriction of attendance was necessary because German was the exclusive language of both audience and performance during these events.
Those without a secure knowledge of German could not have understood
the evening, either from a linguistic standpoint or from the symbolic level
that Goethe signified for the ethnic community. For the members of the
community such an event also honors their cultural values and places the
quarrels over the role of the German language at a momentary distance. It
is an event that only they can share among themselves, and therefore they
must take pains to restrict it as much as possible to their own community.

If there is a sense of restriction that attends evenings such as those
honoring Goethe on the anniversary of his death, it is because the German
cultural activities of the ethnic community have at times suffered greatly
due to outside pressures on the community. Prejudice and public derision
have occasionally forced the musical activities of some community members
to retreat from any form of public scrutiny. Felix Sulman and his amateur
choral society were forced to harden the boundaries of their musical activities
in this way. At times, *Hausmusik* provides the seclusion necessary to block
public attacks on the community's most value-laden repertories.

The Central European community has had to restrict other types of
music in such a way that they do not conflict with the larger society. For
example, there exists in Jerusalem a loosely organized group of musicians
calling itself the Israel Bach Society. This society sponsors a variety of
chamber concerts at the International Evangelical Church in Jerusalem every
Saturday at 8:30 P.M.. The physical setting for the concerts is necessary, for
the Israel Bach Society performs a considerable amount of baroque music
requiring the church's organ. Because much of the music has its basis in
Christian liturgy, religious critics regard it as inappropriate for other concert
halls in Jerusalem, and concerts never take place outside a Christian facility,
effectively removing this genre of concert and music from Israeli society.

The German Protestant church in the Old City of Jerusalem, the

Erlöserkirche, performs a similar role for music that might be offensive outside the Central European community. Generally regarded as possessing the best organ in Jerusalem, if not in Israel, the *Erlöserkirche* sponsors weekly organ recitals during much of the year. It also opens its doors to chamber music recitals and especially recitals of German *Lieder.* Such recitals draw almost completely from the Central European community, even though the church lies outside the Jewish portion of the city. This transplantation of the concerts also deflects pressure from outside forces by resituating the community's boundaries even farther from direct confrontation with religious segments in Israeli society.

The Wagner question remains the *cause célèbre* for those seeking to limit the encroachment of the boundaries of the Central European musical culture into Israeli society. Ironically, it has not been the ethnic community, but outsiders who have given the Wagner question such weight. For the outsiders, Wagner's guilt derives specifically from his Germanness, which in this sense is a political manifestation of ethnicity. For the Central European community, Wagner is no less German, but his ethnic meaning for the community is only coincidentally and tangentially political. The question is not a matter of identifying Wagner as anti-Semitic or not; no one doubts that Wagner was an anti-Semite, but combing the annals of European history to point fingers at anti-Semites and establishing them as cultural straw men in Israel is a thankless task with little significance for many in the Central European community.

And so too does the Wagner battle wage at a considerable distance from the community. In the most recent skirmish of national proportion the combatants came not from the community at all, and the principal participant not even from the country. In October 1981, the Israel Philharmonic Orchestra planned to perform the "Prelude" and "Liebestod" from *Tristan und Isolde* as an encore for one of its concerts in Tel Aviv. Zubin Mehta necessarily consulted with the orchestra's musicians before making the choice, and they concurred that perhaps the moment was right for a public performance of Wagner; indeed, they had performed the work in Europe on a recently concluded tour. The audience was unaware of the choice of encore, at least so one would expect, but it seems evident from the ensuing reaction that many audience members were aware that an excerpt from *Tristan* would follow the regularly programmed works. During the performance shouting broke out, and considerable disturbance in the auditorium marred the performance. The press debate that followed raged for weeks. Neither side yielded; pro- and contra-Wagner attitudes changed not at all.

There would be no reevaluation of the ethnic meaning of his music, nor would the ethnic boundaries of the Central European community shift in any new direction.

The music of Wagner occupies a particular place in nineteenth- and twentieth-century music history. For the Central European community the values inherent in that history transcend the specific contribution of Wagner. These values have accrued to the history because the community recognizes its own musical past ineluctably bound to it. As an ethnic community Central European Israelis share these musical values with many other ethnic and national groups that participated in the urbanization of European cultural history in the nineteenth and twentieth centuries. It was the admixture of these various groups, the interrelation of the arts and humanities, and the interaction of myriad composers and musicians that established the course of this history. In some ways this course effected an unrivaled flourishing of culture for the Central European community; it also led inevitably toward the community's most tragic moment. But Central European Jews had participated in the shaping of this course in disproportionate numbers. To deny this cultural history—even through the simple exorcism of Wagner from it—would be also to deny fundamental values of their own ethnic community in Israel.

Central European Jews in Israel have fostered a musical culture in which the primary expressions of their ethnic values have directly formed from their attitudes toward and intense cultivation of Western art music. A repertory of classical music, especially that of eighteenth- and nineteenth-century Central European composers, functions as ethnic music for the community. But it is not so much the music—that is, individual works associated with specific customs—that has symbolized ethnic values. Rather, it is the ways whereby the performance of Western art music in diverse settings has the ability to organize the German-speaking community as a group and to distinguish that group from the rest of Israeli society. Ethnic meaning derives from the patterns of organization that the community has developed to preserve certain musical practices and change others. These various patterns of organization, because of the conscious role they play in the expression of ethnic values, have resulted in the intensive institutionalization of the community's musical life.

Musical change in the Central European community is therefore only secondarily related to repertory. One could not properly understand the community's musical culture simply by "collecting" music. One would discover certain predilections for Beethoven and Schumann in some settings, but there would be no fundamentally distinctive approaches to the performance of piano works by the two composers. When Wagner is performed in Israel, it does not sound measurably different from a German or American performance. But the attitudes toward performance, the values symbolized by the inclusion of Beethoven or Wagner in a particular setting, these are of central importance to the ethnic group.

To evaluate musical change it is therefore necessary to examine the shifting patterns of organizing musical events in the community. The continuity of the Central European musical culture has been possible only because a broad spectrum of cultural processes has characterized both the centripetal pull of preservation and the centrifugal acceleration of change. The diverse responses within these larger processes of change range from virtual marginal survival to intricate patterns of syncretism.

Musical activities that have experienced relatively little change since transferral to Israel have undergone institutionalization so as to permit very little contact with other ethnic groups; at this level the boundaries of the Central European community are quite impermeable. One of the clearest examples of an institution with impermeable boundaries that do not overtly exclude the national culture is Felix Sulman's amateur choral society. Not only was Sulman an ardent Zionist prior to his immigration to Palestine, but the choral tradition that he and his choristers continue to maintain arose from an explicitly Zionist cultural agenda. But the musical tradition could not win public favor in Israel. First of all, the German language, in which many of its choral texts were set, hardened the tradition's boundaries. Second, the choral tradition included certain types of German secular and Christian religious music that were unacceptable to some segments of Israeli society. Third, the tradition depended on the practice of amateur music-making in the home, which thrives in the Central European community, but only because it has attracted, rather than excluded, other ethnic groups. Thus, the Sulman choir continues to cultivate its particular choral traditions, but this cultivation is of a private nature and exists nowhere else in Israel or Central Europe. The fixed nature of this tradition has, in effect, produced institutional marginal survival.

Other musical institutions have demonstrated similar cases of relatively impermeable boundaries. German cultural evenings in honor of German poets or composers continue to hold special significance for those from the earlier immigrant generations, but the ability of the third generation to take part has sharply diminished simply because of the great difficulty one faces in order to study German systematically in Israel. The boundaries erected by the Wagner question buttress the larger society from the music of Wagner with a fortitude that can yield only to the passage of considerable time. The religious music of conservative Central European Jews has also survived only marginally in Israel. A tradition marked by a rich and extensive history in Central Europe, fewer and fewer practice the tradition in Israel, where some sectors of the more orthodox religious communities would unequivocally dismiss it as unreligious.

Patterns of preservation have also formed within institutions whose boundaries were permeable, but only in one direction, namely allowing entrance into the ethnic community. These institutions find no support in the larger society and would thus disappear if their boundaries became distended at the point of cultural interaction. This, for example, was the case for the organist Max Lampel, who, because of the nature of his particular musical craft, was dependent on very specialized performing facilities and audiences willing to support the tradition of German organ music, which stood outside the general cultural life of Israeli society. Certain composers, such as Hanoch Jacoby, also chose not to direct their new works toward the general public. Jacoby continually refined his compositional style in order that the tradition he inherited from a German musical upbringing might serve the broader cultural goals of Israeli society. That society, however, demanded the expansion of style and the sacrifice of certain elements from the Central European values. Some immigrant composers were willing to accept the conflicting concepts of compositional technique; most, like Hanoch Jacoby, were not.

A few musical institutions, though conservative in nature, have succeeded in attracting considerable interest from musicians outside the Central European community. Despite boundaries that would seem at first glance to be impenetrable, these musical institutions permit flexibility of entrance and exit. The most notable of these is the tradition of *Hausmusik* in Israel. Potentially an institution that could restrict itself to the Central European community, new participants from many ethnic groups and nationalities constantly rejuvenate this tradition. The tradition of *Hausmusik* has managed this achievement by responding with tremendous flexibility to whoever chooses to participate. Language limitations are circumvented; age differences are unimportant; ethnic background is diverse. Certain aspects of the tradition, however, continue unchanged. The repertory of chamber music from the eighteenth and nineteenth centuries remains relatively fixed. Participants must be willing to share in certain recurrent topics of conversation, such as German arts and letters. The institution of *Hausmusik* bears marked similarity to its Central European predecessors, but its participants are today quite different.

The transferral of many elements of a highly urbanized ethnic community to Palestine at the time of immigration enabled the Central Europeans to institutionalize much of their musical culture in order to facilitate change. Whereas the Central Europeans carefully defined the boundaries of many new musical institutions, they were also careful to expand these boundaries constantly so that they could encompass ever larger segments of Israeli society. The many music education programs established by the immigrants of the German *aliyah* usually formed from Central European models and served, during the initial decades, younger musicians who had immigrated from Central Europe, sometimes even by providing instruction in German. Gradually, support for the music education programs became more widespread, and students from all ethnic groups attended the music schools and academies. As musicians from other nations immigrated in the years after Israeli independence, they too joined the faculties of these institutions. The institutions themselves, however, continued to maintain the same function and structure that they possessed at their inception. The continuity provided by these programs affected other areas of musical life in Israel and also encouraged the interdependency of other institutions. The immigrant generation of musicians from Central Europe thus laid the foundations of the music education programs of Israel. Although other aspects of these programs have changed and continue to change, the foundations remain intact and provide a necessary and resilient stability.

The concert life of urbanized Israel also formed from the initial contributions of the Central European community. It has, nevertheless, continually undergone change. A major problem faced by performing groups in the years prior to the German *aliyah* was the dearth of audiences able and willing to patronize concert life consistently. This problem quickly disappeared upon the arrival of German immigrants, who, in accordance with new musical groups, institutionalized concert life during the 1930s. Subscriptions now supported the orchestras; new concert halls appeared; orchestras and chamber ensembles found enthusiastic audiences wherever they traveled in the country. Although bearing the tradition of Central European musical life — indeed, a musical life that consolidated as a response to Nazi pressures on German Jews to organize musical activities within the boundaries of their own community in the *jüdischer Kulturbund* — the new concert life became an immediate vehicle for other ethnic groups to participate in the nascent consolidation of musical life in the cities. The distinctive German character of the orchestras evaporated as performers from many ethnic groups entered their ranks, and today one can only observe a more broadly based diversification, which is itself characteristic of an immigrant culture. The audiences bear witness to the same process of change. The modern concert life in Israel, though founded by the immigrants of the German *aliyah,* has gained support from all areas of Israeli society and has thus fully demonstrated the ability of the initial institutions to change.

Perhaps the most striking contribution of the Central European community to the musical life of Israel is that the institutions fostered by the community have come to serve all parts of the national musical culture. Immigrant composers from Central Europe have contributed important works in many styles, have worked in the cities as well as the kibbutzim, and have embarked on careers as performers, teachers, and critics. The music education programs have produced an abundance of fine students, indeed far in excess of the young nation's size. Chamber concerts of all sorts take place in the homes of the community as well as in the concert halls of the universities. Such pervasiveness indicates that the boundaries of these institutions have always demonstrated relative flexibility and that this flexibility has served both the Central European community itself and the nation as a whole.

The success of Central European institutions has further revealed the full acceptance of a pluralistic culture by the community. Never has that community forced its values on the national musical culture. One may only claim that certain phases of the development of an institution, such as the initial period of building the infrastructure, bear the imprint of Central European culture. Nor have the contributions of other ethnic groups been excluded. As new groups of immigrants entered the country, so also did they enter into the activities of Israeli musical life. Within the institutions themselves, ethnic differences often emerged as forces of consolidation from which the institution as a whole could benefit. Even those institutional boundaries that were seemingly the most impermeable became that way in response to pressure from the larger society, rather than to shifts in internal function. The history of the Central European musical culture in Israel in this sense parallels a history of continually evolving pluralism, these histories together yielding the two cultural streams so essential to the German-Israeli senses of community and nation.

Attesting to the strength of Central European musical institutions is the dramatic speed with which they transformed the musical life of Palestine during the 1930s. In a matter of a few years, a society in which only a few pioneer musicians struggled to find support and audiences developed into one with a wealth of talented musicians and an abundance of public support. This transformation was possible only through the extensive urbanization of the musical life of the Central European community. Not only could this community boast many excellent musicians and a large audience willing to support music actively, but it also contained individuals who were used to organizing the institutions necessary for an urbanized musical culture. Thus, one of Germany's former leading music educators, Leo Kestenberg, became general manager of the Palestine Orchestra in the late 1930s and guided it successfully through the trying years of World War II. The music department of the Palestine Broadcasting Service was also nurtured by German hands, thereby allowing the PBS to become a successful and far-reaching venture in only a few years. German leadership is also evident in the choice of Josef Tal to offer lectures in music history at the Hebrew University and later to head its first program in musicology. The dramatic transformation of the German *aliyah* produced a remarkable degree of successful musical activity within only a few years and provided the foundation for its maintenance through the trials of subsequent years.

Although one can find ethnic boundaries that restrict interaction between the ethnic community and the larger society, most ethnic boundaries have historically expanded into other sectors of Israeli society. Such expansion, too, is a quality of both cultural pluralism and consolidation. Because many of the boundaries depend on the activities of the first generation of immigrants, these boundaries will probably disappear as this generation passes. Those institutions that have responded conservatively to the pressures of Israeli society are also likely to disappear slowly, for many of these have been maintained solely by members of the first generation of immigrants. In contrast, some institutions have increasingly turned with interest in the direction of Central Europe. The wounds opened by the Holocaust, though still unhealed if not too deep ever to be healed, are at least relegated to the acts of another generation. Cultural interchange between Germany and Israel, especially involving music and musicians, will likely increase during the coming decades. This, too, can only be possible because of the responsiveness of cultural institutions in the Central European community.

The musical culture established by Central European immigrants during the 1930s and 1940s will inevitably reflect the whole of Israeli society at an ever increasing pace. In this way, the general structure of that musical culture will remain intact, while its façade will change to meet the different needs of new generations of Israeli musicians. Those musical activities in which the German language has played an essential role will gradually recede, and the technique and methodology stressed by Central European teachers and composers will yield to different and more contemporary approaches. Inevitably, the sense of Central European community will also grow increasingly nebulous and then disappear. In Israel, nevertheless, the legacy of the musicians from the German *aliyah* will leave its mark permanently on musical life. That legacy will not be immediately obvious from a quick glance at the surface characteristics of Israeli musical life. Instead, it will exist just beneath the surface, inextricably bound to the institutions that the Central European immigrants established and that serve as testaments to the renascent cultural life of the Jewish community in pre-Holocaust Europe. The two cultural streams of the land will continue to flow and to enrich musical life, if indeed both community and nation have channeled them toward an ineffable confluence.

APPENDIX

Consultants during Fieldwork,
July 1980–July 1982

Haim Alexander, *Jerusalem, Israel*
Oskar Althausen, *Mannheim, West Germany*
Bathja Bayer, *Jerusalem, Israel*
Yohanen Boehm, *Jerusalem, Israel*
Hannah Brik, *Tel Aviv, Israel*
George Dreyfuss, *Jerusalem, Israel*
Kitty Frank, *Jerusalem, Israel*
Edith Gerson-Kiwi, *Jerusalem, Israel*
Siegfried Gerth, *Mannheim, West Germany*
Miriam Getter, *Ra'ananah, Israel*
Evi Gilles, *Mannheim, West Germany*
H. Goldschmidt, *Tel Aviv, Israel*
Moshe Gourali, *Haifa, Israel*
Peter Gradenwitz, *Tel Aviv, Israel*
Dieter Heck, *Mannheim, West Germany*
Manfred Heinzelmann, *Mannheim, West Germany*
Joachim Hemmerle, *Mannheim, West Germany*
Hanoch Jacoby, *Tel Aviv, Israel*
Gurit Kadman, *Tel Aviv, Israel*
Felix Klein-Franke, *Jerusalem, Israel*
Max Lampel, *Jerusalem, Israel*
E. Levine (Mrs.), *Mannheim, West Germany*
Wolfgang Levy, *Tel Aviv, Israel*
Shabtai Petrushka, *Jerusalem, Israel*
Magalai Philippsborn, *Jerusalem, Israel*
Raphael Philippsborn, *Jerusalem, Israel*
Erika Reis, *Jerusalem, Israel*
Yohanen Ron, *Ramat ha-Sharon, Israel*
Gérard Rosenfeld, *Mannheim, West Germany*
Esther Sachs, *Jerusalem, Israel*

No'am Sheriff, *Tel Aviv, Israel*
Amnon Shiloah, *Jerusalem, Israel*
Ya'akov Shiloh, *Jerusalem, Israel*
Alice Sommer Herz, *Jerusalem, Israel*
Felix Sulman, *Jerusalem, Israel*
Josef Tal, *Jerusalem, Israel*
Uri Toeplitz, *Tel Aviv, Israel*
Shulamit Unna, *Jerusalem, Israel*
Karl Otto Watzinger, *Mannheim, West Germany*

SELECTED BIBLIOGRAPHY

1. Ethnicity, Immigration, and Musical Change

Barth, Fredrik, ed. *Ethnic Groups and Boundaries: The Social Organization of Ethnic Groups*. Boston: Little, Brown, 1969.

Beals, Ralph. "Acculturation." *Anthropology Today: Selections*. Edited by Sol Tax. Chicago: University of Chicago Press, 1962.

Clemmer, Richard O. "Truth, Duty, and the Revitalization of Anthropologists: A New Perspective on Cultural Change and Resistance." *Reinventing Anthropology*. Edited by Dell Hymes. 1969. New York: Vintage, 1974.

Danielson, Larry. "Introduction." *Studies in Folklore and Ethnicity*. Special edition of *Western Folklore* 36/1 (January, 1977): 1-5.

Dégh, Linda. "The Study of Ethnicity in Modern European Ethnology." *Journal of the Folklore Institute* 12/2 and 3 (1975): 113-29.

De Vos, George, and Romanucci-Ross, Lola, eds. *Ethnic Identity: Cultural Continuities and Change*. 1975. Chicago: University of Chicago Press, 1982.

Eisenstadt, S. N. "Institutionalization of Immigrant Behaviour." *Human Relations* 5/4 (1952): 373-95.

Glaser, Nathan, and Moynihan, Daniel Patrick. *Beyond the Melting Pot*. 2nd edition. Cambridge: MIT Press, 1970.

Gordon, Milton M. *Assimilation in American Life*. New York: Oxford University Press, 1964.

———. *Human Nature, Class, and Ethnicity*. New York: Oxford University Press, 1978.

Hamilton, William B., ed. *The Transferral of Institutions*. Durham: Duke University Press, 1964.

Herskovits, Melville J. *Acculturation: The Study of Culture Contact*. New York: J. J. Augustin, 1938.

Klymasz, Robert B. "From Immigrant to Ethnic Folklore: A Canadian View of Process and Transition." *Journal of the Folklore Institute* 10/3 (1973): 131-39.

Merriam, Alan P. *The Anthropology of Music*. Evanston: Northwestern University Press, 1964.

Nettl, Bruno. "Some Aspects of World Music in the Twentieth Century: Questions, Problems, and Concepts." *Ethnomusicology* 22/1 (January, 1978): 123-36.

———. *The Study of Ethnomusicology: Twenty-nine Issues and Concepts*. Urbana: University of Illinois Press, 1983.

——. *The Western Impact on World Music: Change, Adaptation, and Survival.* New York: Schirmer, 1985.

——, ed. *Eight Urban Musical Cultures: Tradition and Change.* Urbana: University of Illinois Press, 1978.

Parsons, Talcott. *Societies: Evolutionary and Comparative Perspectives.* Englewood Cliffs, N.J.: Prentice-Hall, 1966.

——. *The System of Modern Societies.* Englewood Cliffs, N.J.: Prentice-Hall, 1971.

Porter, James, ed. *Selected Reports in Ethnomusicology,* Vol. 3, No. 1. Los Angeles: University of California, Program in Ethnomusicology, 1978.

Redfield, Robert; Linton, Ralph; and Herskovits, Melville J. "Memorandum for the Study of Acculturation." *American Anthropologist* 38 (1936): 149-52.

Royce, Anya Peterson. *Ethnic Identity: Strategies of Diversity.* Bloomington: Indiana University Press, 1982.

Social Science Research Council. "Acculturation: An Exploratory Formulation." *American Anthropologist* 56 (1954): 973-1002.

Steward, Julian H. *Theory of Culture Change.* Urbana: University of Illinois Press, 1976.

2. JEWISH HISTORY AND COMMUNITY IN CENTRAL EUROPE

Adler-Rudel, S. *Jüdische Selbsthilfe unter dem Naziregime 1933-1939.* Tübingen: J. C. B. Mohr [Paul Siebeck], 1974.

Arad, Yitzhak; Gutman, Yisrael; and Margaliot, Abraham. *Documents on the Holocaust: Selected Sources on the Destruction of the Jews of Germany and Austria, Poland, and the Soviet Union.* Translated by Lea Ben Dor. Jerusalem: Yad Vashem, 1981.

Aschheim, Steven E. *Brothers and Strangers: The East European Jew in German and German Jewish Consciousness, 1800-1923.* Madison: University of Wisconsin Press, 1982.

Assall, Paul. *Juden im Elsaß.* Moos: Elster, 1984.

Augstein, Rudolf, et al. *"Historikerstreit": Die Dokumentation der Kontroverse um die Einzigartigkeit der nationalsozialistischen Judenvernichtung.* Munich: Piper, 1987.

Bach, H. I. *The German Jew: A Synthesis of Judaism and Western Civilization, 1730-1930.* New York: Oxford University Press, 1984.

Bloch, Ernst. *Erbschaft dieser Zeit.* Zurich: Oprecht, 1935.

Cohen, Stuart, ed. *Germany.* Jerusalem: Keter, 1974.

Fliedner, Hans-Joachim. *Die Judenverfolgung Mannheim, 1933-1945.* Vol. 1: *Darstellung.* Vol. 2: *Dokumente.* Stuttgart: W. Kohlhammer Verlag, 1971.

Fraenkel, Josef, ed. *The Jews of Austria: Essays on Their Life, History, and Destruction.* London: Valentine, Mitchell, 1967.

Freeden, Herbert. *Jüdisches Theater in Nazideutschland.* Tübingen: J. C. B. Mohr [Paul Siebeck], 1964.

Friedländer, Saul. *When Memory Comes.* Translated by Helen R. Lane. New York: Farrar, Straus and Giroux, 1979.

Gay, Peter. *Freud, Jews and Other Germans: Masters and Victims in Modernist Culture.* New York: Oxford University Press, 1978.

Geisel, Eike, ed. *Im Scheunenviertel.* Berlin: Severin und Siedler, [1981?].

Geissmar, Berta. *Musik im Schatten der Politik.* Zurich: Atlantis, 1945.

Goldscheider, Calvin, and Zuckerman, Alan S. *The Transformation of the Jews.* Chicago: University of Chicago Press, 1984.

Gordon, Sarah. *Hitler, Germans, and the "Jewish Question."* Princeton: Princeton University Press, 1984.

Grab, Walter, ed. *Deutsche Aufklärung und Judenemanzipation.* Vol. 3: *Jahrbuch des Instituts für deutsche Geschichte.* Ramat-Aviv: Tel Aviv University Press, 1980.

Grunfeld, Frederic V. *Prophets without Honour: A Background to Freud, Kafka, Einstein and Their World.* New York: McGraw-Hill, 1980.

Herrmann, Klaus J. *Das Dritte Reich und die deutsch-jüdischen Organisationen 1933-1934.* Cologne: Carl Heymanns Verlag, 1969.

Hertz, Deborah. *Jewish High Society in Old Regime Berlin.* New Haven: Yale University Press, 1988.

Karas, Joža. *Music in Terezín, 1941-1945.* New York: Beaufort, 1985.

Katz, Jacob. *Out of the Ghetto: The Social Background of Jewish Emancipation, 1770-1870.* 1973. New York: Schocken, 1978.

Klemig, Roland, ed. *Juden in Preußen: Ein Kapitel deutscher Geschichte.* Dortmund: Die bibliophilen Taschenbücher, 1981.

Labsch-Benz, Elfie. *Die jüdische Gemeinde Nonnenweier: Jüdisches Leben und Brauchtum in einer badischen Landgemeinde zu Beginn des 20. Jahrhunderts.* Freiburg im Breisgau: Verlag Wolf Mersch, 1981.

Lichtenstein, Erwin. "Der Kulturbund der Juden in Danzig, 1933-1938." *Zeitschrift für die Geschichte der Juden* 10 (1973): 181-90.

Low, Alfred D. *Jews in the Eyes of Germans: From the Enlightenment to Imperial Germany.* Philadelphia: Institute for the Study of Human Issues, 1979.

Militärgeschichtliches Forschungsamt. *Deutsch jüdische Soldaten: 1914-1945.* Rastatt: Militärgeschichtliches Forschungsamt, 1981.

Mosse, George L. *The Crisis of German Ideology: Intellectual Origins of the Third Reich.* 1964. New York: Schocken, 1981.

———. *German Jews beyond Judaism.* Bloomington and Cincinnati: Indiana University Press and Hebrew Union College Press, 1985.

———. *Germans and Jews: The Right, the Left, and the Search for a "Third Force" in Pre-Nazi Germany.* New York: Howard Fertig, 1970.

von der Osten-Sacken, Peter, ed. *Juden in Deutschland: Zur Geschichte einer Hoffnung.* Berlin: Selbstverlag Institut Kirche und Judentum, 1980.

Pollack, Herman. *Jewish Folkways in Germanic Lands (1648-1806): Studies in Aspects of Daily Life.* Cambridge: MIT Press, 1971.

Reinharz, Jehuda. *Fatherland or Promised Land: The Dilemma of the German Jews, 1893-1914.* Ann Arbor: University of Michigan Press, 1975.

Reinharz, Jehuda, and Schatzberg, Walter, eds. *The Jewish Response to German Culture: From the Enlightenment to the Second World War.* Hanover, N.H.: University Press of New England, 1985.

Richarz, Monika. *Jüdisches Leben in Deutschland.* 2 volumes. Stuttgart: Deutsche Verlagsanstalt, 1976-79.

Rosenzweig, Franz. *Zweistromland: Kleinere Schriften zu Glauben und Denken.* 1926. Dordrecht, the Netherlands: Martinus Nijhoff, 1984.

Rozenblit, Marsha L. *The Jews of Vienna, 1867-1914: Assimilation and Identity.* Albany: State University of New York Press, 1983.

Scholem, Gershom. *On Jews and Judaism in Crisis: Selected Essays.* Edited and translated by Werner J. Dannhauser. New York: Schocken, 1976.

———. *Von Berlin nach Jerusalem.* Frankfurt: Suhrkamp Verlag, 1977.

———, ed. *Walter Benjamin/Gershom Scholem Briefwechsel, 1933-1940.* Frankfurt: Suhrkamp Verlag, 1980.

Watzinger, Karl Otto. *Geschichte der Juden in Mannheim 1650-1945.* Stuttgart: Verlag W. Kohlhammer, 1984.

Weltsch, Robert, ed. *Deutsches Judentum, Aufstieg und Krise: Gestalten, Ideen, Werke.* Stuttgart: Deutsche Verlags-Anstalt, 1963.

Zweig, Stefan. *Die Welt von Gestern: Erinnerungen eines Europäers.* Stockholm: Bermann-Fischer Verlag, 1944.

3. Immigration to Israel

Bachi, Roberto. "A Statistical Analysis of the Revival of Hebrew in Israel." In *Scripta Hierosalymitana Publications of the Hebrew University.* Jerusalem: Magnes Press of the Hebrew University, 1956.

Bar-Yosef, Rivkah, and Ramot, Tamar. *Immigrants in Jerusalem: Patterns of Absorption.* Jerusalem: Work and Welfare Research Institute, Hebrew University, [1973?].

Chertoff, Mordecai, and Curtis, Michael, eds. *Israel: Social Structure and Change.* New Brunswick, N.J.: Transaction Books, 1973.

Eisenstadt, S. N. *The Absorption of Immigrants: A Comparative Study Based Mainly on the Jewish Community in Palestine and the State of Israel.* London: Routledge and Kegan Paul, 1953.

———. *Israeli Society.* New York: Basic Books, 1967.

———, ed. *Comparative Perspectives of Social Change.* Boston: Little, Brown, 1968.

Friedlander, Dov, and Goldscheider, Calvin. *The Population of Israel.* New York: Columbia University Press, 1979.

Gil, B., and Sicron, M. *Rishum ha-toshavim.* ("Registration of Inhabitants"). Jerusalem: Ha-lishkah ha-merkasit le-statistika, 1956.

Oring, Elliott. *Israeli Humor: The Content and Structure of the Palmah.* Albany: State University of New York Press, 1981.

Poll, Solomon, and Krausz, Ernest, eds. *On Ethnic and Religious Diversity in Israel.* Ramat Gan: Institute for the Study of Ethnic and Religious Groups, Bar-Ilan University, 1975.

Smooha, Sammy. *Israel: Pluralism and Conflict.* London: Routledge and Kegan Paul, 1978.

Willner, Dorothy. *Nation-Building and Community in Israel.* Princeton: Princeton University Press, 1969.

4. THE CENTRAL EUROPEAN COMMUNITY IN ISRAEL

Beling, Eva. *Die gesellschaftliche Eingliederung der deutschen Einwanderer in Israel: Eine soziologische Untersuchung der Einwanderung aus Deutschland zwischen 1933 und 1945.* Frankfurt: Europäische Verlagsanstalt, 1967.

Bohlman, Philip V. "The Archives of the World Centre for Jewish Music in Palestine, 1936-1940, at the Jewish National and University Library, Jerusalem." *Yuval* 5 (1986): 238-64.

Elcott, David Martin. "The Political Re-Socialization of German Jews in Palestine, 1933-1939." Ph.D. diss., Columbia University, 1981.

Erel, Shlomo. *Aus dem Tagebuch eines Kibbuz-Sekretärs.* Gerlingen: Bleicher Verlag, 1979.

Faerber, Meir M., ed. *Stimmen aus Israel: Eine Anthologie deutschsprachiger Literatur in Israel.* Gerlingen: Bleicher Verlag, 1979.

Feldman, Lily Gardner. *The Special Relationship between West Germany and Israel.* Boston: Allen and Unwin, 1984.

Hitachduth Olej Germania. *Die Deutsche Alijah in Palästina: Bericht der Hitachduth Olej Germania für die Jahre 1936/1937.* Tel Aviv: Hitachduth Olej Germania, 1937.

———. *Der Weg der deutschen Alijah: Rechenschaft, Leistung, Verantwortung.* Tel Aviv: Hitachduth Olej Germania and Olej Austria, 1939.

Petzold, Günther, and Petzold, Leslie. *Shavei Zion: Blüte in Israel aus schwäbischer Wurzel.* Gerlingen: Bleicher Verlag, 1978.

Simon, Ernst. *Aufbau im Untergang.* Vol. 2: *Schriftenreihe wissenschaftlicher Abhandlungen des Leo Baeck Instituts.* Tübingen: Leo Baeck Institut, 1959.

Turnowsky-Pinner, Margarete. *Die zweite Generation mitteleuropäischer Siedler in Israel.* Tübingen: J. C. B. Mohr [Paul Siebeck], 1962.

Wilder-Okladek, F. "Austrian and German Immigration in Israel." *Integration and Development in Israel.* Edited by S. N. Eisenstadt et al. New York: Praeger, 1970.

Wormann, Kurt D. "German Jews in Israel: Their Cultural Situation since 1933." *Year Book: Leo Baeck Institute* 15 (1970): 73-103.

Zweig, Arnold. *Bilanz der deutschen Judenheit: Ein Versuch.* Cologne: Joseph Melzer Verlag, 1961.

5. THE MUSICAL CULTURES OF JEWISH COMMUNITIES AND ISRAEL

Adaqi, Yehiel, and Sharvit, Uri. *Otzar n'imut yehudeh temen* ("A Treasury of Jewish Yemenite Chants"). Jerusalem: Israeli Institute for Sacred Music, 1981.

Avishur, Yitzhak. *Shirat ha-nashim: Shireh 'am be-'aravit-yehudit shel yehudeh 'irak* ("Women's Folk Songs in Judaeo-Arabic from Jews in Iraq"). Or Yehuda: Iraqi Jew's Traditional Culture Center, Institute for Research on Iraqi Jews, 1986.

Bayer, Bathja. "Israel, State of (Cultural Life): Music and Dance." *Encyclopaedia Judaica*. 2nd ed. 1971. Vol. 9.

Bezalel, Itzḥak, ed. *Ha-masorot ha-musikah shel yehudeh sfarad ve-mizrah* ("The Musical Traditions of Sephardic and Eastern Jews"). Special issue of *Pe'amim* 19 (1984).

Bohlman, Philip V. *Ha-historia ve-metodologia shel etnomusikologia* ("The History and Methodology of Ethnomusicology"). *Ha-moreshet ha-musikalit shel ha-k'hilot yisrael* ("The Musical Traditions of the Communities of Israel"), Unit II. Edited by Amnon Shiloah. Ramat Aviv: Everyman's University Press, 1985.

——. "The Musical Culture of Central European Jewish Immigrants to Israel." Ph.D. diss., University of Illinois, 1984.

Bohlman, Philip V., and Slobin, Mark, eds. *Music in the Ethnic Communities of Israel*. Special issue of *Asian Music* 17/2 (Spring/Summer 1986).

Brod, Max. *Die Musik Israels.* 1951. Revised and expanded by Yehuda Walter Cohen. Kassel: Bärenreiter, 1976.

Directory of Music Institutions in Israel. Jerusalem: The Israel Section of the International Music Council, 1977.

Gerson-Kiwi, Edith. "Musicology in Israel." *Acta Musicologica* 30 (1958): 17-26.

Gerson-Kiwi, Edith, and Shiloah, Amnon. "Musicology in Israel, 1960-1980." *Acta Musicologica* 52/2 (1981): 200-216.

Gradenwitz, Peter. *Music and Musicians in Israel.* 3rd edition, revised and enlarged. Tel Aviv: Israeli Music Publications, 1978.

Hirshberg, Jehoash. *Ben-Ḥaim, ḥaiav ve-yitzirtoh* ("Ben-Ḥaim, His Life and Works"). Tel Aviv, 1983.

——. "Heinrich Schalit and Paul Ben-Haim in Munich." *Yuval* 4 (1982): 131-49.

Hirshberg, Jehoash, with Sagiv, David. "The 'Israeli' in Israeli Music: The Audience Responds." *Israel Studies in Musicology* 1 (1978): 159-73.

Huberman, Bronislaw. *Bronislaw Huberman Builds the Palestine Orchestra.* Tel Aviv: [Americans for a Music Library in Israel], 1966.

Idelsohn, A. Z. *Hebräisch-orientalischer Melodienschatz.* 10 volumes. Berlin: Benjamin Harz [et al.], 1914-32.

——. *Jewish Music in Its Historical Development.* 1929. New York: Schocken, 1967.

Keren, Zvi. *Contemporary Israeli Music.* Ramat Gan: Bar Ilan University Press, 1980.

Kestenberg, Leo. *Bewegte Zeiten.* Wolfenbüttel: Moseler, 1961.

Lachmann, Robert. 1940. *Gesänge der Juden auf der Insel Djerba.* Yuval Monograph Series, Vol. 7. Jerusalem: Magnes Press of the Hebrew University, 1976.

Musica Hebraica 1-2 (1938).

Ringer, Alexander L. "Musical Composition in Modern Israel." *Contemporary Music in Europe: A Comprehensive Survey.* Edited by Paul Henry Lang and Nathan Broder. 1965. New York: W. W. Norton, 1968.

Shaḥar, Natan. "Ha-malḥin ba-kibbutz, makomo be-seder ha-ḥevrateh ba-kibbutz ve-yatzirato ha-musikalit" ("Musical Life and the Composer in the Kibbutz:

Historical and Socio-Musical Aspects"). M.A. thesis, Bar Ilan University, Ramat Gan, Israel, 1978.

Shiloah, Amnon. *Ha-masoret ha-musikalit shel yehudi baval* ("The Musical Tradition of Iraqi Jews: Selection of Piyyutim and Songs"). Or Yehuda: Iraqi Jew's Traditional Culture Center, Institute for Research on Iraqi Jewry, 1983.

Shiloah, Amnon, and Cohen, Erik. "The Dynamics of Change in Jewish Oriental Ethnic Music in Israel." *Ethnomusicology* 27/2 (May, 1983): 227-52.

Stutschewsky, Joachim. *Ḥaim bli p'sharot: Korot ḥaiav shel musikai yehudi* ("Life without Compromise: Memoirs of a Jewish Musician"). Tel Aviv: Sfarit poalim, 1977.

Thalheimer, Elsa. *Five Years of the Palestine Orchestra*. Tel Aviv: Palestine Orchestra, 1942.

Werner, Eric. *A Voice Still Heard.... The Sacred Songs of the Ashkenazic Jews.* University Park: Pennsylvania State University, 1976.

INDEX

Abileah, Arieh, 188
Abrahamssohn: as possible version of "Brahms," 3
Absolute music, 2
Abu Ghosh, 171
Abu Ghosh Festival, 171-72
Academies, music: in Germany, 24, 156, 208; historical development in Israel, 148-50; in Israel, 12, 19, 112, 140, 148, 161, 185, 191, 201, 208, 222, 235
Acculturation, 104-5, 109-10, 142, 150, 183-84, 193-94, 207-8, 209
Acculturative response. *See* Acculturation
Adler, Hugo, 79, 91, 93-94, 96, 134-35, 197. Compositions: *Balak und Bilam,* 94, 134, 197; *Licht und Volk,* 96
Adorno, Theodor W., 212
Alexander, Ḥaim, 193, 210n
Aliyah: definition of, 29n
Aliyah, fifth. *See Aliyah,* German
Aliyah, German, 9-12, 15, 17-18, 22-23, 29n, 33, 74, 80, 96, 116-17, 127, 138, 140, 142, 146-48, 151, 161-62, 162n, 172, 182, 184, 192, 210n, 227-28, 235-38; definition of, 29; periods during, 17, 29, 139
Aliyah germanit. See Aliyah, German
Allgemeine deutsche Lieder, 52, 67
Amateurism: as a quality of chamber music performers, 222-24, 233
Anti-Semitism, 4-5, 7, 12n, 13n, 37, 80-81, 231
Antwerp, 93
Art song. *See Lieder*
Arvel, Ḥaim, 159
Ashkenazic Jewish traditions, 152
Assimilation: of German-Jewish community, xii, 20-21, 32, 37, 40-42, 47, 59, 77,
103, 110; musical, 110, 182. *See also* Emancipated society; Emancipation
Aufklärung. See Enlightenment, the

Bach, Johann Sebastian, 175, 201, 213
Baden-Baden, 94
Bar Kochba Turnverein, 61-63
Bartók, Béla, 122, 189
Basel, 54
Beethoven, Ludwig van, 27, 213-14, 233
Beling, Eva, 22, 26
Ben Tsissy, Fordhaus, 120, 142; conductor of the first Palestine Orchestra, 142
Ben-Ḥaim, Paul, 186, 189, 192, 196-201, 203
Benjamin, Walter, 43
Berger, Jean (Arthur Schloßberg), 91
Berlin, 10, 39, 57-59, 61, 113, 122, 144, 149, 162, 170, 173, 193, 200, 227
Berlin State Opera, 142
Bernstein, Arthur, 136
Bildung, 16, 20-21, 28, 29n, 100, 148, 174, 214, 223; definition of, 15
Binyon Zion, 153
Bismarck, Otto von, 49
Bläse, Wilhelm von, 173
Blau-Weiß, 37, 51, 58, 63-67, 70, 163n, 170
Bloch, Ernest, 122, 128, 135
Bonn, 35
Boundaries, ethnic. *See* Ethnicity: boundaries
Brahms, Johannes, 2-3, 6
Breslau, 13n
Brod, Max, 25, 185, 190, 193
Brün, Herbert, 193
Buber, Martin, 43

Censorship, 4-5, 13n

A Note on the Author

PHILIP V. BOHLMAN is Assistant Professor of Music at the University of Chicago, where he is also a member of the Center for Middle Eastern Studies. He is the author of *The Study of Folk Music in the Modern World* and the co-editor, with Mark Slobin, of *Music in the Ethnic Communities of Israel,* a special issue of *Asian Music.* He has written numerous articles on ethnic musical traditions in the American Midwest, Central Europe, and Israel, including the essay on music in Israel for the *New Grove Handbook of World Music.* "The Land Where Two Streams Flow" was selected as a winner in the 1985 Post-Doctoral Publication Program of the National Foundation for Jewish Culture.